JUDEANS AND JEWS

Four Faces of Dichotomy in Ancient Jewish History

The Kenneth Michael Tanenbaum Series in Jewish Studies

The Kenneth Michael Tanenbaum Book Series features outstanding research on topics in all areas of Jewish Studies. This interdisciplinary series highlights especially research developed within the framework of the University of Toronto's Centre for Jewish Studies. The Centre is an interdisciplinary research and teaching unit with a large and diverse cohort of affiliated faculty and an impressive roster of annual conferences, symposia, and lectures. Reflecting the Centre's vibrancy, the series highlights the best new research by local and international scholars who contribute to the intellectual life of this interdisciplinary community. The series has been enabled by a generous donation from Kenneth Tanenbaum, whose family has long supported the Centre and helped make it a leader globally in Jewish Studies.

General Editor: Jeffrey Kopstein, Director, Centre for Jewish Studies, and Professor of Political Science, University of Toronto

Judeans and Jews

*Four Faces of Dichotomy in Ancient
Jewish History*

DANIEL R. SCHWARTZ

UNIVERSITY OF TORONTO PRESS
Toronto Buffalo London

ISBN 978-1-4426-4839-5

Printed on acid-free, 100% post-consumer recycled paper with vegetable-based inks.

Library and Archives Canada Cataloguing in Publication

Schwartz, Daniel R., author
Judeans and Jews : four faces of dichotomy in ancient Jewish history /
Daniel R. Schwartz.

(Kenneth Michael Tanenbaum series in Jewish studies)
Includes bibliographical references and indexes.
ISBN 978-1-4426-4839-5 (bound)

1. Jews – Historiography.   2. Jewish diaspora – Historiography.
3. Jews – Identity – Historiography.   4. Judaism – Historiography.
I. Title.   II. Series: Kenneth Michael Tanenbaum series in Jewish studies

DS115.5.S38 2014   909'.04924   C2014-903759-7

University of Toronto Press acknowledges the financial assistance to
its publishing program of the Canada Council for the Arts and the
Ontario Arts Council, an agency of the Government of Ontario.

 Canada Council   Conseil des Arts
for the Arts   du Canada

 ONTARIO ARTS COUNCIL
CONSEIL DES ARTS DE L'ONTARIO
an Ontario government agency
un organisme du gouvernement de l'Ontario

University of Toronto Press acknowledges the financial support
of the Government of Canada through the Canada Book Fund
for its publishing activities.

In memory of Martin Hengel (1926–2009)
A scholar, a gentleman, and a friend

Entrance to the Jewish cemetery in Rhodes, Greece. The old sign
on the right calls it the cemetery of the "Israelite" community, but the more
recent sign, formulated when "Israel" had become the name of a country,
refers to the cemetery as "Hebraic" in Greek and as "Jewish" in English.
Photo courtesy of Jonathan Kremer, 2009.

Contents

Preface

The first three chapters of this volume are based upon the Shoshana Shier Lectures I gave in Toronto early in 2010. I am very grateful to Prof. Derek Penslar who, during his tenure as academic director of the Jewish Studies Program at the University of Toronto, invited me to give these lectures as the Shoshana Shier Distinguished Visiting Professor in Jewish Studies. A fourth lecture, on Heinrich Graetz, which was presented as work-in-progress, burgeoned into larger proportions and took a different direction and so was published separately.[1] In its stead, I have included here, as the fourth chapter, an essay based upon an earlier Hebrew article that laid the groundwork for my work on Graetz and focuses on the same general issue as the other chapters. I have also included, as an appendix, a debate with Steve Mason – an honoured friend and serious sparring partner these many years – about the use of "religion" and "Judaism" with regard to Jews in antiquity.

I am very grateful to the Centre for Jewish Studies at the University of Toronto, especially to its director during my semester there, Professor Hindy Najman, for the wonderful hospitality and working conditions with which I was provided, and to Professors Sol Goldberg and Jeffrey Kopstein, who arranged for the Centre's generous subsidy for the publication of this volume. I would also like to thank the Shier family for its warm hospitality, and especially Mr. Joseph Shier for the time he took to debate with me about several of the issues raised in these lectures and their modern analogues. Again, my thanks to my undergraduate students at the University of Toronto, and to the participants in a 2009 adult education course I gave at the Zalman Shazar Center for Jewish History in Jerusalem, who contributed to earlier attempts of mine to sort out the several polarities this volume addresses and to understand what basic dichotomy they reflect. Finally, my thanks to Professors Karl P. Donfried and Steve Mason, who read and commented on various drafts of this volume; to the anonymous readers for the University of Toronto Press, whose comments were quite incisive and helpful; to Steven Ben-Yishai and Ian MacKenzie, who helped with the copy editing; and to Len Husband and Wayne Herrington of the Press, who saw the book through all the hurdles along the way.

At the risk of stating the obvious, I will note that whether or not *historia* manages to be a *magistra vitae*, the histories that historians write are certainly influenced by their lives. My interest in the ancient topics addressed by this volume has everything to do with the fact I grew up in the Diaspora (in the USA) but have lived in Israel for the past four decades and more. In particular, my sensitivity to the question of "Judeans" vs. "Jews" in antiquity, and my resistance to the trend to use "Judeans" alone in discussions of the Second Temple period, have a lot to do with my sensitivity to tendencies in our contemporary world that would identify being Israeli (the modern version of "Judean") with being Jewish, with all the problems that entails vis-à-vis non-Jews in Israel, Judaism in Israel, and Jews in the Diaspora.

More particularly, the way this volume is framed has everything to do with the fact that when I look around me I see that the clearest paths chosen by Jews in Israel are quite dichotomous. At the one pole there are numerous ultra-religious Jews who take their Judaism very seriously but have little interest in the state, living as best they can as if they were in the Diaspora, under foreign rule. At the other pole, correspondingly, there are numerous secular Israelis who are Jews by descent but have little to no interest in Judaism. Both of those extreme options are quite natural and easy to understand, and although relatively few people adhere consistently to either pole, and many are quite consciously seeking some position between them, it seems that – as with any use of "ideal types" – the various options can best be understood by assessing them and locating them in light of those two poles. It is probably too much to hope that any study of the ancient expressions of these polar alternatives can both steer away from anachronism and contribute to the clarification of the modern issues as well, but I have done my best to serve both desiderata.

Put in a nutshell, what this book argues is that we should identify polar contrasts in each of three separate corpora of evidence from the ancient Jewish world – between 1 Maccabees and 2 Maccabees, between priestly and rabbinic law, and between early and later works of Josephus – and also understand them to be three expressions of one basic split, between Judea and Judaism. Accordingly, already at the outset, I should make two observations about the use of such broad generalizations and polar contrasts. After all, it is obvious that there is something quite schematic and reductionist about them, for such analyses of diverse historical data perforce marginalize nuances, gradations, mixtures, and idiosyncrasies. What might outweigh such liabilities?

My first observation is that sometimes there is, nevertheless, no choice, and that the present volume derives from such a situation. As is noted at the opening of ch. 3, I have undertaken to translate for a new series, from Greek into English, the last three books of Josephus' *Antiquities*. Among other things, that requires me to decide how to translate *Ioudaios*, the standard Greek term for the main figures of the work, into English – "Jew" or "Judean"? The problem is that where Greek has one term, English has two, but only two. Had English too only one term (as, for example, it has only "Greek"[2] and "Roman" for *Hellēn* and *Rhomaios*, although they too have various senses), life would have been simpler; I would use that term and leave it to readers to interpret it.[3] As it is, however, since English has two terms, of which one clearly refers to Judea while the other does not, I have to choose between them (just as one would have to choose if English offered words like "Greekist" or "Romist") – but the fact is that, the way things are today, the use of either term amounts to a statement that the other is less appropriate. That is because "Judean" is so rare in general English usage that any use of it immediately makes readers realize it is being used instead of "Jew," but in scholarly usage "Judean" has become so widespread that any use of "Jew" requires an explanation; this is certainly the case for someone who is preparing a volume for a series in which all the volumes that have hitherto appeared have adopted "Judean." This situation more or less required me to examine to what the two (no more!) options might refer when we use them concerning antiquity, and the present volume, and the fact that it presents its materials between two poles, is the result.

My second observation is that, apart from being forced upon us by the facts of Greek and English vocabulary, dichotomies such as those identified in this book can also be useful. True, it is clear that constructing them requires schematization and running roughshod over details, and so it is standard procedure that, whenever a dichotomous contrast is proposed, critics point out cases in which the evidence associated with each pole is less than univocal and less than consistent. Some would go so far as to say that such difficulties – the gaps between the neat "ideal types" that figure in dichotomies and the evidence concerning real people and events – are so weighty as to render the former worthless. Indeed, in 1981 W. D. Davies characterized the state of the study of ancient Judaism as "the eclipse of dichotomies,"[4] just as S. J. D. Cohen, in a perspicacious survey of our field published in 1990, categorized scholars as either "unifiers" or "separators" and noted that, by and large, the latter had the upper hand.[5]

However, the refusal to generalize, which of course precludes the second-story move of contrasting generalities one to another, can reduce historians to antiquarian list-makers; by and large historians rightly resist that; and what is in fact required is care about context and resolution. Thus, for example, it is clear that anyone interested in learning about Anglicanism would be better served by literature that compares Anglicanism to Presbyterianism (for example) than by literature that compares Protestantism to Catholicism (not to mention Christianity to Judaism). But if someone who lumps Anglicans and Presbyterians together in comparing Protestantism to Catholicism is urged not to overlook the differences between Anglicans and Presbyterians, he or she would be justified in responding that if the English language sees fit to use "Protestantism" for both, then it is legitimate and useful for us to focus, *in this context*, on what they have in common. So too in the present case, if we are to make sense of our usage of "Jews" and "Judeans" with regard to antiquity, we need to focus on what those we would denote by each term had in common, however clear it is that there were differences among those whom we lump together and similarities among those we contrast one to another.[6] The challenge, according to which historians will be judged, concerns their success, when going through masses of evidence, at identifying the major factors of similarity, upon which generalizations should be built, as opposed to minor points that must be sidelined to allow more important commonalities to become salient.

Indeed, a few lines after referring to the "eclipse of dichotomies" Davies – conceding their usefulness – went on to leave the door open, predicting that dichotomies would doubtless return and expressing the confidence that "they will be described with a more refined scholarly sensitivity than in the past."[7] The present work definitely fulfils his prediction and I hope it justifies his confidence. It was written in the general conviction that a dichotomous scheme is a useful way to analyse the major options and parameters within which nuances and details can be understood, and particularly in the hope that recognition of the basic dichotomy between Judean and Jew proposed here – between land and religion, or between land-based religion and non-land-based religion – will help us make better sense of much of the evidence for Jews and Judaism in antiquity than has hitherto been possible.

I dedicate this volume to the memory of the late Professor Martin Hengel of Tübingen. He was one of the great modern scholars of ancient Judaism, one of the great German contributors to the restoration of German-Jewish relations after the Holocaust, and a gentleman I was honoured to count among my friends.

This book was completed early in 2011. Since then I made various revisions, but did not attempt to relate to all subsequent scholarship.

Daniel R. Schwartz
The Hebrew University of Jerusalem,
March 2014

Note on Translations and Abbreviations

Chapter and verse references, in biblical and apocryphal works, are according to those in the New Revised Standard Version of the Bible. References to the Mishnah are according to the numbering in H. Danby, *The Mishnah* (Oxford: Oxford University Press, 1933). All translations in this volume are my own, unless otherwise noted. Citations and abbreviations follow, by and large, those of the *Society of Biblical Literature Handbook of Style*. The following abbreviations are used:

AGJU	Arbeiten zur Geschichte des antiken Judentums und des Urchristentums
AJEC	Ancient Judaism and Early Christianity
BDAG	F. W. Danker, ed., *A Greek-English Lexicon of the New Testament and Other Early Christian Literature* (3rd ed., 2000)
BJS	Brown Judaic Studies
BZAW	Beihefte zur *Zeitschrift für die alttestamentliche Wissenschaft*
CBET	Contributions to Biblical Exegesis and Theology
CBQ	*Catholic Biblical Quarterly*
CBQMS	*Catholic Biblical Quarterly* Monograph Series
CEJL	Commentaries on Early Jewish Literature
CRINT	Compendia rerum iudaicarum ad Novum Testamentum
CTM	*Concordia Theological Monthly*
DSD	*Dead Sea Discoveries*
EBib	Études bibliques
EncJud	*Encyclopaedia Judaica* (1972)
FJTC	Flavius Josephus, Translation and Commentary
FRLANT	Forschungen zur Religion und Literatur des Alten und Neuen Testaments

JUDEANS AND JEWS

Four Faces of Dichotomy in Ancient Jewish History

Introduction

Judæan, Judean. [adjective] Of or pertaining to Judæa or southern Palestine. [noun] A native or inhabitant of this region.[1]

Jew. A person of Hebrew descent; one whose religion is Judaism; an Israelite.[2]

Judean, also *Judaean.* [adjective] Of, relating to, or characteristic of ancient Judea. [noun] An inhabitant of ancient Judea.[3]

Jew. A person belonging to the worldwide group constituting a continuation through descent or conversion of the ancient Jewish people and characterized by a sense of community; *esp.* one whose religion is Judaism.[4]

Judean. [adjective] of or pertaining to Judea. [noun] a native or inhabitant of Judea.[5]

Jew. 1. A person whose religion is Judaism. 2. one of a scattered group of people that traces its descent from the Biblical Hebrews or from post-exilic adherents of Judaism; Israelite.[6]

As the central guides to English usage on both sides of the Atlantic unanimously agree, our language distinguishes very clearly between "Judean," which denotes people by linking them to the region called Judea, and "Jew," which entails no territorial linkage and refers, instead, to one or two other parameters – descent and religion. In antiquity, in contrast, texts in Greek (as some other languages, including Hebrew, that will not concern us in this volume) employ only one

cognate term – *Ioudaios* (plural: *Ioudaioi*).[7] What created the need for a
second term in English, as in other modern languages, is the fact of
exile: Since for nearly two millennia the descendants of the ancient
Ioudaioi had no state of their own and most of them lived in the
Diaspora, it made little sense to define them as Judeans – but since
the memory of the ancient Judeans lived on, another term was needed
to define those descendants in their current situation. "Jews" fits that
bill. Moreover, throughout that period the other groups to whom the
descendants of the *Ioudaioi* were usually compared, Christians and
Muslims, were defined neither by a link to any country nor by one to
any common descent, but by their religion – by their common beliefs
and practices vis-à-vis God.[8] That, of course, reinforced the tendency
to understand the Jews similarly and, accordingly, the need for non-
territorial nomenclature.

In recent years, in contrast, especially in light of the existence of the
modern state of Israel, there has been much renewed appreciation of
the territorial dimension of the *Ioudaioi* in antiquity.[9] For the Second
Temple period, upon which this volume focuses, the importance of that
dimension is quite easily documented: it is a period of history that began with a "Return to Zion"; was punctuated in its midst by the establishment of a sovereign Judean state ruled by high priests whose seat of
authority was in a "holy city," Jerusalem, and, more particularly, who
were defined by their right to administer the holiest area of Jerusalem,
namely, the Temple Mount, and to enter the holiest place in the Temple
of Jerusalem on the holiest day of the year; and ended, in 70 CE, with
the destruction of that Temple. Correspondingly, numerous texts indicate that the *Ioudaioi* of the period were understood as Judeans – the
residents of that land. Thus, for examples from both ends of the period,
Aristotle was quoted as stating that *Ioudaioi* are called by that name
"due to the place, for the place they live is called Judea," and Josephus
thought it made sense to write that Agrippa I, grandson of Herod the
Great, was a *Ioudaios* and one of the most prestigious people "there."[10]

However, that is only one aspect of the Second Temple period, for if
that period began, in the sixth century BCE, with the Return to Zion
and the re-establishment of a Jewish community (although not yet a
Jewish state) in Judea, that same century also saw the birth of a phenomenon that has been characteristic of the Jews ever since: Diaspora.
Many or most Judeans did not return to Judea but remained in
Babylonia, just as the subsequent centuries witnessed the establishment of numerous and often substantial communities of *Ioudaioi* all

around the Graeco-Roman Diaspora – and the question arises, how did they understand themselves? To provide an answer today, in English, requires us to decide whether to call them Judeans or Jews. Moreover, given the fact that Diaspora is not only a matter of geography but also – even primarily – a political situation, namely life under foreign rule, we must recognize that, even regarding the *Ioudaioi* in Judea, which was under foreign rule during most of the Second Temple period, the same question could arise – all the more so, given the fact that they belonged, to some significant extent, to the same people as the *Ioudaioi* of the Diaspora.

The past two decades have been witness to something of a paradox in scholarship. On the one hand, there has been a boom in the study of the Diaspora in the Hellenistic-Roman period. Sources have been collected,[11] and numerous monographs,[12] collections of studies,[13] and surveys[14] have been published; the Hellenistic-Roman Diaspora is now on the map in a way, and to an extent, it never was before. But paradoxically, although that might have been expected to foster the recognition of non-Judean types of *Ioudaioi*, it has in fact become popular, during the same recent period in scholarship, to use "Judean" rather than "Jew" as the standard designation of the subjects of Jewish history in this period.

As noted above, the latter is often quite warranted. However, an across-the-board application of that can result in apparent absurdities. Thus, for example, when Josephus refers in *War* 2.487 and *Antiquities* 19.281 to *Ioudaioi* who were, for centuries, residents of Alexandria who enjoyed there a status equal to that of the other Alexandrians, and their long-term residence in Alexandria is in fact the main point Josephus underlines in his account, if we render *Ioudaioi* as "Judeans" and then replace that term by the definition supplied by our standard dictionaries (cited above), the result is a self-contradiction. By definition, century-long inhabitants of Alexandria could not be natives or inhabitants of Judea, and to use "Judeans" in translation here would also be to write at cross-purposes to Josephus.[15]

I know of two ways of dealing with that problem. A very current way is to avoid it by ascribing to the English term "Judean" a broader "ethnic" sense, one that adds to its geographical meaning the element of common descent and then, with regard to Jews of the Diaspora, emphasizes that latter element. Thus, for example, S. J. D. Cohen opens his discussion of this issue with the heading "A *Ioudaios* is a Judaean (A Function of Birth and/or Geography)" and goes on to say, "As an ethnic-geographic term, *Ioudaios* is parallel to terms like Egyptian, Cappadocian, Thracian, Phrygian, and so forth, which are both ethnic and geographic ... As an ethnic-geographic term, *Ioudaios* is best translated as 'Judaean.'"[16]

So too Mason:

> One frequently meets the observation that in some passage (e.g., in Josephus) *Ioudaios* may mean "Judaean" (i.e., in or belonging to the territory of greater or proper Judaea), but in other passages the word has *no such geographical constraints and therefore* should be rendered "Jew." The foregoing analysis, however, has tried to show that "Judaean" does not have a geographical restriction, any more than other ethnic descriptors do. Such a restriction *in our minds* arises from the absence of a political entity called Judaea today, so that when we hear the word we think first of an ancient place and not of the people. But just as "Roman," "Egyptian," and "Greek" (etc.) had a wide range of associations beyond the geographical, and they do not require us to substitute other terms when we refer to "Roman citizens" or call Lucian a "Greek," so too "Judaean" should be allowed to shoulder its burden as an ethnic term full of complex possibilities.[17]

Two details in Mason's phrasing of the second sentence point up the issue quite plainly: (1) It states that "the foregoing analysis" shows something about "Judean," but that is an English word, while Mason's detailed foregoing analysis in fact dealt with a Greek one, *Ioudaios*. (2) While his use of the past tense in the fourth sentence ("But just as 'Roman,' 'Egyptian,' and 'Greek' [etc.] had a wide range of associations beyond the geographical") is quite appropriate, his use of the present tense in the second sentence ("'Judaean' does not have a geographic restriction") simply contradicts the English dictionaries in assuming an answer to the question we are discussing: should our modern usage, in English, be governed by modern usage or by ancient usage?

Moreover, apart from conflicting with English usage, the addition of "birth" (Cohen) or "ethnic"/"people" (Mason) to the geographic sense of "Judean" runs up against three additional problems:

1. It ignores the fact that English associates the element of common descent with another term, "Jew."
2. It can deal only with difficulty with the fact that the Graeco-Roman period saw the rise of proselytism, that is, the widespread phenomenon of people of non-*Ioudaios* descent becoming *Ioudaioi*.[18]

3. The other terms, to which Cohen and Mason compare "Judean," such as "Egyptian," "Greek," and "Roman," have no alternatives comparable to "Jew," and they are in fact quite usual in English, so use of them does not amount to a statement that they are more appropriate than other ways of viewing the people in question. Indeed, scholars and others do have varying notions about what most or best characterized "Greeks" (e.g.) in some given place and time,[19] but their use of "Greek" does not commit them to any particular notion because they have no choice. Writers in English, in contrast, a language that supplies two terms, must decide which to use, and a decision to use "Judean," which is quite a rare term,[20] amounts to a demonstrative statement that the other alternative, "Jew," is not appropriate.[21]

The other way to evade the territorial meaning of "Judean" is to expand the English definition of "Judean" to include not only "natives" and "residents" of Judea but also people defined by shared historical memories of roots in Judea and/or a shared common focus upon Judea. That is, just as we may understand references to "Puerto Ricans" or "Italians" in the United States as including people who have been residing in the United States for generations but nevertheless define themselves, and are defined by others, in a significant way, by reference to their ancestors' homeland, we could do the same for *Ioudaioi* of the ancient Diaspora as well. That is indeed a possibility, although normally we should hesitate before we allow historians to dictate the meanings of the words they use. Usually we expect them to choose the words that bear the meanings they want, and if it is difficult to do so, that itself may be the springboard for research to explain why.

Apart from that, however, there is the more basic problem that this volume addresses: the assertion that *Ioudaioi* should be understood as "Judeans" in the Second Temple period begs the question and directs us away from recognizing that, in fact, a good bit of what was happening and what was interesting among *Ioudaioi* in the Second Temple period was oriented to what we call "Judaism," a religion – an element firmly located by the dictionaries in the domain of "Jews," not "Judeans." Indeed, the word *Ioudaïsmos* itself appears for the first time in the midst of this period and precisely where we would expect to find it: in a work, the Second Book of Maccabees, written by a *Ioudaios* of the Hellenistic Diaspora in the second century BCE – perhaps one of the *Ioudaioi* of Alexandria who, as Josephus underlined in the passages cited above (at n. 15), lived there for centuries. And investigation of that work shows, as the first chapter of the present volume argues, that in other ways as well, and not just in the use of that term, it bespeaks interests and values that we normally define as having to do with religion, rather than as being land- or state-oriented. To impose the use of "Judean" upon that book, and those similar to it, when the English language offers us a more appropriate alternative, would be terribly misleading. True, the currently popular move to prefer "Judean" has spawned attempts to make *Ioudaïsmos* in 2 Maccabees mean something other than "Judaism" – arguments to which I shall respond in the appendix to this volume.

As stated above, however, it was not only life abroad that could devalue the territorial component of the identity of the *Ioudaioi*. The very lack of home rule in Judea throughout most of the Second Temple period, during which Judea was, in turn, a province of Achaemenid Persia, Ptolemaic Egypt, Seleucid Syria, and the Roman Empire, undercut the meaning of saying "I am a *Ioudaios* because I live in Judea." And that was reinforced all the more by the real expressions of foreign rule: taxes sent abroad, laws imposed from without, foreign garrisons, and visible paganism. Moreover, the very fact of living in the Hellenistic world, in which the main and most successful and prestigious others, namely the "Greeks," were as a rule not from Greece, nor did they live in Greece, undercut the notion that people should meaningfully define themselves by countries. Although processes of Hellenization were naturally more pronounced in the Hellenistic Diaspora, clearly they affected Judea as well.[22]

For all those reasons, then, it should not surprise us that the Second Temple period saw the appearance and development, even in Judea, of orientations and values that played down the importance of the land and, instead, linked being a *Ioudaios* (or its Hebrew or Aramaic equivalent – *Yehudi, Yehudai*) with religion. Just as the Greeks adhered to Hellenism (the things they valued and did, qua Greeks), and it became apparent that *Ioudaioi* could become Greeks by doing the same, so would *Ioudaioi* who did not want to become Greeks come to understand that they were *Ioudaioi* not because of where they lived but because they chose to adhere to something parallel to Hellenism but different from it: what we, and some of them, called "Judaism." That, in turn, would mean that we should tend to understand those *Ioudaioi* as "Jews." In the second chapter of this volume I suggest that differences between some ancient Jewish sects should be understood, mutatis mutandis, as another version of the basic Judean/Jewish split, pitting priestly Judeans against rabbinic Jews – of whom the former, quite appropriately, lost their place in the world with the destruction of the Second Temple, while the latter, just as appropriately, went on to flourish outside Judea and, eventually, to create their chief oeuvre, the Talmud, in the Diaspora.

The third chapter of this volume is basically a test case, focusing on the works of Flavius Josephus, the first-century Jewish historian whose works are so basic to any study of the Second Temple period. Josephus was born in 37 CE and died around 100, so the destruction of the Second Temple, in 70 CE, split his life into two approximately equal parts. Moreover, in the first half of his life he was very Judean: he was a priest, Yoseph ben Mattityahu of Jerusalem and eventually one of the generals in the Judeans' revolt against Rome – a revolt that strove to restore Judean rule in Judea. In the latter half of his life, in contrast, he was very Roman: beginning in 67 CE he was, while still in Judea, under the wing of the imperial family, and beginning in 71 CE he lived (as he reports in *Life* 423) in Rome itself, as the Roman citizen Flavius Josephus, in a residence supplied (along with financial assistance) by Vespasian. And it was there, in Rome, that Josephus took up his career as a historian. Whatever notes or drafts he had brought with him from Judea, Josephus composed his works in Rome, where there was a large community of Jews used to the values and conditions of Jewish life in the Diaspora for more than a century,[23] and he wrote at a time when the Temple no longer existed, which means there was no longer anything in the world that even looked like it was a Jewish place. True, things do not happen overnight; it takes time to digest the meaning of such changes. Nevertheless, comparison of Josephus' first work, *The Judean War*, written in the seventies, shortly after he got off the boat from Judea and before he had learned to think like a diasporan Jew, to his *Antiquities*, written some fifteen or twenty years later, gives manifold reason to believe that, in time, Josephus did metamorphose from a Judean into a Jew and that, accordingly, the title of his later work should be not *Judean Antiquities* but, rather, as it always used to be, *Jewish Antiquities* or *Antiquities of the Jews*. If that creates some dissonance when put alongside Josephus' other work, *The Judean War*, that dissonance will be a useful reminder of the dichotomous nature of the different worlds the two books reflect.

Finally, the fourth chapter is devoted to the way our issues were reflected in the historiography of Heinrich Graetz, the great Jewish historian of the nineteenth century who, beginning with the third (1878) edition of his volume on the latter half of the Second Temple period, replaced – without stating any reason – all references to "Jews" and "Jewish" (*Juden, jüdisch*) with "Judea" and Judean" (*Judäa, judäisch*). My attempt to ascertain the reasons for this strangely unexplained and unnoticed switch led to an appreciation of the way Graetz struggled to define the period as basically religious or as basically political but eventually recognized it was impossible to do either. That recognition illustrates the point that the present little volume is meant to spotlight, namely, that in fact the latter half of the Second Temple period was the stage for a basic dichotomy, one that can be ironed out by unitary nomenclature only at the price of hiding a good deal of what is most interesting and essential about the history of the *Ioudaioi* in this crucial period.

1

Judean Historiography vs.
Jewish Historiography:
The First and Second Books of Maccabees*

As opposed to the biblical books of 1–2 Samuel, 1–2 Kings, and 1–2 Chronicles, which are each single works divided into two volumes, of which the second continues the first, the First and Second Books of Maccabees are totally separate works. Indeed, to some extent they tell the same story, from different points of view.[1] Both begin, after some obviously introductory material,[2] with the accession of Antiochus IV Epiphanes to the Seleucid throne in 175 BCE, and both proceed to recount that king's dealings with the Jews, including the Hasmonean revolt against him. However, in contrast to 2 Maccabees, which concludes with events of 161 BCE, 1 Maccabees, which gets that far halfway into the book (ch. 7), continues to bring the story down to 135/134 BCE. Both works bear witness to the history of that eventful and even critical period, and historians use them in tandem, or use one to correct the other, in order to reconstruct the period and interpret it.

In the present study, however, my purpose is different. Rather than using these works as evidence for the events they recount, I focus on them as witnesses to the worlds of their respective authors, for their authors very obviously represent different poles of the ancient Jewish world – they wrote in different languages, in different contexts, with different values, and with different purposes. As such, they afford us a rich view of the polarity in the Jewish world as early as the second century BCE, when they were written. These differences between the two books can be grouped easily under three rubrics, moving from externals to the most fundamental level.

---

* This chapter draws upon more detailed discussions in D. R. Schwartz, *2 Maccabees* (CEJL; Berlin: De Gruyter, 2008).

I. Hebrew Book vs. Greek Book

Although today both books survive in Greek alone (in the Septuagint), along with secondary translations made from the Greek, and 2 Maccabees was indeed composed in Greek, 1 Maccabees was originally composed in Hebrew. The latter point, attested explicitly by St. Jerome, is also obvious, given its non-Greek "translationese" vocabulary and style, to any reader of Greek who is familiar with biblical Hebrew.[3]

That most obvious difference between the two books, which evidently reflects differences between the education and culture of their authors, has various immediate implications. One has to do with style: 1 Maccabees, as the Hebrew Bible, typically has a very restrained style, whereas 2 Maccabees, following a popular style of Hellenistic literature of its day, is often quite "pathetic." That is, it aims at arousing the feelings (*pathos*) of the readers, whether by using high-flying diction or by explicitly pointing out the feelings that the events should arouse.[4] Another implication has to do with the respective "bookshelves" from which the authors drew their allusions: if 1 Maccabees draws frequently upon the Hebrew Bible,[5] 2 Maccabees – while not without allusions to the Hebrew Bible[6] – does so much less frequently, but often employs standard tropes and allusions from Greek literature.[7]

II. Judean Book vs. Diasporan Book

That obvious linguistic difference between the two books points to one that is only a little less obvious: 1 Maccabees is a Judean work, 2 Maccabees is one by a Jew of the Hellenistic Diaspora. That 2 Maccabees is a work of the Diaspora is indicated explicitly at 2:23, where the author of the work as we have it (sometimes termed the "Epitomator") informs us that the work is his abridgement of a longer original written by one Jason of Cyrene (Libya). But it is also indicated by several other points, concerning which the contrast with 1 Maccabees shows just as clearly that the latter is a Judean work.[8]

1. 1 Maccabees shows great interest in and knowledge about Judean geography; there is next to none of that in 2 Maccabees. Note, for example, that the long battle scenes in 2 Macc 8 and 15 give no indication of where the battles took place; contrast 1 Macc 3–6. This corresponds to what we would expect from authors living, respectively, in the Diaspora and in Judea.

2. Correspondingly, 2 Maccabees is interested in the Hellenistic world and well at home in it, much more than 1 Maccabees. Thus, for example, 1 Maccabees (1:18; 10:51–11:18) refers to Ptolemy VI as "Ptolemy," but 2 Maccabees (4:21; 9:29; 10:13) cares to distinguish him from the others by calling him "Philometor"; 1 Macc 7:1 says Demetrius I arrived at "a city by the sea," but 2 Macc 14:1 finds it interesting to specify that he came to Tripolis; 1 Macc 3:32 says wrongly (deliberately or not) that Lysias was "of the royal family," which reflects the etymo-logical meaning but not the real import of *syggenēs*, which was a rank of a prestigious courtier in a Hellenistic court and is prop-erly reported by 2 Macc 11:1; etc.

3. The structure of 1 Maccabees takes us from ch. 1, where Hellenistic rulers are terrible, to ch. 16, where Hasmonean rule is established firmly. Its entire story is built in sections portraying the successive Hasmonean rulers who, step by step, solve the problem portrayed by ch. 1: ch. 2 on Mattathias, chs. 3–9 on Judas, chs. 9–12 on Jonathan, chs. 12–16 on Simon (in whose days the dynasty is formally established – ch. 14), end of ch. 16 on John, who takes over after the death of Simon, his father. That is, the whole work functions as a dynastic history, explaining how bad Seleucid rule was, how it happened that the Hasmoneans established native rule instead of Seleucid rule, and why it was warranted that the Hasmoneans (especially the line of Simon[9]) should rule the state they established. That is a message well at home in Hasmonean Judea, and we should understand the work, basically, as one written on behalf of the Hasmonean court in Jerusalem.[10]

4. The story of 2 Maccabees, in contrast, focuses on the history of Jerusalem, which it characterizes as the Jews' polis – which starts off in wonderful circumstances (3:1–3) and ends up in wonderful circumstances (15:37). Thus, the book's story amounts to an account of the city's troubles and tribulations, down to the nadir in the middle of the book, and then back up to the restoration of its fortunes by the end.[11] This point of view permeates the book: the wicked king forbids the Jews to "live as citizens of the city" (*politeuesthai*) according to Jewish law (6:1); the book's villains persecute their "fellow-citizens" (*politai* – 4:50; 5:6, 8, 23) but the book's heroes look out for them (4:2; 14:37; 15:30). That is, the book is the history of the Jewish polis – but that means the book is applying to the Jews the central category of culture in the

Hellenistic world, the polis. That is a point of view well at home in the Hellenistic Diaspora.[12]

5. 1 Maccabees assumes that Gentiles and their kings are, by and large, wicked and hostile.[13] For 2 Maccabees, in contrast, the opposite is the case. It is enough to contrast the first ten verses of 1 Maccabees, which open by portraying Alexander the Great as an arrogant conqueror and conclude by summarizing the legacy of his successors over the next century and a half as "and they multiplied evils in the world," to the first three verses of the prologue of 2 Maccabees (3:1–3),[14] which illustrate just how wonderful things were to begin with. There, the book's opening statement, that "once upon a time" things were just fine in Jerusalem, is fleshed out by underlining that the Greek kings in general and Seleucus IV in particular showed exemplary respect for Jerusalem and the Temple – a point reiterated at 5:16 where, when Antiochus robs the Temple, the author emphasizes how exceptional he was by reporting that much of what he stole consisted of votive offerings given to the Temple by Gentile kings. Or, for another example, contrast the way 1 Maccabees assumes that "the nations around us" attack us without provocation, whether things are going well with us (5:1) or badly with us (12:53), while 2 Maccabees takes it for granted that Gentiles in general, and Greeks in particular, are outraged when Jews are murdered (4:35–6, 49); after all, a Jew is a "man" (4:35), just like each of them.[15] This distinction is one between the point of view of Judeans proud of themselves for having established sovereign home rule instead of Gentile rule, on the one hand, and Jews used to living among Gentiles and under Gentile rule, in the Diaspora, who prefer to believe that it is just fine to live that way, on the other.

6. 2 Maccabees evinces relatively little interest in the Temple cult in Jerusalem. Of course, the Temple is not ignored; the very story focuses on the Temple, which is robbed in ch. 4, robbed and defiled in ch. 5, and defiled even more severely in ch. 6, but then rededicated in ch. 10 and defended in the subsequent chapters; note especially the way the book ends with the threat to the Temple expressed at 14:33 being overcome precisely tit for tat at 15:32–3. Nevertheless, it is clear that the Temple is secondary to the polis. So it is already in the idyllic "once upon a time" (3:1–3), which begins with the city and works its way to the Temple; so it is at 4:48, where those who protest the theft of vessels from the Temple

are characterized as defenders of "the city and the populace and the holy vessels"; so it is at 5:17–20, where the author, in an aside to readers, heavy-handedly explains that the people is more important than the Temple, so when the residents of the city (of Jerusalem) sin, the Temple suffers too, just as when God and the Jews are reconciled, the Temple too is restored; and so it is at 6:1, where Antiochus' decrees are said to forbid the Jews to "conduct their civic behaviour [*politeuesthai*] according to the divine laws," so when the defilement of the Temple is reported in the next verses, it understood only as an aspect of what happened under that more general, civic, rubric.

Again, the secondary status of the Temple is underlined in another way in ch. 3: although that chapter focuses upon the famous scene in which God most impressively protects the Temple against violation by a high Seleucid official, Heliodorus, the latter is portrayed as having drawn the conclusion that the God *who lives in heaven* keeps special watch over the Temple (3:39). That is, even here it is important for the author to underline that the Temple is not the House of God. Similarly, at 2 Macc 14:34–5 the priests respond to a threat to the Temple by raising their hands to heaven in prayer, and although they ask God to protect the Temple, they first emphasize that he has no need of it; contrast the parallel at 1 Macc 7:36, where the author carefully specifies that it was while standing in front of the altar and the Temple that the priests prayed to God, and says nothing about their raising their hands to heaven or about God's lack of need of the Temple. While it may well be that priests of Jerusalem were also aware of biblical statements about the transcendence and universal accessibility of God, the facts of their lives did not make such teaching very functional – but for Jews of the Diaspora it was essential. Indeed, the way the author of 2 Maccabees tells these stories is just as we would expect from a diasporan author – who needs to be assured that God of Israel is the God of Heaven, equally accessible to all Jews.[16]

The same author's relative lack of interest in the Temple cult is also very obvious in 5:16, where he has only two general words, "holy vessels," to describe what Antiochus stole from the Temple, along with many words to note that much of what he took had been donated by Gentile kings; contrast 1 Macc 1:21–3, where there is great detail about the cultic items that Antiochus stole from the Temple but not a word about any gifts from Gentiles or their kings. Scenes such as 1 Macc 3:49, where Jews are desolated because they are unable to bring sacrifices, or 1 Macc 10:21, which is enthusiastic over Jonathan's appearance in high-priestly robes, are not found in 2 Maccabees, nor are they to be expected there – no more than we might expect 1 Maccabees to tell us as easily as 2 Maccabees about negligent priests (2 Macc 4:14) and wicked high priests (2 Macc 4:7–13; 4:32–50). Only a Jew from the Diaspora, who is used to living Jewishly without the Temple cult, can easily live with such stories about the institution's bankruptcy.[17]

III. Judea vs. Judaism

In the wake of those brief observations about the differences between a Hebrew book and a Greek one, and between a Judean book and a diasporan one, we will now turn to more fundamental differences between the two books. As we shall see, they are far-reaching but may be understood as arising out of those discussed above.

First and foremost, if we ask what problem is addressed by 1 Maccabees and how it is resolved, the answers are clear: foreign rule is the problem (ch. 1), Hasmonean rule is the solution (chs. 2–16). Nothing is said, anywhere, about *why* the Hellenistic rulers were formerly able to rule the Jews, only about how. Rather, the book simply indicates that Alexander the Great and his successors successfully conquered and ruled the East; they did it because they were able to do so. For 2 Maccabees, in contrast, the problem is Jewish sin. That is what explains the Jews' suffering at the hands of Antiochus, and the solution is atonement for that sin. This point – of which there is nothing of the kind in 1 Maccabees – is made pointedly in authorial excurses at 4:16–17, 5:17–20, and 6:12–17, as also in the whole structure of the story: the explicit turning point of the book comes at 8:5, when, with atonement achieved, God's wrath turns to mercy and, therefore, Judas Maccabaeus can begin to be victorious in his battles against the Greeks.

Second, note that, according to 2 Maccabees, what made for atonement was the death of martyrs, which is why the two long martyrdom chapters (chs. 6–7) precede the turning point at the beginning of ch. 8.[18] When, in contrast, we turn to 1 Maccabees and ask what it thinks of martyrs, the answer is plain: not much. Rather, in the three places it mentions martyrs it uses them as foils to show that their naive piety brought them nothing but death, in contrast to the path of rebellion chosen by the Hasmoneans:

- At the very end of ch. 1, 1 Maccabees briefly reports the death of some martyrs but they have no result; they only demonstrate how bad things are. Immediately thereafter, from the outset of ch. 2, the author pointedly turns his and our attention to Mattathias and his sons – that is, to rebellion – as the real solution to the problem posed by foreign rule.
- Next, in the midst of ch. 2, after the author reports that some pious Jews let themselves be killed rather than violate the Sabbath to defend themselves (vv. 29–38), he goes on immediately to report that Mattathias and his men decided not to behave that way but, rather, to defend themselves even on the Sabbath (vv. 39–41). That is, the choice of pious death rather than violation of the divine laws gets you nowhere. What is needed, and what works, is valiant and persistent rebellion – the path the Hasmoneans took.
- Finally, in ch. 7 (vv. 10–18) pious Jews (called *Asidaioi* ["Pious"] or "scribes") who accept Seleucid overtures of peace turn out to be fools and are massacred, while the world-wise and open-eyed Hasmoneans know whom they can trust – themselves.

This difference between a book that holds that Jewish sins bring on divine wrath but the blood of martyrs can work atonement and thus influence God to change the course of history, on the one hand, and a book that holds that our enemies succeed because they are strong and heroic but we can beat them off if we are stronger and more heroic, and holds that martyrdom is naive and pointless, on the other hand, corresponds to several other differences between the two books that all amount to an absence of God in 1 Maccabees as opposed to his centrality in 2 Maccabees:

1. *Miracles and apparitions*: 1 Maccabees reports nothing supernatural – no miracles, no divine apparitions. 2 Maccabees is full of them: from the horse and rider who descend from heaven (along with two handsome enforcers) to punish Heliodorus in 3:25–6, to the heavenly army over Jerusalem in ch. 5:2–4, the heavenly horsemen who descend to protect Judas in 10:29–30 and another who leads his troops in 11:8, and finally to the appearance of Onias and Jeremiah in Judas Maccabaeus' dream reported at 15:12–16, which was so real that Judas actually received from Jeremiah the sword he then goes on to use to defeat the Syrian general, God is visibly active in the story from beginning to end. Nothing like those

episodes appears in 1 Maccabees, and although it too reports that Judas once acquired a special sword, it says he took it from a fallen enemy general after killing him in battle (3:11–12).

2. *Poetic justice*: The assertion that the fate of villains corresponds to their crimes is a more subtle way of asserting God's providential and just control of events – and it too is absent from 1 Maccabees but frequently found in 2 Maccabees. Thus, a temple-robber was killed by an angry Jewish mob near the Temple treasury (4:42);[19] Jason was exiled because he had exiled others (5:9);[20] Antiochus had persecuted the innards of others (by forcing them to eat impure foods) and so he died "very justly" with great pains in his innards (9:6); the only Jews who died in battle were discovered to have been wearing idolatrous amulets under their tunics, which shows that God "judges righteously and makes the hidden things visible" (12:40–1); and Menelaus died "very justly" in ashes because he had defiled the ashes of the altar (13:7–8).

3. *Prayer*: Here the picture is not as totally one-sided, for there are some prayers and references to prayer in 1 Maccabees. However, beginning with ch. 5 they are very few and far between, and usually no more than a brief reference that is not much more than pro forma or window-dressing.[21] In 2 Maccabees, in contrast, prayers are numerous and often long, and they are answered,[22] just as the martyrs of ch. 7 all express their certainty that God will restore the Jews' fortunes and punish their enemies. This, of course, corresponds to the book's emphasis upon God's active providence; time and again the book points out explicitly that it was God who made things happen.[23]

4. *"Luck/fate"*: In contrast, 1 Maccabees clearly states, at three important junctures, that something blind exerts control over events. The term it uses for such luck or fate is *kairos*, literally "point in time, moment." Thus at 9:10 Judas refuses to flee the field of battle despite overwhelming odds against him, saying that if his *kairos* had come to die, he would rather do so without staining his honour; at 12:1 Jonathan realizes that the *kairos* was going his way and so he seized the opportunity to send ambassadors to Rome; and at 15:33–4 Simon explains that at some past *kairos*, others had conquered the Jews' ancestral lands but now, when "we have the *kairos*," his forces were able to retake them. Whether *kairos* is conceived of as blind uncontrolled luck, or astrologically, or some other way,[24] what is important for the contrast with 2 Maccabees is that *kairos* has nothing to do with a providential God.

What all these points amount to is quite simple: 2 Maccabees, a diasporan work by Jews who, qua Jews, have no army and can depend only upon God to protect them, tells a story that focuses on the Jews' covenant with God. According to the book, God providentially looks after the Jews and protects them as long as they observe his laws, and although he suspends his protection when they sin, he resumes it when they atone for their sins via suffering and martyrdom.[25] 1 Maccabees, in contrast, written on behalf of a dynasty that undertook to rebel and put an end to foreign domination of Judea, successfully did so, was very impressed with its own accomplishments, and saw them as justifying its claim to rule the newly established Jewish state, tells a story that focuses upon that dynasty and leaves God, by and large, out of the picture. Indeed, beginning with ch. 5 the book hardly mentions him.[26]

More than a century and a half ago Carl Ludwig Wilibald Grimm, a professor of theology in Jena, included, in the introduction to his erudite commentary on 1 Maccabees, a comparison of the book to biblical historiography:

> Since the book's character and the tone of its story are, like its language, simple and similar to those of the Old Testament, the book is usually compared, in this respect, to the Books of Samuel and Kings. Only in one not insignificant point (*Nur in Einem* [sic] *nicht unwesentlichen Puncte*) does it differ from the old Israelite historiography and align itself rather with the post-exilic Books of Ezra and Nehemiah: in contrast with the old theological pragmatism[27] it no longer presents events in a supernatural light and no longer allows God, following a specific plan, to direct events in miraculous ways, moving in and out through the webs of natural causation.[28]

Eighty years later, in contrast, Abraham Kahana, one of the great Hebraists and scholars of Jewish Palestine,[29] wrote of the author of 1 Maccabees, "He wrote the book *in Hebrew* and specifically in the style of the biblical books, with which he was very familiar and whose spirit filled him. On that basis he managed to write a book which, as it were, grows organically out of the Holy Scriptures."[30]

Both commentators agree, of course, about the book's affinity with classical biblical historiography insofar as language and style are concerned; that is obvious. But they differ radically about its agreement with the basic spirit of biblical historiography. For Grimm, a theologian, it was important to note that although biblical historiography assumes that God follows his own plans and purposes – directing events in miraculous ways, moving in and out with sovereignty through the webs of natural causation (what modern scholars term "double causality" – people do what they do for their own reasons, but God makes things happen, or allows things to happen, for his[31]) – 1 Maccabees, after the first few chapters, does not.[32] This is such an important distinction that one can only wonder how far Grimm's tongue was pressed into his cheek when he wrote that it was a "not insignificant point." As for Kahana, in contrast, it is remarkable that a highly literate Zionist writer in the formative age of a Jewish state did not recognize, or refused to acknowledge, the yawning chasm that divides 1 Maccabees from biblical historiography, and instead declared that the author of 1 Maccabees was full of the Bible's spirit. Is there something about the pursuit of a sovereign Jewish state, in the twentieth century CE just as much as in the second century BCE, that makes it difficult for Jews to understand the Bible or accept its message about God's providential involvement in the world?

Be that as it may, we are left with the conclusion that, of the two books, the Judean one imitated the Bible's language and literary style but lacks its central premise and teaching, while the diasporan one, which is linguistically and literarily far removed from the Hebrew Bible, preserves that premise and teaching. 2 Maccabees is not a biblical book, but it is a Jewish book; 1 Maccabees is neither. Rather, 1 Maccabees is a Judean book. Two books are not a broad enough sample to allow the contrast between them to establish that Judaism is a diasporan phenomenon and cannot survive the conditions of a sovereign Jewish state. But they certainly are suggestive.

2

Priestly Judaism vs. Rabbinic Judaism: On Natural Religion and Religion of Choice

About twenty years ago I published two articles on what I considered, and still consider, a significant difference between the ways ancient priests and rabbis typically understood Jewish law: I characterized the former as tending to realism and the latter to nominalism.[1] Since then, three things happened: (1) those studies elicited responses, pro and con, and they engendered additional thought; (2) I spent more than a decade exploring 2 Maccabees, work that spawned, inter alia, the comparison with 1 Maccabees suggested in the preceding chapter – and thus the ground was laid to consider the relation between the Judea/ Diaspora dichotomy and the one between priests and rabbis; (3) I spent three years as a vice-chargé of discipline at my university, and another six as chairman of its committee on instructional rules and procedures, which entailed adjudicating students' appeals of decisions made throughout the university. Both judicial positions gave me intensive hands-on experience with the way law works, especially with the relationship between procedures on the one hand and facts and rights on the other, and that has affected my understanding of ancient legal issues. In what follows, I will (I) set out my understanding of the basic distinction between priestly and rabbinic Judaism; (II) outline a basic difference between the ways members of each camp typically approached Jewish law; (III) respond to the major criticism of my original statements of this thesis, and revise it accordingly; and finally (IV) suggest that, mutatis mutandis, this distinction is basically the same one exemplified, although via historiography rather than law, in the contrast between 1 and 2 Maccabees. The last point implies that although priestly and Pharisaic-rabbinic Judaism both flourished in Judea, and although there is no explicit evidence for Pharisaic Judaism as such in the Diaspora, nevertheless Pharisaic-rabbinic Judaism should be understood in a meaningful way as diasporan.

I. Priestly Judaism and Rabbinic Judaism

As if they were created especially in order to illustrate the sociologists' classic distinction between ascribed status and achieved status,[2] the two most salient types of religious leaders among Jews of the Second Temple period drew their prestige and authority from two very different roots. Priests (*kohanim*) were born; sages (*hakhamim*), later known as rabbis, were made.[3] Then as now, *only* a man whose father was a priest – assumed by tradition to be a descendant of such priests all the way back to Moses' brother Aaron – was a priest, and *all* such men were priests, even if they had no interest in priestly affairs and never participated in them. Sages, in contrast, were made by their learning and charisma. They were sages only to the extent their teachers, peers, disciples, and followers accepted them as sages.

True, Josephus frequently refers to ancient Jewish sects, which he terms "philosophies" (*Ant.* 18.9, 11, 23) or "schools" (*War* 2.118–19), and he consistently divides them into three groups (Pharisees, Sadducees, and Essenes[4]), not two. And Josephus' tripartite division has generally maintained itself in modern discussions of varieties of ancient Judaism.[5] However, the two other major corpora of relevant evidence – the New Testament and rabbinic literature – fail to mention the Essenes but do speak frequently of the contrast between Sadducees and Pharisees.[6] That, already, gives us reason to wonder whether Josephus' triad should really be the basis for our understanding of the divisions among ancient Jews. Another reason to do so is the fact that Josephus loves to present triads, balancing them neatly with one position in the middle and the other two at either pole. Thus, when Josephus tells us in *Ant.*13.171–3 that the Essenes attributed everything to fate, the Pharisees some things, and the Sadducees nothing, we might well wonder whether this is not simply a schematic and congenial construction of the familiar "three little bears" type, similar to his statement in *Life* 32–6 that there were three parties in Tiberias in 66 CE, of which one wanted war, one wanted peace, and one was bent on war but pretended to hesitate.[7]

Be that as it may, even before the discovery of the Dead Sea Scrolls scholars regularly treated the Sadducees and the Pharisees as a pair, with the Essenes being an oddity to be discussed separately.[8] And since the discovery of the Scrolls it has become common to introduce the Essenes into that basic binary discussion by associating them with the Sadducees as part of a larger priestly camp. That happened in three steps: first the Qumran sect was identified as Essene; then the basically priestly nature of the Qumran sect was recognized; and then, since the priestly nature of the Sadducees had long been recognized, and since texts showing some agreement between Qumran law and that of the Sadducees became available, the result was the merging of the Sadducees and Essenes into one camp under the rubric "priestly Judaism" – which was then left in contrast with the Pharisees, the predecessors of rabbinic Judaism.[9] Of course, there were differences between the Essenes and the Sadducees (just as there were differences between the Pharisees and the later rabbis), just as there were tensions among the Essenes themselves,[10] but it seems that at the level of general analysis of trends in ancient Judaism it is very justified, today, to talk about the contrast between priestly Judaism and rabbinic Judaism.

Each step of this chain has, of course, been subject to debate, but they are all, today, quite mainstream. Concerning the first point, suffice it to say that (1) detailed comparisons of the Qumran Scrolls to Josephus' and other ancient evidence on the Essenes continue to support the identification;[11] (2) works that express doubt about the identification generally admit the similarity but urge us to avoid full identification only because there is room to imagine more than one similar group;[12] and (3) recent works that have at times been taken to deny that the Essenes ever existed do not in fact do so.[13] As for the second point – the basically priestly nature of the Qumran sect – it is demonstrated by such considerations as the numerous texts that ascribe authority and prestige to priests qua priests,[14] by texts such as the *Temple Scroll* that evince detailed interest in matters of priestly concern (Temple cult, purities), and by the identity of the sect's enemies ("the Wicked Priest and the last priests of Jerusalem" of cols. 8–12 of *Pesher Habakkuk*[15]); usually one can characterize a group by the enemies it chooses to hate. That is, whatever the differences between the Qumran sect and the Sadducees, the very fact the former took the latter seriously enough to hate them associates them together as having major commonalities.[16] The third point, the priestly nature of the Sadducees (which allows for its alignment alongside the Qumran sect as a type of priestly Judaism), has long been recognized.[17] It is indicated already by the name "Sadducees" (Hebrew: *Zadduqim*), which points to Zadok, the high priest in the days of David and Solomon (2 Sam 15:24–9; 1 Kings 2:26–7), whose descendants supplied the high priests down to the Babylonian exile (see 1 Chr 6:3–15) and then again until the Hasmonean period (see Josephus, *Ant.* 20.234). When anything goes on for that long, it is bound to be thought of as sanctified by tradition (see esp. Ben-Sira 51:12, "Give praise to him who has chosen the sons of Zadok to be priests, for his steadfast love endures forever"[18]), and so it is likely that a group that appeared in the Hasmonean period and called itself "Sadducees" at least began as a party supporting the traditional line of legitimate high priests as opposed to Hasmonean usurpers.[19] Again, at Acts 4:1 Luke associates "the priests, the captain of the temple, and the Sadducees" as working together to try to squash the preaching of the apostles, and at 5:17 he roundly reports that "the high priest and all who were with him, that is, the sect of the Sadducees," persecuted the apostles;[20] similarly, Josephus reports at *Ant.* 20.199–200 that a Sadducean high priest saw to the arrest and execution of Jesus' brother, James. Finally, the priestly nature of the Sadducees is bespoken by some rabbinic texts,[21] and, as we shall see, it is also reflected in some of the legal positions held by the Sadducees, according to rabbinic literature.

Pharisaic Judaism, which was to become rabbinic Judaism, was, in contrast, eminently non-priestly. True, priests could be Pharisees and rabbis.[22] Nevertheless, the typical opposition between the two camps is obvious in a large number of New Testament and rabbinic texts that pit Sadducees and Pharisees one against the other, as also in numerous rabbinic stories that portray competition between sages or rabbis, on the one hand, and priests, on the other – even when the latter are not designated as Sadducees but, rather, as "Boethusians" (see n. 6), "the sons of the high priests," or, simply, "priests."[23] Eventually, as P. Schäfer has shown, this type of antagonism would spawn rabbinic efforts to erase the memory of the priests' former status and roles.[24]

In concluding this section, I offer a pair of sources that illustrates wonderfully the respective orientations of the two camps.[25] These texts are especially significant insofar as essentially they both posit the same law; the difference is in their formulations. Both texts address the following problem: Leviticus 13 unambiguously, and in almost every verse, assigns to the priests the full and exclusive authority to determine whether someone has a skin disease and, if so, to put the person into quarantine. However, the making of such decisions – which today we would entrust to physicians – requires knowledge and training. Obviously, ancient Jews would have taken care to include such training in the education of priests,[26] but it could nevertheless happen that in a given time and place no capable priest was available. Of course, one could allow someone else, who was properly trained, to make the diagnosis and ensuing decisions – but the Bible requires that a priest do that. Both of the following texts offer the same obvious solution: a non-priestly expert (e.g., a physician) makes the decision, but the priest pronounces it, thus allowing it to be, formally, the priest's decision:

Damascus Document **13:4–7**[27]	**Mishnah,** *Nega'im* **3:1**[30]
And if a man has a judgment involving the Torah of skin disease, then the priest shall come and stand in the camp. And the Examiner shall explain to him the interpretation of the Torah; even if he[28] is an imbecile, he shall cause him[29] to be confined, for they [the priests] have the judgment.	All are qualified to inspect leprosy signs, but only a priest may pronounce them unclean or clean. They [that are skilled] say to a priest, "Say, Unclean!" and he shall say "Unclean!," or [they say to him] "Say, Clean!" and he shall say, "Clean!"

For our characterization of the basic difference between the two camps, what is important here is the fact that the *Damascus Document*, a Qumran text, assumes that, as a rule, a priest will handle the whole process, and it also emphasizes that a priest retains his status and prerogatives even in the extreme case in which he is an imbecile. The rabbinic text, in contrast, makes no effort to limit the involvement of non-priestly experts to the exceptional case in which no capable priest is available. Moreover, the Mishnah's portrayal of the priest as repeating automatically whatever he is told makes no effort to maintain any respect for the priest; experience shows it is difficult to read this paragraph of the Mishnah to an audience without engendering smirks or even laughter at the priest's expense. This difference between a text that leans over backward to underline the priest's authority qua priest, even when nothing beyond his pedigree justifies it, and one that irreverently reduces even normal priests to no more than rubber stamps or ventriloquists' dummies, eloquently illustrates the difference between the two camps.

II. Priests or Rabbis: What Difference Did It Make?

Usually, and with obvious logic, the difference between priests and rabbis has been followed to a distinction between attitudes towards the Temple and the sacrificial cult. Given the fact that only priests had access to the inner precincts of the Temple of Jerusalem and only priests officiated at the altar, it makes sense to assume they ascribed great value to the Temple and its cult, which validated their own prestige and authority. Pharisees and rabbis, in contrast, might be expected to prefer types and sites of religion to which they had equal access – such as study and prayer in houses of study and synagogues, or simply homes or town squares.[31] This is, for example, the basis of such classic discussions as Leo Baeck's "The Pharisees," which focused on the distinction between the Sadducean "men of the Temple" and Pharisaic "men of the synagogue."[32]

There is much to be said for this, and certainly, taking a broad view, it is borne out by the fact that Pharisaic/rabbinic Judaism survived the destruction of the Temple while priestly Judaism did not.[33] However, just as in one important way that distinction went too far (positing that Pharisees strove to democratize the priesthood and themselves become priests, whereas in fact it seems they tried instead to marginalize the priests[34]), it seems that in another important way it did not go far enough.

To understand the latter point, we should revert to the basic distinction between priests and rabbis. Priests are born, rabbis are made – first by their own decisions to study and devote themselves to religion, then by the decision of their teachers, peers, disciples, and followers to accept them as rabbis. If we were to imagine a debate between partisans of the two camps, arguing about the relative merits of the two types of leaders, it seems that inevitably the argument would turn, in short order, into one about the relative importance of nature, on the one hand, and human decisions, on the other. Those who take priesthood seriously must take nature seriously and ascribe it authority, just as they deny that any human decision could make a priest into a non-priest or vice versa. Those who take rabbis seriously will probably tend to the opposite position, denying the notion that priestly birth, or anything natural, comes along with legal authority.[35]

That distinction, however, applies to much more than the question of who will enjoy religious authority and access to the sacred. The question whether nature endows anything with legal authority arose not infrequently in other contexts as well – with regard to the calendar, for example. The calendar – so all ancient Jews agreed – had everything to do with nature: years corresponded to the movement of the sun, and months to those of the moon.[36] Nevertheless, rabbinic literature quite openly and even demonstratively invests the rabbis with authority to make decisions that deviate from what nature dictates in two types of cases. Both derive from the fact that a lunar month – the time between the appearance of the first crescent of the moon one month and (after waxing and waning and disappearing) its reappearance the next month – is around 29.5 days. This created two problems:

(1) Since months were assumed to be composed of whole days, a court had to decide every month whether the preceding month had had twenty-nine or thirty days. As detailed in the mishnaic tractate *Rosh Hashanah*, a month was declared to have had only twenty-nine days if witnesses reported to the relevant court – about whose identity priests and "sages" could differ, according to 1:7 – that they had seen the new crescent during the night following the twenty-ninth day; if not, the preceding month was declared to have had thirty days. Obviously, such a procedure could entail errors, for, deliberately or not, led astray by clouds or by some axe to grind, witnesses might mislead the court into making a decision that did not conform to nature.

(2) Given the fact that twelve lunar months total only 354 days, i.e., about eleven days fewer than a solar year, the need arose to intercalate the year every two or three years by adding a thirteenth month to take up the shortfall; if that were not done, holidays (which have fixed dates) would not be coordinated with particular seasons, as they should (Passover is a spring holiday, Tabernacles celebrates the autumn harvest – Exod 23:15–16). The decision, whether or not to intercalate a given year by the addition of a thirteenth month, was made ad hoc, according to the court's assessment, late in the winter, as to whether or not it was necessary to add a month so as to ensure that Passover would come in the spring.[37]

For us, it is very important to note that rabbinic literature is demonstrative about the rabbis' authority to make both type of decisions, insisting in the first case that even erroneous decisions must be obeyed[38] and, in the second case, not only setting down the criteria by which decisions concerning intercalation should be made but also preserving epistles in which prominent sages set down their considerations for making such decisions.[39] In contrast, Qumran literature insists that such adjustment of the calendar is completely illegitimate: the very first column of the *Manual of Discipline* is emphatic that the demand "not to move up their times nor to move back their festivals" is among the basic tenets of the sect. Indeed, it is worthwhile to look closely at the wording of that passage (*Manual of Discipline* 1:11–15):

> (11) ... all those devoting themselves to His truth bringing all their knowledge, and their strength, (12) and their property into the Community of God in order to strengthen their knowledge by the truth of God's statutes, and discipline their strength (13) according to the perfection of His ways, and all their property according to His righteous counsel, and in order not to deviate from any single one (14) of all the commands of God in their times, and in order that they not be early [in] their times, nor late (15) from all their seasons, and in order not to turn aside from His true statutes [by] walking either [to] the right or [to] the left ...[40]

The wording of this passage obviously echoes Deut 17:11 – part of a passage discussing the way difficult cases are to be referred to a supreme court. What is interesting in the present context is that although the biblical text repeatedly underlines, in vv. 9–11, that what the court "says" is to be followed, and so one "may not deviate" from what it "declares," "neither to the right nor to the left" (a point the rabbis used to teach that the court's decisions must be followed, even if objectively wrong[41]), the Qumran text omits the words about the court's declarations. Rather, it insists that the holidays and festivals have fixed times and prohibits changing them – which would amount to deviating from "His true statutes."[42] Indeed, although there are many calendrical texts from Qumran, we hear nothing of any panel or court there making decisions about the calendar.[43]

Differences in approach to the calendar thus supply clear cases of the distinction between priestly Jews who ascribe significance to nature rather than to the human decision-making followed by Pharisaic-rabbinic Jews. Another simple illustration of this type of distinction is supplied by the Mishnah's discussion, in *Ketub.* 13:2, of the case of a married man who went abroad and his neighbour – rightly or wrongly under the impression that the husband had not left his wife sufficient funds – gave the wife money to support herself. Upon the husband's return, the neighbour asked the husband to reimburse the funds, but the husband refused. After all (we may assume the husband argued), there was no promissory note, no letter from him to the neighbour asking him to lend his wife the money, no declaration or documentation that the money was given as a loan, not as a gift. According to the Mishnah, in such a case "the sons of the high priests" found for the neighbour, holding that if the fact that the money had been transferred could be established, the neighbour was entitled to be reimbursed, but Rabban Johanan ben Zakkai, one of the most prestigious spokesmen of Pharisaic Judaism, found for the husband. According to R. Johanan ben Zakkai, the law recognizes no debt in this case. Rather, the neighbour is comparable to a careless person who "left his purse on the antler of a deer" and has only himself to blame if it disappeared.

In my experience, the great majority people who hear this story *feel* for the neighbour. It seems to be *unfair* to deny him his money. After all, the husband should have provided for his wife, and if the neighbour was nice enough to do so in his stead, he should not lose out because he did not first consult with a lawyer about how to do it. However – and this is my point here – what we "feel" is a fact of nature, seated in our hearts or stomachs or thereabout, not in anything verbal; the notion of "unfair" applies to things that we feel are wrong, whether or not they violate any law formulated by some appropriate legislature or lawgiver.[44] Those who ascribe legal authority to such a feeling, those who in our case are willing to view the money as an enforceable debt, ascribe authority to nature – and the Mishnah ascribes that position to "the sons of the high priests." R. Johanan ben Zakkai, in contrast, is willing to tolerate a gap between nature and law, just as much as other rabbis tolerated another variety of the same gap concerning the calendar.

Two examples from the realm of marital law will illustrate the same distinction, and an important ramification of it. The first issue is simple: may a Jew marry more than one wife? The Torah reports that the patriarchs did, a legal text in the Torah takes it for granted (Deut 21:15), it was practised to some extent in antiquity, and ancient rabbinic law allowed it,[45] but a Qumran text, quoting not a legal text but, rather, one that refers to the origin of nature, forbids it roundly. Namely, the *Damascus Document* (4:20–1) condemns non-sectarians as those who "are caught in two respects in whoredom: (a) by marrying two women in their lifetime, although the principle of nature [*yᵉsod habᵉriah*] is 'a male and a female he created them'" (Gen 1:27).[46] This text clearly insists that nature is a source of law: the fact that humanity began with a monogamous couple means that is the way things must be.[47]

The question that creates the other snare that entraps sinners, according to this text, is somewhat more complicated: may a Jew marry his niece? The Torah says not a word against it, we know that it was allowed by ancient Jews,[48] and rabbinic literature indicates that the ancient rabbis even recommended it, apparently as a type of benevolence ("charity begins at home").[49] In contrast, a few lines after it condemns bigamy, the *Damascus Document* condemns uncle-niece marriage too:

> (b) and they marry each one his brother's daughter or sister's daughter. But Moses said, "To your mother's sister you may not draw near, for she is your mother's near relation" [Lev 18:13]. Now the precept of incest is written from the point of view of males, but the same [law] applies to women, so if a brother's daughter uncovers the nakedness of a brother of her father, she is a [forbidden] close relationship.[50]

That is, (1) since Lev 18:13 forbids a man to marry his aunt, who precedes him by one generation and is one space over in the family tree, and (2) since, although the Torah's laws of incest are addressed to men, they apply equally to women, (3) it follows that a woman too may not marry someone who precedes her by one generation and is one space over in the family tree – i.e., her uncle. That amounts to forbidding a man to marry his niece. Q.E.D.

The obvious question here is, what justifies the second stage of that argument? What entitled the Qumran exegete to assert that whatever the Torah forbids for men is forbidden for women too? That is a difficult question, and the only answer I have found is based upon the following comparison. Suppose that, on a certain highway, the Highway Department put up two signs: the first reads "Dangerous Curve – Slow Down!" and the second, a mile or two later, reads "Dangerous Curve." If a driver were to fail to slow down for the second one, reasoning that, had such an obligation existed, the Highway Department should have told him, we would understand that the driver has mistakenly understood a prohibition *pointed out* by the Highway Department as if it were *created* by the Highway Department. The truth is, of course, that the Highway Department did not create, at the first curve, the obligation to slow down. Nature – the combination of velocity and curves – created that obligation, and all the Highway Department did is point that out. An intelligent driver, once having been told that a dangerous curve requires slowing down, should be able to infer such an obligation whenever a dangerous curve is brought to his or her attention. Similarly, if a parent tells a child not to touch the frayed electric cord of a radio and the child touches the frayed cord of a television and gets a shock, the parent should realize the child is perhaps not yet capable of realizing that the prohibition was not created by the warning but only pointed out by it, and that, accordingly, it could and should be expanded by analogy to all similar cases.

But not all rules are part and parcel of nature, and regarding those that are not, but, rather, are created by a legislator's will, one cannot assume that they may and should be expanded by analogy. Some may, and should; some not. If, for example, a driver assumed that the sign "Right Turn Only at Intersection" reflected the nature of intersections, and therefore thought the same rule applied to all intersections, or if a child thought that "Don't you dare watch that film" reflected the nature of films and inferred they were all forbidden, we would, just as certainly as in the case of frayed electrical cords, infer that they lacked understanding.

So, similarly, it seems that, concerning marriage with nieces, the Qumran exegete assumed that the Torah's prohibition of marriage with an aunt was pointing out a prohibition *that exists in nature*: there is something naturally wrong about marriages between people related that closely one to another, the Torah pointed out one instance of such kinship, and intelligent readers should generalize it to all cases that are naturally similar. Pharisees and rabbis who refused to make such a generalization assumed, instead, that the prohibition was *created* by the lawgiver.[51] Thus, this case goes further than the preceding one, about bigamy. If in that case there was no formulated law but the priestly legislator thought natural history created a law and his opponents disagreed, now we see that, even when there is a formulated law, those same opponents refused to expand it by depending upon natural logic.

One final dispute, between priestly law and rabbinic law, will illustrate quite clearly what "existing in nature" means. Are animal bones impure? For example, does touching them make a person impure? The Torah says not a word about this, but it does clearly state that *human* bones are impure (Num 19:16). According to a mishnaic text (m. *Yad.* 4:6), the Sadducees held that if human bones are impure, animal bones are too – and the impurity of animal bones is also bespoken by a Qumran text (*Temple Scroll* 51:4–5) and indicated by an interesting archaeological find from Qumran: rather than simply being discarded after meals, animal bones were buried in jugs, apparently to ensure that people would not inadvertently come into contact with them.[52]

The reasoning m. *Yad.* 4:6 attributes to the Sadducees is very interesting. They claim (so the Mishnah reports) that if human bones are impure, animal bones *must* be impure, a fortiori ("all the more so"). The logic of that position appears to be as follows:

1. Human bones have two characteristics: "humanity" and
   "boneness."
2. The Torah states that human bones are impure (Num 19:16).
3. That impurity must be a natural attribute of one of the human
   bones' two characteristics.
4. Since the impurity is obviously not an attribute of "humanity"
   (for humans are generally not impure), it must be an attribute
   of "boneness."
5. Animal bones have two characteristics: "animalness" and
   "boneness."
6. "Humanity" is superior to "animalness."
7. If, as Num 19:16 shows, even "humanity" is not capable of overcoming the impurity of "boneness," so human bones are impure,
   certainly lowly "animalness" is not capable of overcoming the
   impurity of "boneness" – so animal bones are impure. Q.E.D.

That argument depends entirely on the third step – the assumption that
if something is impure, the impurity must be a natural attribute of it. In
contrast, according to the Mishnah, the Pharisees responded that the
impurity of human bones is attributed to them from without, by the
legislator. Their argument is apparently as follows:[53]

1. Impurity is a legal status, not a natural state.
2. Human bones, accordingly, were not impure until the Torah called
   them impure.
3. The Torah called them impure to serve a certain purpose: to
   prevent people from retaining bones of their loved ones as memen-
   tos. The Torah requires that the dead be buried in their entirety,
   and it was to enforce that requirement that it declared human
   bones impure.
4. Since, in contrast, the Torah ascribes no value to the proper burial
   of dead animals, it did not declare their bones impure.

This argument between priests (the Qumran sectarians and the Sadducees of the Mishnah) and rabbis makes it very clear that, in contrast
to the priestly view that held that the bones *are* impure and the law
pointed that out, the rabbinic view was that it was the *calling* of the
bones "impure" that gave them that status – just as calling a transfer
of money a loan makes it a debt, calling a day the first day of a month
makes it the first day of the month, and calling an aunt a forbidden

spouse makes such a marriage forbidden. Priests would hold that all these legal statuses obtained in nature and the Torah simply informed us about them, just as the Highway Department's signs about dangerous curves.[54] But that distinction is basically the same one with which we began, between priests – who are priests naturally, even if no one knows it, and rabbis – who are rabbis only if they are called rabbis by those entitled to do so: their teachers, peers, disciples, and/ or followers.

III. Refinement of the Theory

As noted in the preface to this chapter, I formulated this basic distinction between priestly and Pharisaic-rabbinic Judaism in two articles published some twenty years ago, and over the years they elicited responses. On one major issue in particular I have realized a need to revise my original formulation of the theory, and I am grateful to those who pushed me to do so.

The revision reflects the recognition that some rabbinic laws seem to assume that law conforms to nature. In my articles, and above, I presented a dichotomy between a priestly view (which I termed "realism") that the legal status of things conforms to the way they are and the law points that out, and a rabbinic view ("nominalism") that the legal status of things and actions was imposed upon them by the divine lawgiver or the relevant human authority (who called them by the appropriate *nomen* – "new moon," "prohibited," "required," "impure," "loan," etc.) and prior to that did not obtain.[55] While my characterization of the priestly point of view has found general acceptance,[56] concerning rabbinic law it must be recognized, as especially Jeffrey L. Rubenstein and Vered Noam have argued, that some points seem to bespeak an attitude of the "realistic" type I characterized as typical of the opposing, priestly, camp.[57]

In response it is important to note, first of all, that both scholars agree that the trend of the development of rabbinic law was from realism towards nominalism. Rubenstein argues that this is simply typical of legal systems that survive for a long time, for legal texts that were once formulated to conform with realities as they were then understood remain obligatory even when reality, or notions of it, have changed.[58] Noam correspondingly observes, concerning the subject upon which she focuses, that onto an earlier view of impurity as "a force of nature" the sages/rabbis (already prior to the destruction of the Second Temple) "layered," as "a secondary stratum of sorts comprising exceptions and 'addenda,' a more subtle halakhic tapestry ... severing it from reality and, in doing so, stripping it of its 'natural' substance."[59] That is a major historical point and, as noted, supports the notion that the general trend of rabbinic law was towards nominalism. Nevertheless, the fact remains that rabbinic literature includes laws that appear to be realistic, and we should therefore examine their implications.

True, some of the cases in which that happens are actually exceptions that prove the rule, for the rabbis explicitly recognize that the realistic law is extra-systemic. Thus, for example, Rubenstein points to the rabbinic expansion of the laws of forbidden marriage, by analogy, to include relations not mentioned by the Torah (t. *Yebam.* 3:1 [ed. Lieberman, 8]; b. *Yebam.* 21a), and he compares that expansion to the way the *Damascus Document* prohibits marriage with nieces because the Bible prohibits marriage with nephews, as we have seen.[60] However, it seems very important to note that while that Qumran text asserts that the law of the Torah applies to both, the rabbinic law expressly calls the non-scriptural prohibitions "secondary" (*sheniyyot*) and says they are "of the words of the scribes" (not of the Torah), explicitly viewing them only as a "fence" meant to keep people far from what the law itself forbids.[61] Similarly, although various rabbinic texts note that at times rabbis or other Jewish officials did or should impose punishments although the usual laws and rules of procedure do not allow it (in exceptional cases in which they did not want to ignore egregious discrepancies between the system's ability to call a person "guilty" and the real truth), they recognize these too as extra-systemic "fences" around the law.[62] I would definitely agree with Rubenstein's conclusion about material of this kind: "Such statements reflect a belief that many unions are wrong, not that the only prohibited relationships are those called wrong by the Torah"[63] – just as I expect that R. Johanan b. Zakkai thought that the returning husband was wrong not to reimburse his nice neighbour (above, 29), that R. Gamaliel was not happy about celebrating the Day of Atonement on the day that was really wrong (below, 36), and that no one was happy about letting a murderer off scot-free because there was only one witness to his crime and the Bible requires two (Deut 17:6; 19:15).[64] But in all such cases the difference concerning the legal status of such notions is not to be overlooked.

Nevertheless, there are cases in which rabbinic law seems to treat Torah laws "realistically." This has been urged particularly with regard to the laws of impurity, which often treat it as a real substance that either is found somewhere or is not, that can or cannot enter a given space or container, or escape from such, etc.[65]

In refining the theory, I have three main points to make. The first is that rabbinic Judaism was a movement made up of numerous individuals, and given the fact that it is obvious that there is room in the world for both positions, it is not surprising that rabbinic literature will give voice, at times, to a tendency that I have identified as characteristic of the rabbis' priestly competitors. But it should also be noted that rabbinic literature, in prominent cases, takes care not to endorse those views. Thus, for three examples:

1. Rubenstein points to b. *Ḥul.* 27b, where "a Galilean traveller" explains that the ways in which different types of animals are to be slaughtered correspond to the matter from which they were created. However that difficult text is to be understood, it is, as Rubenstein notes, very reminiscent of a Qumran text that asserts that locusts are to be killed by fire or water "because this is the law of their nature" (*Damascus Document* 12:14–15)[66] – an evidently realist position. Accordingly, it is true that, as Rubenstein comments with regard to this source, "we find seemingly realist ideas in rabbinic sources."[67] But the fact that we find such a view in rabbinic sources is not the end of the story, for we should also note that if the Talmud ascribes this view to no one more respectable than "a Galilean traveller," it is not at all endorsing it as authoritative; compare, for example, the similarly mnemonic teaching ascribed to "that Galilean" in b. *Shabbat* 88a (the Jews, who have three castes [priests, Levites, Israel], received a three-part Bible on the third day of the third month), which sounds like something the real professionals ascribe to a well-meaning amateur. Indeed, even R. Jose the Galilean is said once to have been rebuked as "you stupid Galilean," a passage preserved at the end of a page that includes several other disdainful statements about uncouth and unlearned Galileans (b. *'Erub.* 53a–b). Although, as Oppenheimer urges, this should not be taken as objective evidence for general ignorance of Torah in the Galilee (any more than the statement at b. *Ned.* 48a that "the Galileans were cantankerous" should be taken as plain fact), it does, as he admits, bespeak the antagonism usual among competing schools.[68] That means, however, that the ascription of a

view to a Galilean may function, in the Babylonian Talmud, as an expression of disdain and should not be assumed to represent a view endorsed by the rabbis who stood behind that work.

2. Similarly, Vered Noam has shown that R. Eliezer b. Hyrcanus, among the early rabbis, often adopted the realistic stance I found to characterize the priests – *a point that has everything to do with the fact that the other rabbis excommunicated him.*[69]

3. The Mishnah presents another early sage, with a remarkably similar name, R. Dosa b. Hyrcanus, as the flag-bearer for the realistic point of view, in each case rejecting it:[70]

    a. He agrees with the "sons of the high priests" that the neighbour's loan to the wife is a collectible debt, but is overruled by R. Johanan b. Zakkai (m. *Ketub.* 13:2).

    b. He angrily rejects a court's calendrical decision that conflicted with the moon's true situation, but is ignored by R. Gamaliel, who insists the court's decision be followed even with the result of observing the Day of Atonement (the holiest day of the Jewish year) on the wrong day (m. *Rosh Hashana* 2:8).

    c. With regard to the sages' decision that Rosh Hashanah (New Year's Day, 1 Tishri) be celebrated for two days rather than the biblical one day (Lev 23:24) because of a doubt as to which day was meant,[71] he insists that the liturgy must be formulated conditionally so as to reflect the point that only one day was "really" Rosh Hashanah – "but the sages [who did not want to recognize a difference between the days' legal status and their real status, DRS] did not agree with him" (m. *'Erub.* 3:9).

    d. Within the context of a rule that pieces of food must be of a certain minimum size to be susceptible to impurity, Dosa insists that if several pieces are each too small, then the fact that we use the same name for them (e.g., "raisins") does not unify them and make them large enough to become impure (m. *'Ed.* 3:2) – in contrast to the sages' majority view that holds, with explicit nominalism, that "this is the rule: all things that have the same name [*shem*] are [in the aggregate] impure; but if they have two names – they are pure" (3:1).[72]

    e. With regard to the law of Deut 14:25 that allows tithes to be redeemed by "money," Dosa insists that one may use an unminted planchet (slug; Hebrew *'asimon*, from the Greek "unlabelled"; m. *'Ed.* 3:2). That is because the metal has its value despite the fact that it has not been minted; minting amounts only to labelling the coin as having the value that it has. Given the fact that probably not many people had such slugs, this is a particularly demonstrative expression of Dosa's point of view that things are, legally, what they *are*, not what they are called – but the Mishnah (ibid.) goes on to report that the sages rejected his view.

Thus, although the Mishnah and other early rabbinic sources recognize that such an attitude towards law exists, it frequently takes the opportunity to reject it, insisting instead that it is the giving of the *nomen* ("loan," "new moon," "new year," "impure," "shekel") that has legal significance.

That, however, does not account for the fact that mainstream rabbinic laws of impurity seem to assume a significant measure of realism, as noted above.[73] That is undeniable. What I would point out, however, as my second response, is that it appears to be impossible to decide whether the authors of such texts thought impurity was a real substance or, rather, thought of it as merely notional but the notion compared it to a real substance.

To clarify this point, let us consider an explicit case of nominalism: the diasporan Jewish author of the *Letter of Aristeas*, writing late in the second century BCE,[74] has a wise spokesman of Judaism first say that although with regard to their physical nature (*pros ton physikon*) all types of meat are composed similarly (§143), Moses nevertheless *called* (*prosonomasas*, lit. "named") the meat of predatory birds "impure" in order to teach us the moral lesson that we should not live by preying upon others (§§145–50). That is, every time we deliberately pass up the opportunity to eat a predatory bird, it serves to remind us to avoid such behaviour. That statement, however, although it focuses upon moral teaching, has its practical implication: it requires us to abstain from eating certain types of birds and, accordingly, will have entailed, no less than would the alternate assumption that such birds *really are* impure, rules about the details of such abstinence (such as, precisely which birds are forbidden? what about crossbreeds? mixtures? minimal quantities?). I see no reason to think that anyone examining those rules, or observing Jews who followed them, would have been able to discern which premise they adopted; indeed, some Jews may have followed one, some the other. Once the basic decision was taken that something is to be treated as if it is impure, it will have been treated the way impure things are treated, and the presence or absence of the words "as if" in the legislator's or practitioner's mind will not have practical importance or visible implications.

In this context, I would briefly discuss three laws discussed by M. Silberg in a 1962 article that was the original impetus for the application of "realism" and "nominalism" to the study of Jewish law.[75] Silberg pointed to three legal principles that can be understood as if they correspond to natural facts: (1) a promissory note may not be reused, even if all the data in it are still true (so, for example, if I lent my neighbour money in the morning and he gave me an IOU noting the date of the loan, then at noon he repaid the debt and received the IOU in return but later that same day again borrowed the same sum, a new IOU must be written); (2) one cannot transfer ownership of something (e.g., next year's harvest) that does not yet exist; (3) one prohibition cannot be added to another.[76] Silberg shows that these rules can be understood as treating the legalities involved as if they were physical: (1) the promissory note expended its force on the first loan; (2) the legal act of transferring ownership has nothing to take hold of if the object of the transfer does not exist; (3) the second prohibition cannot take hold of its object because the first one covers it and prevents the second from being able to reach it and take hold of it.

Indeed, one can understand these laws that way. However, there is nothing that requires us to do so.[77] The first two can be understood as procedural rules meant to ensure the good regulation of society, and the third as a matter of legal formalism:

1. The rule that a promissory note may not be reused serves to reinforce the demand that it be destroyed upon repayment of the debt, a demand that is important because failure to destroy the note upon repayment might engender confusion or even allow for fraud.
2. One may not transfer property that does not yet exist, because that would engender too great a risk of lack of clarity as to what was transferred, and/or risk of lack of full commitment by one party or both.
3. Prohibitions apply only to things or actions that are otherwise allowed.[78]

But even if we choose to understand these rules on the basis of the physical analogy, as Silberg suggested, I see nothing that indicates whether those who formulated these rules thought the processes are physical rather than that we may consider them as if they were physical.

Similarly – turning to some laws discussed by Noam – I see no way to decide whether the law (m. *Ohal.* 3:6) that says that impurity cannot pass through something smaller than a square handbreadth assumes and teaches that impurity cannot come in pieces smaller than that. As Noam puts that view, this law offers "a highly 'tangible' conception of impurity: It moves through space, seeks to disseminate itself, and is blocked by barriers."[79] Perhaps, however, this law assumes and teaches only that impurity is to be treated *as if* it had such characteristics. Indeed, perhaps some readers of the Mishnah, and observers of its law, took it one way while others took it the other way.

In fact, the nominalistic understanding of m. *Ohal.* 3:6 might well seem likelier, for the very same paragraph of the Mishnah opens with another law that is usually, and reasonably, interpreted nominalistically: it rules that if there is a corpse in a room with several closed doors, all that is in their doorways is defiled, but if one (of sufficient size) is open, that "saves" all the other doorways from impurity. True, taken alone that could be interpreted realistically, as if the presumption were that impurity flows out the easiest way available. However, the phrasing of this law in 3:6 echoes that of a paragraph a few chapters later (m. *Ohal.* 7:3), and there we read explicitly that not only the opening of a door, but even the *decision* to do so, "saves" the other doorways from impurity. It is quite reasonable to assume that that principle governs 3:6 too,[80] but that principle is a prime example of what Noam means when she writes that "the laws governing openings also contain distinctly nominalist elements that sever impurity from any form of 'natural existence' and make it contingent on human subjectivity."[81] But if the first law of 3:6 thus views impurity nominalistically, it is difficult (if not impossible) to imagine that the very next clause of the Mishnah, which seems to imply that impurity is real and does not come in pieces of less than a square handbreadth, assumes and teaches the opposite view.

However, although traditional commentators of course take such a harmonistic approach, importing intention from 7:3 into their interpretation of 3:6,[82] critical readers might urge us to abstain from such harmonization – and taken as is, 3:6 could be read realistically as meaning that impurity flows out the easiest way possible but not through aper-

tures smaller than a handbreadth. If we go that route, I can respond
only that, as stated above, I see no way to determine whether, taken by
themselves, passages such as 3:6 should be understood as stating something about the nature of impurity or, rather, only that the law treats it
as if it that were its nature. Above, in section II, therefore, my attempt to
distinguish between the two approaches focused on the preceding
stage: the identification of what is treated as impure or forbidden and
what is not. At that stage we can identify the willingness to use natural
analogy (such as from forbidden aunts to uncles, or from impure human bones to animal bones) as clear evidence of the realistic approach,
and refusal to use it as evidence of nominalism. But once the decision
has been taken that something is impure, rabbinic discussions and laws
that assume that impurity behaves *as if it were real* do not at all prove
that they thought it *is real*.

Nevertheless, it is clear that realism is to be found in rabbinic law.
Thus, for example,

- although the rabbis are at times willing to assume that even a person's body will change in response to the rabbis' decision to intercalate a year,[83] and
- although they were willing to relate to people who were condemned to execution as if they were already dead (see n. 99), and
- although they were willing to assert that a widow's remarriage, on
  the basis of a court's decision that her first husband was dead, was
  valid, even if the first husband reappeared,

they would nevertheless not go so far, in the last-named case, as to consider the first husband dead and thus allow the woman to remain with
her second husband.[84]

Accordingly, my third and main response to such criticism is to refine
my theory by admitting that, as originally presented, it overstepped the
database upon which it built.[85] Namely, I built the theory on the basis
of cases in which ancient Pharisees/rabbis argued with Sadducees/
priests, and in those cases the positions taken seem indeed to be as I
portrayed them.[86] But that need not govern rabbis when, especially in
generations after the destruction of the Temple and the disappearance
of priestly sects, they were discussing things among themselves. That is,
in understanding the differences between priests and Pharisees/rabbis
we should first focus upon them when they were competing with one

another. That was a situation that demanded they be consistent, one in which any willingness to depart from their own principles would have constituted a dangerous (or face-losing) concession to the competition.[87] Later, with no priestly parties to pounce upon them whenever they allowed some realism into their system, the rabbis could do so when it seemed warranted, or formulate things as if they had.[88]

Arguments a fortiori: Natural Arguments

An examination of rabbinic willingness to build law on the basis of arguments a fortiori will, allow us to see this point quite clearly. Arguments a fortiori ("all the more so," what the rabbis called *qal vahomer* – "light and heavy"), such as the one the Sadducees applied concerning animal bones and human bones (above, 31–2), are very natural: we use them intuitively all the time (e.g., if I don't have enough money for my own bus fare, then it is all the more clear that I do not have enough for my companion too, but if I have enough for the two of us, it is all the more clear that I will have enough if my companion decides to walk), without any need to learn about them or even to realize we are using them. And they are very cogent arguments: if the facts as to what is "light" and what is "heavy" and as to what the relevant status of one of them is, the conclusion about the relevant status of the other follows ineluctably.

It is, therefore, no accident that the central rabbinic text that focuses on the Pharisees versus the Sadducees, a string of disputes recorded in the Mishnah, *Yadayyim* 4:6–7, focuses on the use of arguments a fortiori, and the central point made by this text is that such arguments are characteristic of the Sadducees but are not, in fact, a valid basis for law.[89] Those paragraphs of the Mishnah, as also the next one (§8, where the villain is not a Sadducee but, rather, a "Galilean heretic"[90]), deal with a hodgepodge of legal issues, ranging from rules concerning the impurity of scrolls, bones, and liquids, to legal responsibility for damage done by one's animal or slave, to rules applying to the date-formulas in legal documents, and it is obvious that what gives the text its unity is the fact that in each case the Pharisees out-argue their opponents. That is, this text's main agenda is to underline the superiority of its Pharisaic heroes as opposed to their "heretical" opponents – which makes it a central text for our quest, especially since, as we shall now see, the texts all turn on the question of the authority of arguments a fortiori:

1. Complaining about the Pharisees' rule that contact with a biblical
    scroll makes one's hands impure, the Sadducees claim that since
    contact with a profane book like Homer does not impart impu-
    rity, it should be clear, all the more so, that contact with a holy
    book does not. To that the Pharisees respond that to deem profane
    Homer pure and the holy Bible impure is no more illogical than
    to deem the bones of lowly donkeys pure but those of humans
    impure – but since that is the law, our conclusion must be that
    arguments a fortiori have no legal force.[91]
2. Similarly, when the Sadducees then complain against the Pharisaic
    rule that if someone pours water from a pitcher into a pail that has
    (for example) a human bone in it the water in the connecting
    stream and therefore the water left in the pitcher remains pure,[92]
    the Pharisees respond that if that were really a problem then the
    Sadducees should be upset all the more about something similar
    but much worse: an aqueduct that goes through a cemetery.[93] The
    fact that the Sadducees are willing to use water from that aque-
    duct[94] means either that their complaint about the pitcher is
    baseless or else that they themselves are not consistent in their
    adherence to their own principle – that arguments a fortiori are
    valid sources of law.
3. Then the Sadducees complain that the Pharisees impose legal
    responsibility upon the owner for damage done by one's animal,
    but not for damage done by one's slave. In this case too they
    phrase their complaint as an argument a fortiori: since the owner
    has more obligations concerning his slave than concerning his
    animal, if he has any particular obligation concerning his animal
    he should have it all the more concerning his slave. (To understand
    the logic of this complaint, imagine what we would think about
    people who are scrupulous about vaccinating their dogs but not
    their children.) The Pharisees respond by offering a reason why the
    law for slaves should differ in this case from the law for animals[95]
    – thus showing, again, that arguments a fortiori are not a reliable
    basis for law.
4. Finally, in §8 a "Galilean heretic" complains that the Pharisees
    write the name of the temporal ruler alongside the name of God.
    Apparently the reference is to the use in religious documents
    (such as bills of divorce), which mention God, of dating formulae
    that mention the ruler – a juxtaposition the Galilean considered
    disrespectful.[96] The Pharisees' response is that if that were really

a problem, the Galilean should see a much worse problem in the Torah itself, for Exod 5:2 juxtaposes "Pharaoh" and "God" and even mentions Pharaoh first. That is, as in the case of pitchers and aqueducts, the point is either that the heretic's original complaint was baseless or else that he is not a consistent adherent of what is supposed to be *his* basic principle: that arguments a fortiori are a valid basis for law.

This basic difference between the two camps is also made very clear in another argument reported elsewhere in the Mishnah, one that concerns the punishment of "conspiring witnesses," who, according to Deuteronomy, are to suffer, tit for tat, the punishment they attempted to bring wrongly upon their victim:

> If a malicious witness rises against any man to accuse him of wrongdoing, then both parties to the dispute shall appear before the Lord, before the priests and the judges who are in office in those days; the judges shall inquire diligently, and if the witness is a false witness and has accused his brother falsely, then you shall do to him as he had meant to do to his brother . . . it shall be life for life, eye for eye, tooth for tooth, hand for hand, foot for foot. (Deut 19:16–21, RSV)

This means, for example, that since conviction for murder entails the death penalty, witnesses who falsely testified that someone was guilty of murder are themselves to be executed. What is important for us in the present context is the fact that although the law in Deuteronomy clearly contemplates such punishment of false witnesses if the fact they were perjurious was already discovered under cross-examination, prior to any verdict, the Mishnah (*Mak.* 1:6) reports that both the Pharisees and the Sadducees departed from that position: the Pharisees limited the punishment to cases in which the falsity of the testimony was discovered only after the innocent victim was *convicted*, while the Sadducees went even further and limited the punishment to cases in which the innocent victim was in fact *executed*.

The Mishnah gives no indication of the reasons for the differing opinions, apart from some obviously unserious citation of biblical prooftexts,[97] but it seems that we can easily understand the two positions according to the basic approaches we have posited for the two groups. The Sadducean position[98] seems to have been that in prescribing the death penalty for a witness who falsely testified that someone had perpetrated a capital crime, the Torah treats the witness as a murderer (who, as it were, used the court as his weapon) – and we cannot treat someone as a murderer if the intended victim is still alive. The Pharisees, in contrast, held that when a court decides to convict someone and condemns him to death, its proclamation has effect (just as would its erroneous proclamation about a new moon), and so whoever misled the judges into making that decision committed an act tantamount to murder and is deserving of the punishment for murder.[99]

Here, first of all, we see that the Sadducees' position is that the intended victim's natural state (the fact that he is alive) governs the matter, while the Pharisees insist that what the court said about him does; that is the basic distinction we have posited. Moreover, the discussion of this law in the Babylonian Talmud (b. *Mak.* 5b) rubs the point in by quoting an otherwise unknown tannaitic sage named Beribbi, who declares that "if they did not kill they are to be killed, but if they did kill they are not to be killed," i.e., the "conspiring witnesses" are to be killed *only* if their victim was convicted but not yet executed; if he was already executed, the conspiring witnesses are not to be killed. That, of course, contradicts all natural logic. Indeed, as the Talmud itself reports (ibid.), Beribbi's father angrily responded that what he said is ridiculous, excluded by a natural argument a fortiori: if we execute witnesses who only tried to bring about the death of an innocent victim, but failed, certainly we should execute those who succeeded! To that Beribbi responded, however, "Our rabbi, you yourself have taught us that arguments based upon logic alone are not a sufficient basis for imposing punishment!" That is, since the Bible speaks of the case of *unsuccessful* conspiring witnesses, those are the only ones we may punish, however logical it admittedly would be to punish successful ones all the more. And Beribbi's position is defended in the ensuing discussion and accepted as authoritative.

Thus, if the series of arguments in m. *Yad.* 4 shows that the rabbis focused on use or non-use of arguments a fortiori as distinguishing Sadducees from Pharisees, the present case shows how far the Pharisees and rabbis were willing to go, in the context of conflict with the Sadducees, to deny the validity of the Sadducees' basic principle: the Sadducees hold, in consonance with nature, that no murder occurred if the victim is still alive, but the Pharisees are willing to punish, as murderers, those who wrongly made a court declare that someone should be executed. More generally, if the Sadducees hold that natural logic requires us to go beyond the language of the Torah and execute conspiring witnesses who not only gave false testimony but actually succeeded in having their victim killed, the sages, at least after Beribbi perfected their position, insist that natural logic – even the most cogent type of natural logic, an argument a fortiori – is not a sufficient basis for such a law. To impose a punishment we need an express statement by the lawgiver.[100]

The fact that later, and/or when among themselves and not competing with others, the ancient rabbis too were often willing to employ arguments a fortiori, using them to generate laws and even punishments,[101] just as they were willing to expand other biblical laws on the basis of the assumption that the Bible pointed out only one example of something broader,[102] does not undermine the basic point that when they wanted to be consistent, in the face of competitors, they eschewed such arguments. It is to the arguments between the two camps that we should look when attempting to discover the essential differences between them.

IV. Priests vs. Rabbis ≈ Judea vs. Diaspora

Finally, I note that, whatever the numerous differences, at a very basic level the distinction we have set out in this chapter is the same as the one we set out in the preceding chapter. Indeed, already a century and a half ago, Abraham Geiger argued that 1 Maccabees was a Sadducean work and 2 Maccabees a Pharisaic one.[103] True, such a specific characterization of those two works cannot be maintained, if only because neither work mentions either sect, and we have in fact no evidence for Pharisees and Sadducees in the Diaspora.[104] Nevertheless, it seems to me that Geiger had a basic intuition that points in the correct direction.

Let us begin by noting again, at the level of historical events, that priestly Judaism disappeared with the destruction of the Second Temple, while rabbinic Judaism survived that catastrophe and eventually flourished outside of Judea – first in the Galilee[105] and later in Iraq, where the Babylonian Talmud, "the Talmud" par excellence, the basic document of rabbinic Judaism, was produced. That seems to indicate some affinity between rabbinic Judaism and the Diaspora.

Moreover, if above I characterized 1 Maccabees as bespeaking a providence-less world, one in which what you see is all there is, while the world of 2 Maccabees is one governed by divine providence, now I would add that, according to Josephus, the Sadducees denied the existence of divine providence while the Pharisees posited it;[106] the latter point is, of course, amply borne out by rabbinic literature.[107] And the same goes for 2 Maccabees' emphatic insistence upon the belief in resurrection,[108] which is not mentioned in 1 Maccabees but – according to Josephus, the New Testament, and rabbinic literature – the Pharisees/rabbis affirmed it while the Sadducees denied it.[109] Beyond that basic agreement, I also note that the notion that the soul can exist apart from the body, which is more or less a prerequisite for belief in resurrection (which supposes that the soul waits somewhere for reunification with the body[110]), posits for the individual what Diaspora does for the nation.

Again, when discussing 2 Maccabees I underlined that it evinces relatively little interest in the Temple cult *per se*, preferring to view it only as an aspect of the Jewish polis. Although rabbinic literature, for its part, had little interest in the polis (which was so important for Hellenistic Jews[111]), it too put together a way of understanding the Jewish world in which the Temple/priesthood/sacrifice complex was secondary to what was important for them: Torah.[112]

Most basically, however, note that while it was natural to be Judean in Judea, it was unnatural to be Jewish abroad. Just as the natural default for a baby born in Judea was to be Judean, the natural default for a baby born in Egypt was to be an Egyptian, for one born in Cyprus, a Cypriot, and for one born in Rome, a Roman. To raise a child as Judean in Judea required – just as raising a child to be a priest – only noninterference with nature; to raise a child as a Jew in Egypt, Cyprus, Rome, or anywhere else in the Hellenistic-Roman Diaspora, entailed – just as with raising a child to be a rabbi – the *decision* to do something that was not at all natural. If, as proposed in parts II–III of this chapter, the basic distinction between the priestly attitude towards Jewish law and the rabbinic one is between the notion that law conforms to nature and the notion that law bespeaks *decisions*, the basic orientation of rabbinic Judaism conforms to that of Diaspora Judaism. Indeed, if the first figure of the Second Temple period mentioned in the rabbinic chain of transmission in ch. 1 of Mishnah *Avot* was a high priest, it is not surprising that the next one had a Greek name, Antigonus, and that the major figure in that chain, Hillel,[113] is said to have moved to Palestine from Babylonia and to have been characterized by an apothegm that demonstratively undercuts the importance of priestly birth.[114]

For many rabbinic Jews that seems, finally, to have reflected a yet more basic stance, according to which they were not really "at home" anywhere in the world. Rather, they taught that, as opposed to "the peoples of the world" ('*ummot ha'olam* – the typical name for Gentiles in rabbinic literature[115]) – note: not "the *other* peoples of this world"! – for Jews this world is only an anteroom. The R. Jacob quoted in m. *Avot* 4:16–17, whose statements focus upon the next world, including "This world is like a vestibule before the world to come: prepare thyself in the vestibule that thou mayest enter into the banqueting hall" (trans. Danby), was, in the late second century CE,[116] not only a contemporary but also a soulmate of the author of the *Epistle to Diognetus*, who wrote of true Christians, in ch. 6, that they are "in the world but not of the world." For rabbinic Jews of that type, which was so widespread, and which, for Jews as for Christians, went so well together with an appreciation of the willingness to depart from this world via martyrdom,[117] life anywhere in this world is life in the Diaspora.

3

From Joseph b. Mattathias, a Priest of Judea, to Flavius Josephus, a Jew of Rome

In 1965 Prof. Louis H. Feldman published, in the Loeb Classical Library, a volume titled Josephus: Jewish Antiquities, Books XVIII–XX. *In 2000, in contrast, he published, in the new FJTC series, a volume titled* Flavius Josephus: Judean Antiquities 1–4, *and since then more volumes of the "Judean Antiquities" have also appeared in that series. Nevertheless, as Steve Mason, the editor of that series, has noted, the question of "Jews" vs. "Judeans" is one about which different translators have different tendencies.[1] I am currently working on the last volume in that series, which is to include* Ant. 18–20 *– the books Feldman handled in his 1965 volume. The present chapter is part of my deliberation as to whether to go on using "Jewish" and "Jews," as Feldman once did, rather than "Judean," which has been adopted in his and other volumes of the new series.*

Joseph b. Mattathias was born in Jerusalem in 37 CE.[2] Born as he was into Jerusalem at the height of its glory, "the most illustrious city of the entire East" (as it was termed by a somewhat older contemporary of Josephus[3]), we may well understand that he took being a Jerusalemite very seriously.[4] And the Temple was at the centre of the city – the renovated Temple, as Herod had grandiosely expanded and renewed it. Moreover, Josephus was a priest; he proudly alludes to his priestly descent in every one of his books, pointing to it to explain his expertise in things Jewish.[5] Thus, we may well understand that being a Judean, a Jerusalemite, and a priest were three concentric and interlocked elements in the identity with which Josephus grew up – and which would, to some degree, remain with him his entire life. The continued lustre of the Jerusalem priesthood in his eyes, despite the destruction of

Jerusalem and the Temple, is well illustrated, for example, by the fact that as late as the nineties Josephus, in paraphrasing the biblical story of Uzzah who died because he touched the Ark of the Covenant in his effort to save it from falling off a wagon (2 Sam 6:6–7//1 Chr 13:9–10), noted – as the Bible does not – that Uzzah was not a priest (*Ant.* 7.81–2). Evidently, Josephus thought that fact sufficiently justified Uzzah's fate: even the best and most holy intentions cannot allow a non-priest to touch what only priests may touch.[6]

However, Josephus lived the latter half of his life in very different circumstances. If until 67 he was a Jerusalemite priest, eventually ending that part of his life by serving as military commander of the Galilee on behalf of the Jerusalemite rebel government, which was out to reclaim, as the Hasmoneans long before, Judean sovereignty, from the summer of 67 on he was in the Roman camp – first as an honoured prisoner, then as freedman and client and, to a significant extent, as the house historian of the Flavian emperors.[7] Moreover, beginning in 71, when he accompanied Titus to Rome, and until his death no earlier than the mid-nineties, he resided in the imperial capital.[8] Thus he was transformed, at midlife, from a Jerusalemite into a diasporan Jew. Indeed, the destruction of the Temple and Jerusalem in the summer of 70 meant that not only erstwhile Jerusalemites, but all Jews, had to deal with the loss of a geographical centre. That compounded the new diasporan situation in which Josephus found himself.

In this chapter we shall see that this polar turnabout in Josephus' circumstances, as those of the Jews at large, engendered some salient changes in his views as represented by his writings. To understand this, we must realize that of Josephus' four works, the *War* was written in the seventies, while the other three – his twenty-volume *Antiquities* and two smaller works: *Against Apion* and *Vita* (an autobiography of sorts) – were concluded and published fifteen to twenty years later, in the nineties.[9] This allows us to compare his later writings to his earlier ones and draw inferences about changes in his orientation and values. In particular, the fact that the *War* first covers the period from 175 BCE to the outbreak of the war in 66 CE before opening its detailed account of the war, while *Antiquities* covers the entire period from Creation until 66 CE, means that Josephus wrote about the period from 175 BCE to 66 in both of his works. That allows us to make various fairly specific comparisons of his parallel narratives.

Let us begin with a comparison of Josephus' narratives concerning some troublemakers who appeared in Judea in the fifties of the first century, in the days of the Roman governor Felix. The violence associ-

ated with these events was part of the deterioration that led, a decade
later, to the outbreak of the rebellion. In both works, the passage we
cite follows immediately upon Josephus' report about "brigands"
called Sicarii ("dagger-men") – Jewish terrorists who murdered their
enemies.[10]

War 2.258–65, trans. Thackeray, JLCL[11]	*Antiquities* 20.167–72, trans. DRS
(a) (258) Besides these [Sicarii] there arose another body of villains, with purer hands but more impious intentions, who no less than the assassins ruined the peace of the city. (259) Deceivers and impostors, under the pretence of divine inspiration fostering **revolutionary** changes, they persuaded the multitude to act like madmen, and led them out into the desert under the belief that God would there give them tokens of **deliverance [= "freedom"]**. (260) Against them Felix, regarding this as but the **preliminary to insurrection**, sent a body of cavalry and heavy-armed infantry, and put a large number to the sword.	**(a)** (167) The doings of the brigands filled the city with such unholiness, and the impostors and the deceiving men wheedled the multitude to follow them out to the desert. (168) For, they said, they would show them clear signs and wonders that would happen through the providence of God. Many were convinced and paid the penalty for their lack of sense, for Felix had them arrested and punished.
(b) (261) A still worse blow was dealt at the Jews by the Egyptian false prophet. A charlatan, who had gained for himself the reputation of a prophet, this man appeared in the country, collected a following of about thirty thousand dupes, (262) and led them by a circuitous route from the desert to the mount called the mount of Olives. From there he	**(b)** (169) But at that time there came to Jerusalem from Egypt someone who said he was a prophet, and he urged the urban masses of Jerusalem [to go with him] to the mountain that was called "of Olives," which is located vis-à-vis the city at a distance of five furlongs. (170) For, he said, he wanted to show them from there

proposed to **force an entrance into Jerusalem and, after overpowering the Roman garrison,** to set himself up as tyrant of the people, employing those who poured in with him as his bodyguard. (263) His attack was anticipated by Felix, who went to meet him with the Roman heavy infantry, the whole population joining him in the defence. The outcome of the ensuing engagement was that the Egyptian escaped with a few of his followers; most of his force were killed or taken prisoners; the remainder dispersed and stealthily escaped to their several homes.

that **at his command the walls of Jerusalem would fall,** through which he promised them entry [into the city]. (171) But Felix, when he learnt of these things, ordered his soldiers to take up their weapons and with many cavalrymen and infantry stormed out of Jerusalem and attacked the Egyptian's men, killing four hundred of them and taking two hundred alive. (172) The Egyptian himself escaped from the battle and disappeared.

(c) (264) No sooner were these disorders reduced than the inflammation, as in a sick man's body, broke out again in another quarter. The **impostors and brigands, banding together,** incited numbers to revolt, exhorting them to assert their independence, and threatening to kill any who submitted to Roman domination and forcibly to suppress those who voluntarily accepted servitude. (265) Distributing themselves in companies throughout the country, they looted the houses of the wealthy, murdered their owners, and set the villages on fire.

(c) But again **the brigands** incited the people to war against Rome, calling upon them not to be subject to them and setting afire and looting the villages of those who did not obey them.

Turning first to the stories in parts (a) and (b), we may note that readers of both accounts no doubt understand that Josephus condemns the Jewish troublemakers he describes, and justifies the Roman governor who moved against them. However, readers of the accounts in *Antiquities* may well wonder why, indeed, Felix moved against them. What was criminal or threatening about promising signs and wonders in the desert? Or why should anyone have taken seriously the Egyptian prophet's threat that by his order the walls of Jerusalem would fall? Why didn't Felix just ignore such kooks or laugh at them? Why send out the troops against them?

Of course, we could easily imagine answers to these questions. Mass movements can always get out of hand, and maybe these did, or maybe the governor was wise to nip them in the bud. But my point is that Josephus did not offer any such answer in *Antiquities* – although he had done so, quite explicitly, in his earlier account. There, in the *War*, he had reported that the promised signs and wonders were "tokens of freedom," and that Felix had, quite properly, taken them to be "the preliminary to insurrection." The Roman governor, Josephus thus reports, was faced by a rebellious movement and dealt with it as required by his mandate – the maintenance of Roman law and order in Judea. Similarly, concerning the Egyptian prophet, according to the account in *War* he did not promise merely to order the walls of Jerusalem to fall. Rather, he planned to storm the city with thousands of armed followers and overpower the Roman garrison. All that, which Josephus reported quite clearly in the seventies, is absent from his account in the nineties. Why?

When we attempt to formulate our problem with the accounts in *Antiquities* more generally, we realize that the issue is the relationship between religion and state: in his versions of these stories in *Antiquities*, Josephus does not tell us *why* the representative of the Roman state found it necessary to move against virtuosi of the Jewish religion. His account in *War* clearly told about people claiming special status in the Jewish religion who were making promises that directly threatened the Roman state, but in *Antiquities* he avoided that connection as best as possible.

That this was Josephus' concern is shown strikingly by section (c) as well. For here, where *War* reports that "the brigands" (= the Sicarii of whom Josephus wrote just prior to our stories) joined forces with "the impostors" (= the false prophets of parts a and b) in terrorizing those who abstained from rebellion, in *Antiquities* only the "brigands" engaged in such terrorism. Here too, in other words, Josephus has leaned over backwards to distance Jewish religious figures from anti-state violence. This is especially striking insofar as the Jewish religious figures of whom Josephus is speaking in these paragraphs are ones that he despises; nevertheless, in the *Antiquities* he is concerned to distance them from affairs of state. In the *War*, in contrast, written within a few years of his arrival in Rome, he still spoke freely about the involvement of religious figures in affairs of state, namely, about their role in fomenting rebellion.

Historically speaking, we should probably learn from both accounts. Josephus' account in *War* tells us more or less how things really were in pre-war Judea: Jews rebelled against Rome on the basis of their belief that God was on their side and would support their efforts to put an end to Roman rule in his land. Josephus' account in *Antiquities*, in contrast, shows us that Josephus had, by the nineties, learned the basic rule of Jewish existence in the Diaspora: the Romans could and did tolerate and even protect the Jewish religion and its institutions, but only on condition that they made no claims in the state's sphere and therefore posed no threat to Roman rule. Around the same time Gospel writers were making sure to report that Jesus taught his followers to render unto Caesar what belongs to Caesar and unto God only what is God's (Matthew 22:21 and parallels),[12] Josephus was making sure, in his own way, as best he could, that adherence to the Jewish religion would not be suspected of entailing any opposition to Roman rule – or, indeed, of any involvement in affairs of state qua Jews. While he could not, of course, deny that there had been Jewish rebels against Rome, he could do his best, even at the price of crippling a story by omitting integral elements, to argue that those Jewish rebels were only bad apples who did not even pretend to represent the Jewish religion. Had he had two terms available, he probably would have preferred to call them Judeans, not Jews.

Note that already in the *War* Josephus had taken a somewhat similar approach, denying the religious legitimacy of the rebels. Thus, for two examples:

(1) When he reports, and complains, at *War* 2.118, that a rebel leader, Judas of Galilee (also known from Acts 5:37), founded a new philosophy, he immediately goes on to claim, in the next paragraph, that in fact the Jews have only three legitimate philosophies – a point he then fleshes out at great length.[13]

(2) When rebels suspend sacrifices on behalf of Rome, a move that Josephus decries as the actual beginning of the rebellion (*War* 2.409), Josephus is careful to parade at *War* 2.411 the Jews' dignitaries, the high priests, and the Pharisees – i.e., the true spokesmen of Judaism, supplemented in §417 by the priestly experts about tradition, who all declare that the decision is a violation of Jewish law and tradition.[14]

However, in both cases Josephus admitted that the rebels claimed a religious program, no matter how much he denied its validity. In the *Antiquities*, in contrast, he went one step further and tried to deny the rebels even that basic claim.

In that comparison of Josephus' early and late versions of events in the days of Felix – which indicates that in *Antiquities* Josephus was, in effect, distinguishing between Judeans (who sought to free Judea from Roman rule) and Jews (adherents of Judaism) – we saw Josephus, in *Antiquities*, recounting episodes, in which religion and state were originally linked, in a way that kept them separate. Here are two more comparisons in which he does the same in a more subtle way:

War 2, trans. Thackeray, JLCL	*Antiquities* 18, trans. DRS
(170) those [Jews] on the spot were in consternation, considering their laws to have been trampled under foot, as those laws permit **no image to be erected in the city** …	(55) Pilate … intended to abrogate Judaic rules by bringing into the city busts of Caesar, which were attached to the military standards, although the law **forbids us to make images**.
(195) When the Jews appealed to their law and the custom of their ancestors, and pleaded that **it was forbidden[15] to place an image of God, much more of a man, not only in their sanctuary but even in any unconsecrated spot through-out the country,** Petronius replied …	(264) "If," they said, "you in any case are determined to bring and erect the statue, do what has been decided upon only after first doing away with us. For we cannot stand by and watch as things happen that are **forbidden to us** by the dignity of our lawgiver and our forefathers, who adopted these [rules] as per-taining to virtue."

These stories are very similar. The top pair are Josephus' parallel reports of the Jews' reaction when Pontius Pilate (Roman governor of Judea in the twenties and thirties) introduced busts of Tiberius Caesar into Jerusalem; the bottom pair are from his parallel reports of the Jews' appeal in 40 CE to Publius Petronius, the Roman governor of Syria, in their attempt to dissuade him from executing Gaius Caligula's order to erect a statue in the Temple of Jerusalem. What is interesting, in the present context, is that in both cases *War* presents their appeal in a way that makes sense and addresses the issue at hand: the Jews say that the introduction of such icons into a Jewish place – the city of Jerusalem, the Temple, or even the entire Jewish country – is totally unacceptable. In the *Antiquities*, in contrast, Josephus' reports make less sense, for in both cases he has the Jews saying nothing about any place and insisting, instead, that *they* are not permitted to make such icons – which was totally a non-issue. Nobody was asking the Jews to make any icons. Of course, one might suspect that Josephus was simply expressing himself carelessly. But the fact is that in the *War* he clearly stated that the problem was a Roman violation of the sanctity of a Jewish place, but that notion does not appear in the parallels in *Antiquities*. In *Antiquities* it is replaced by the notion that Jewish law applies to Jews, not to a place.

In yet another case of this type, with reference to an episode towards the end of Herod's reign, Josephus goes yet another step further. As Josephus reports, Herod had hung a golden eagle – symbol of Rome? or of his own rule?[16] – over one of the gates of the Temple, and that aroused Jewish opposition, whether merely because of the apparent violation of the Second Commandment or also in opposition to his rule and/or Rome's.

War 1, trans. DRS	*Antiquities* 17, trans. DRS
(648) There were in the city two wise men who were thought to be especially accurate concerning the ancestral [customs], and for that reason they enjoyed the highest respect in the entire nation.	(149) There were … the most learned of the Jews and unparalleled expounders of the ancestral laws, men who were loved by the people due to the education (which they supplied) the youth …
(650) For it is [they said] not allowed that there be **in the Temple** any image or bust or any work representing a living being.	(151) For the law forbids those who choose to live according to it [even] to imagine setting up images or to prepare dedications of any living beings.

Here too, as in the appeals to Pontius Pilate and Petronius, the Jews of *War* clearly state that the prohibition of images applies to a particular *place*, the Temple. *Antiquities*, in contrast, just as inappropriately as in those other cases, insists only that Jews may not fashion or erect iconic images. Thus, here too Josephus of the *Antiquities* is now formulating things in a way congenial to a Jew of the Diaspora, whose religious world does not privilege any particular place.

In this case, moreover, Josephus is amazingly explicit about something else of importance to us. If in the *War* (§650) Josephus explains that such images are "not allowed" – using a Greek term, *athemitos*, that, as a standard dictionary of first-century Greek puts it, "refers primarily not to what is forbidden by ordinance but to violation of tradition or common recognition of what is seemly or proper"[17] – in the *Antiquities* he says images are forbidden by Jewish law *"to those who choose to live according to it."* That is, where *War* takes the prohibition for granted as simply natural in a certain country ("that's simply not the way things are done here!"), *Antiquities* candidly admits the artificial and volitional nature of Jewish law. If Judeans observed Judean law in Judea because when in Judea it is natural to do like the Judeans, Jews observe Jewish law in the Diaspora by choice, although it is anything but natural to do so there. As we have seen in the preceding chapter, however, in the contrast of nature vs. decision the priests adhered to the former, the rabbis to the latter, and we suggested aligning the former with Judea and the latter with the Diaspora. Now, precisely in accordance with that scheme, I suggest that comparison of early Josephus to late Josephus exhibits, often enough (if not with total consistency), his transformation from priestly Judean (indeed Jerusalemite!) into a Jew of the Diaspora, whose Judaism is, basically, of the same type as Pharisaic/rabbinic religion.[18]

A few other differences between *War* and *Antiquities* point in the same direction:

1. *Providence*: As especially H. W. Attridge has underlined, divine providence is the major theme of the *Antiquities*. Josephus writes that large in his preface to the work,[19] and he reverts to the theme throughout his work.[20] The theme is much less developed in *War* – to such an extent that when it does appear at the very end of the work (7.453), as if it were the bottom line of the story, that is a reason, along with others, to think that final book of *War* is a secondary addition to the work.[21] As we have seen, however (above, 18–19), providence is very active in the diasporan 2 Maccabees as well, as it is for the Pharisees, although not for 1 Maccabees and the Sadducees.

2. *Reference to God*: More generally, *Antiquities* brings God into the
   story much more than *War* does. Note, for some examples, the
   following cases, that speak for themselves:

War, trans. Thackeray, JLCL	*Antiquities*, trans. Marcus (JLCL) and DRS
1.287: [Herod's brother, Joseph] was on the point of leaving the fortress, when on the very night fixed for his departure, rain fell in abundance …	14.390–1: But he was stopped by a rain which **God** sent in the night, for once the cisterns were filled with water, they no longer needed to flee.
1.340–41: That evening, Herod, having dismissed his companions to refresh themselves after their fatigues, went himself just as he was, yet hot from the fight, to take a bath, like any common soldier, for only a single slave attended him. Before he entered the bath-house one of the enemy ran out in front of him, sword in hand…	14.462: At this point the king ordered his soldiers to have their supper, as it was late, and he himself, being tired out, went into a room to bathe. And here he came into very great danger, but **by the providence of God** escaped it.
1.656: From this time onwards Herod's malady began to spread to his whole body and his sufferings took a variety of forms.	17.168: But Herod's illness became more and more acute, for **God** was afflicting just punishment upon him for his lawless deeds.
2.183: Yielding to these solicitations, Herod presented himself to Gaius, who punished him for his cupidity by banishing him to Spain.	18.255: Gaius, angered by her high spirit, exiled her together with Herod and gave her possessions to Agrippa. This, then, was the judgment with which **God** punished Herodias for her envy of her brother, and Herod for having listened to frivolous womanly words.

Here too, Josephus of the *Antiquities* expresses himself like the author
of 2 Maccabees.

3. *From cult to law*: Finally, in the *Antiquities* we find Josephus – even Josephus, the priest of Jerusalem – doing what the rabbis learned to do: transform the sacrificial cult from something of independent value into simply one complex of observances that are part of Jewish law. To understand this point I will first adduce a rabbinic text promised in the preceding chapter (ch. 2, n. 112), then compare the move it demonstrates to one we can identify in Josephus' parallel narratives. The rabbinic text is quite a central one: the first chapter of the mishnaic tractate *Avot* ("Fathers"), which is something of a curriculum vitae of rabbinic Judaism – a chronological list of the generations of the sages who transmitted the Torah from its very first stage, at Mt. Sinai, to the rabbis' own present in the first or second century CE. Here, after the opening paragraph covers some of the mythic figures (Moses, Joshua, the prophets, and the "men of the Great Synagogue," whoever they were), §2 gets down to earth by naming an individual authority of the early second century BCE: Simon the Just. As all subsequent sages in the list, Simon is characterized by an apothegm associated with him:

> Simon the Just received [the tradition] from them. He used to say: The world stands on three things: on the Torah, on the Temple-service,[22] and on works of loving-kindness.

That is, the Jewish world is comparable to a three-legged stool: it rests upon three pillars, of which one is anchored in the Temple of Jerusalem. That means, however, that the cult is not part of the Torah, but rather parallel to it and of separate and comparable status. That was quite appropriate for Simon the Just, for (as readers of rabbinic literature knew) he was a high priest,[23] so the Temple was the institution that he personified and that endowed him with his authority and prestige. After the report about Simon the Just, however, the chapter goes on first to jar us by listing, as the next link in the chain, a sage who (as noted at the end of ch. 2) bore the eminently Greek name Antigonus. Then, after naming the next bearers of that tradition over eight or nine generations, and after including an apothegm that already undercuts the importance of priesthood in favour of Torah (see ch. 2, n. 114), the list concludes, and the chapter ends, with the entry for a sage whose apothegm contradicts Simon's frontally: "Simon ben Gamaliel said: The world stands/exists[24] on three things: on justice, truth, and peace" (m. *Avot* 1:18).

Now it is very probable that Simon ben Gamaliel (who is explicitly termed a Pharisee in §191 of Josephus' *Life*, just as his father is so identified in Acts 5:34),[25] knew of Simon the Just's statement, and it is absolutely certain that whoever edited this chapter of the Mishnah did. If he chose to bracket the chapter with these two parallel but conflicting statements, he is making a strong statement about what has changed, trumpeting the difference between the pillars of the world in the eyes of a high priest and in the eyes of a Pharisaic sage, and in effect saying, in light of all the generations that separated them, "We've come a long way." That is the opening declaration of this central document of rabbinic Judaism.

I pointed to this statement of *Avot* 1 in order to prepare the way for the following comparison between another two parallel narratives by Josephus. This time the context is Pompey's siege of the Temple in 63 BCE:

War 1, trans. Thackeray, JLCL	*Antiquities* 14, trans. Marcus, JLCL[26]
(146) Indeed, the labours of the Romans would have been endless, had not Pompey taken advantage of the seventh day of the week, on which the Jews, from **religious scruples** [*thrēskeia*], refrain from all manual work …	(63) But if it were not our ancestral custom to rest on the Sabbath day, the earthworks would not have been finished, because the Jews would have prevented this; for the **Law** [*nomos*] **permits** us to defend ourselves against those who begin a battle and strike us, but it does not allow us to fight against an enemy that does anything else.
(148) Just as if the city had been wrapt in profound peace, the daily sacrifices, the expiations and all the ceremonies of **worship** [*thrēskeia*] were scrupulously performed to the honor of God. And at the very hour when the temple was taken, when . they were being massacred about the altar, they never desisted from the **religious rites** [*thrēskeia*] for the day.	(65) And one may get an idea of the extreme piety which we show toward God **and of our strict observance of the laws** [*nomoi*] from the fact that during the siege the priests were not hindered from performing any of the sacred ceremonies through fear, but twice a day, in the morning and at the ninth hour, they performed the sacred ceremonies at the altar, and did not omit any of

	the sacrifices even when some difficulty arose because of the attacks.
(150) Then it was that many of the priests, seeing the enemy advancing sword in hand, calmly continued their sacred ministrations, and were butchered in the act of pouring libations and burning incense; putting the **worship** [*therapeia*] of the Deity above their own preservation.	(67) … nor were they compelled, either by fear for their lives or by the great number of those already slain, to run away, but thought it better to endure whatever they might have to suffer there beside the altars than to neglect any of the **ordinances** [*nomima*].[27]

Here it is very clear, according to *War*, that the Jews take the Temple cult very seriously,[28] and that cult is, with one minor exception,[29] not treated as a part of the larger category of law. In the *Antiquities*, in contrast, while the real contents remain the same, Josephus' formulations repeatedly make it clear that the Jews' devotion to their cult derived from, and was meant to exemplify, their devotion to observance of their law (*nomos, nomoi, nomima*). The way this functioned on the two fronts that would have concerned Josephus is easily understood. First, externally: it would not at all have been functional, in Rome of the nineties, to tell the Romans that the Jews take their sacrificial cult very seriously, even to the point of willingness to die rather than abandon it. The Jews had no sacrificial cult when Josephus was writing, and such statements would at best have amounted to emphasizing just how severe a blow the Romans had dealt the Jews – which would not contribute to fostering conciliation and peaceful coexistence. But to tell the Romans that Jews take their religious law seriously was quite functional, for it would encourage them to allow the Jews to observe whatever elements of it were available to them in their post-70 and diasporan circumstances. Similarly, internally, it would have been just as dysfunctional for Jews to tell their children, or each other, how important the Temple cult was, so important that priests were willing to die rather than abandon it – but quite useful to present that as an instance of a more general willingness of Jews to die rather than abandon Jewish law.

Thus, the way Josephus transformed priests who were willing to be killed rather than abandon the Temple cult into observers of Jewish law willing to be killed rather than violate it[30] is another eloquent example of the way a Judean priest had become a Jew of the Roman Diaspora.[31]

If we now return to the practical question raised in the preface to this chapter, how to translate *Ioudaios* in Josephus, I conclude that it seems appropriate to employ "Judean," with its geographical reference, in the *War*, but "Jew" (and the adjective "Jewish") in the *Antiquities*. True, inevitably there are some passages where the other translation is more appropriate in each work.[32] Nevertheless, in general such a differential usage would properly call attention to the fact that, for Josephus, being a *Ioudaios* had changed, in the latter half of his life, from something that had to do mainly with what it is natural to do in Judea and a type of worship that existed there alone. If in the seventies he was still expressing himself according to the notions of the Judean context in which he grew up, after twenty years abroad and of life in the context of a diasporan Jewish community (although we know nothing of his relation to it), he was now expressing himself differently. Being a *Ioudaios* had turned, for Josephus, from something that related to a particular place, and to what was normally done there, into something that related more to a universal and providential God and to the observance, by choice rather than due to the nature of things, of his laws. In our parlance, accordingly, Josephus had transformed, however inconsistently, from a Judean into a Jew.

4

Judeans, Jews, and the Era
That Disappeared:
On Heinrich Graetz's Evolving Treatment
of the Second Temple Period

The first three chapters of this book discussed examples of a basic dichotomy in ancient Judaism – one between Jews whose identity qua Jews centred on Judea, on the one hand, and Jews whose identity qua Jews centred on no place but, instead, on a more universal Judaism, on the other. In conformance with usual English usage, I term the former "Judeans" and the latter "Jews." That dichotomy raises, for writers in languages such as English that supply two such terms, the question as to whether it is appropriate or useful to use only one of them when writing about the Second Temple period merely because the language of the main sources for the period, Greek, has only one such term, Ioudaios. Ch. 3 addressed one particular case of that issue, that of Josephus, and ended with the suggestion that we render his Ioudaios as "Judean" in his earlier work and "Jew" in the later ones, in recognition of a change in his own self-understanding and emphases in the decades between them. In the present chapter, I would like to expose and analyse some of the difficulties encountered by the foremost Jewish historian of the nineteenth century: Heinrich Graetz (1817–1891), due to his assumption that one should use either "Jews" or "Judeans" but not both.[1]

Heinrich Graetz loved the Second Temple period, as is clearly shown by the fact that of all eleven volumes of his *Geschichte der Juden*, only vol. III, on the 230 years from the death of Judas Maccabaeus in 160 BCE to the destruction of the Second Temple in 70 CE, went into four editions in his own lifetime – of which the second, third, and fourth were each, in turn, billed not only as *"verbesserte"* ("improved") but also as *"stark vermehrte"* ("greatly enlarged"). Indeed, already in 1856, in the first edition of vol. III, he declared that this period is the most interesting, most attractive, and richest of all Jewish history.[2] His continued and ever-growing interest in the period is reflected well in the volume's growth: if the first edition filled 572 pages, and the second (1863) was more or less the same size, by the third (1878) it had grown to 692 pages, and the fourth (1888) and fifth (1905/1906), which needed to be published in two half-volumes, ran to 858 pages, including thirty appendices in small print.[3] It seems that at least part of the fascination derived from the variety and tensions in the period that, as we shall see, in the end caused Graetz both to change his nomenclature for those to whose history the volume was dedicated and to abandon his attempt to define what he called the *Grundcharakter* ("basic character") of this period of their history.

I. From Jews to Judeans

The last nine volumes of Graetz's *Geschichte der Juden*, vols. III–XI, which are devoted to the two millennia from the death of Judas Maccabaeus (160 BCE) to the nineteenth century, appeared before the first two, which cover the biblical period down to the death of Judas Maccabaeus. The last nine appeared by 1870; the first two appeared between 1874 and 1876, after Graetz's visit to Palestine in 1872, which he considered an essential part of his preparation for writing them.[4] As is usual in multi-volume works such as this one, each volume has two title pages: the one on the left gives the name of the full series along with the number of the particular volume, while the main title page, on the right, announces the title of the particular volume. Our point of departure for the present study is the fact that although the entire series is titled *Geschichte der Juden von den ältesten Zeiten bis auf die Gegenwart* ("History of the Jews from the Earliest Times until the Present"), and the individual titles of the nine post-biblical volumes all begin, accordingly, with the words *Geschichte der Juden* and then go on to specify the period in question (e.g., vol. XI, the last in the series, is *Geschichte der Juden vom Beginn der Mendelssohn'schen Zeit [1750] bis in die neueste Zeit [1848]* – "History of the Jews from the Beginning of the Mendelssohnian Period [1750] until the Most Recent Time [1848]"), the individual titles of the first two volumes, on the biblical period down to the death of Judas Maccabaeus, open instead with the words *Geschichte der Israeliten* ("History of the Israelites").[5]

True, at first glance one might think this is not very surprising, given the widespread usage that distinguishes that way between biblical "Israel" and "Israelites," on the one hand, and post-biblical "Judea,"

"Jews," and "Judaism," on the other. Thus, for example, Julius Wellhausen opened his famous history of biblical religion by stating that its goal is to ascertain whether Mosaic law "is the starting point for the history of ancient Israel, or not rather for that of Judaism, *i.e.*, of the religious communion which survived the destruction of the nation by the Assyrians and Chaldæans."[6] The same nomenclature was preserved in the numerous editions of Wellhausen's fuller *Israelitische und jüdische Geschichte*, which began to appear in 1894 and it is still popular today, as we may illustrate by referring to the title and preface of a standard English-language work published a century after Wellhausen's *Prolegomena.*[7]

However, further examination of Graetz's work indicates that the matter is not so simple, and that this detail of nomenclature – Israelites/ Jews – is only the tip of an iceberg that links up with the one that interests us in this volume (Judeans/Jews) and has everything to do with the nature of Jewish history in the Second Temple period. In what follows, I will first set out two more surprising points about the first two volumes of Graetz's *Geschichte*, and then add another four surprises about the next one, vol. III, which, as noted, takes the story from 160 BCE down to the destruction of the Second Temple in 70 CE. All six points reflect a major change in Graetz's presentation of the ancient part of his story. After presenting that change, I will consider, in section II, what may have caused it.

1. *Israeliten vs. Juden*. Graetz's use of *Israeliten* in vols. I–II of his *Geschichte* is quite surprising in light of the fact that earlier, in his programmatic 1846 essay on the structure of Jewish history (henceforth *Structure*), he had condemned such distinctions.[8] In that essay, in which he used *Juden* in speaking of the biblical period as well,[9] he expressed anger that not only non-Jewish historians but also Jews as well, most notably I. M. Jost, used such differential nomenclature that denies the unity of Jewish history.[10]
2. *The second era disappeared, part 1: The Babylonian exile does not open a new era*. According to Graetz's 1846 *Structure*, which was something of a blueprint for his multi-volume *Geschichte*, all of Jewish history is divided into three neat eras (*Zeiträume*), of which the second begins with the return from Babylonia in the sixth century BCE and the third with the destruction of the Second Temple in 70 CE. In accordance with this scheme, p. 1 of vol. I of the *Geschichte* prominently announces that it opens the first era (*Erster Zeitraum.*

Die vorexilische biblische Zeit. Erste Epoche: Die Anfänge ["First Era,
the Pre-Exilic Biblical Period; First Epoch: The Beginnings"]), and
p. 1 of vol. IV just as prominently announces that it opens the third
era (*dritter Zeitraum*), which covers the period from 70 CE until the
nineteenth century; see below, 67, 69. But there is no such major
break with the return from Babylonia. Rather, that episode comes
at no special juncture: as the third chapter of the second half-
volume of vol. II, beginning on its p. 77. And even the Babylonian
exile itself is no such major break: although it opens that half-
volume, the table of contents there lists it only as the second epoch
of the first era, not as the beginning of the second era.

When I first noticed this I suspected it was merely a *lapsus calami*
and that Graetz meant to label vol. II/2, which opens with the
Babylonian exile, as devoted to the second *era* (*Zeitraum*), as in his
Structure,[11] not to the second epoch of the first era. However, that
foundered on four considerations: (1) as noted, it is treated only in
the middle of vol. II, as befits a secondary epoch, rather than at the
beginning of a volume, as would befit an era; (2) the same organization and terminology reappear uncorrected in the second edition
of this volume (1902); (3) there is no introduction (*Einleitung*) to
vol. II/2, which we should have expected were it the beginning of
an era (contrast the introductions in vols. I and IV, each of which
opens an era); and (4) in the 1875 preface to the first edition of vol.
II[12] Graetz declares that the distinction between the two half-volumes is not arbitrary, since the Babylonian exile, which separates
the two, is a watershed just as much as was the death of Solomon
and the concomitant split of the monarchy – with which his vol.
II opened. But that episode, important as it was, was a watershed
within the first era, so his comparisons clearly show that, for Graetz,
the post-exilic period (= first half of the Second Temple period)
covered in vol. II/2 was still part of the biblical era – the first era.
Thus, when he referred to the post-exilic period only as an epoch,
which is a part of an era, he meant what he said. But that is very
different from what he had posited in his *Structure* in 1846.

3. *The second era disappeared, part 2: The period covered by vol. III is
not part of any era.* If, as we just saw, vol. II/2 does not open the
second era, but vol. IV already opens the third, it should follow
that vol. III opens the second era. However, this is not the case. In
very striking contrast to the opening headings on p. 1 of vol. I and
p. 1 of vol. IV, which proudly announce the eras opened in those

volumes, in the first three editions of vol. III (1856, 1863, 1878) the first page simply opens its story *in medias res* (see p. 68): the only heading on the page, apart from "Erstes Kapitel," reads "Jonathan" (the name of the Hasmonean who took over after the death of Judas, which is where the volume begins). And even the fancier heading that was added to the first page of vol. III beginning with the fourth edition (1888) offers only "Die makkabäische und herodianische Epoche" ("The Maccabean and Herodian Epoch")[13] it is termed an epoch, not an era (*Zeitraum*), and there is no attempt to number it as part of any larger scheme. This too, as noted, departs completely from his practice in vol. I and IV, each of which opens an era.

4. *The end of the introduction to vol. III, and the end of vol. III, do not correspond to the volume's contents.* Vol. III deals with the period from the death of Judas in 160 BCE to the destruction of the Second Temple in 70 CE. That fits the statement in the volume's introduction that the period to which it is devoted is "about two centuries" long.[14] However, the end of the same introduction goes on to say that "the era" (*der Zeitraum*) "divides, if we allow it to begin with the return from the Babylonian Exile, into three parts or periods,"[15] of which, as Graetz then details, the first ends with the death of Judas. That is, Graetz simply ignores the awkward point that only the second and third of these periods (160–105 BCE; 105 BCE – 70 CE) are in fact discussed in vol. III. Similarly, in the very last line of the volume, Graetz compares Jeremiah, at the end of the first *Zeitraum*, to Josephus, at the end of the second *Zeitraum* – as if the first era ended in the sixth century BCE and not in the second century BCE.[16] These bits of legerdemain in the volume's introduction and last lines are remnants of the scheme Graetz originally proposed in his *Structure* and call attention to the gap between that 1846 proposal and the way Graetz eventually handled the period when he composed his *Geschichte*.

5. *The introduction's vicissitudes.* Graetz's difficulties with vol. III are also reflected in his repeated rewriting of its introduction (*Einleitung*), in the first three editions, pulling it (as we shall see) this way and that in his attempt to define the period as one that is mainly religious, despite its political aspects. Even more strikingly, they are reflected in the fact that by the fourth edition (1888) he gave up and omitted the introduction altogether.

6. *From "Juden" to "Judäer."* In the mid-1870s, at around the same time that Graetz was preparing his vols I–II, on the biblical period, he

Erster Zeitraum.
Die vorexilische biblische Zeit.

Erste Epoche
Die Anfänge.

Erstes Kapitel.
Die Vorgeschichte.

Die Urbewohner Kanaans. Die riesigen Anakiten und Rephaim. Die Phönicier. Die Ansprüche der Israeliten auf Kanaan. Die Erzväter. Die Erblehre. Wanderung nach Aegypten. Stammkrystallisation. Licht- und Schattenseiten der Aegypter. Mose. Ahron und Mirjam. Prophetenthum. Mose's Berufung zur Befreiung. Widerstand. Auszug aus Aegypten. Durchgang durch den See des rothen Meeres. Wanderung durch die Wüste. Gesetzgebung auf einem der Berge des Sinaï. Das Zehnwort. Rückfall. Zugeständnisse. Kreuz- und Querzüge. Siege über Völkerschaften jenseits des Jordan. Anfänge der hebräischen Poesie. Mose's Tod.

An einem sonnigen Frühlingstage drangen Hirtenstämme über den Jordan in ein Ländchen ein, das nur als ein etwas ausgedehnter Küstenstrich des Mittelmeeres gelten kann, in das Land Kanaan, später Palästina genannt. Dieser Uebergang über den Jordan und der Einzug in dieses Ländchen sollte für das Menschengeschlecht ein höchst wichtiger Akt werden; der Boden, auf welchem diese Hirtenstämme festen Fuß faßten, wurde dadurch für eine geraume Zeit hindurch ein wichtiger Schauplatz, das Land erhielt durch die nachhaltigen Folgen dieses ersten Schrittes den Namen: das heilige Land. Die entfernten Völker hatten keine Ahnung davon, daß der Einzug hebräischer oder israelitischer Stämme in das Land Kanaan auch für sie von so folgenreicher Bedeutung werden sollte, und selbst die dort angesiedelten Stämme waren weit davon entfernt, in diesem Einzuge ein für sie verhängnißvolles Ereigniß zu erblicken. Es war damals eine sich öfter wiederholende Erscheinung, daß Hirtenstämme mit ihren Heerden in dieses Land kamen, da es weidenreich war. Es war eine Zeit der vielleicht

Gräß. Geschichte der Juden. I.   1

Pp. 67–9: Page 1 of the first editions of the first, third, and fourth volumes of Graetz, *Geschichte*. The first and fourth volumes open with explicit and graphically emphatic proclamations of the fact that they open, respectively, the first and third eras (*Zeiträume*) of Jewish history, but the third, which should open the second era, opens only with the laconic local headings: "First Chapter" and "Jonathan."

Erſtes Kapitel.

—

Jonathan.

Zuſtand des Volkes nach dem Tode des Helden Juda Makkabi. Parteiſtellung;
Aſſidäer, Helleniſten, Hasmonäer. Jonathan, Führer der Hasmonäer. Sein
Guerillaskrieg gegen Bakchides. Tod des Hohenprieſters Alkimos. Waffen-
ſtillſtand zwiſchen Jonathan und Bakchides. Jonathan ſtillſchweigend Ober-
haupt des Volkes. Der Streit um den ſyriſchen Thron bringt Jonathan die
Hoheprieſterwürde ein. Seine vorſichtige Politik, ſeine Gefangenſchaft und
ſein Tod.

160—143 v. Ch.

Juda der Makkabäer hatte ſeine Heldenſeele auf dem Schlacht-
felde von Eleaſa ausgehaucht. Die ganze Nation legte Trauer an[1]),
ſie war in der That eine Waiſe geworden. Die hochanſchwellende
Begeiſterung, welche waffenſcheue Dulder zu Helden umgeſchaffen,
jene kühnen Thaten zu Wege gebracht, die man unter dem Namen „die
makkabäiſchen“ bezeichnet, und feurige Sänger geweckt, welche „dem
Herrn neue Lieder ſangen“, konnte, eben weil ſie eine aufgeregte
Seelenſtimmung war, nicht allzulange andauern; es mußte natur-
gemäß allmälig eine Abſpannung eintreten. Ein ganzes Volk, das
auf Ackerbau und Viehzucht angewieſen iſt, kann nicht Jahr aus Jahr
ein unter den Waffen bleiben, um ſich den ſtets erneuernden feindlichen
Heereszügen entgegenzuwerfen. Die Erhebung des jüdiſchen Volkes
zur Abwehr der tyranniſchen Zumuthung, die theuerſten geiſtigen
Güter, Religion und Sitte mit einem fremden, verhaßten Weſen um-
zutauſchen, hatte den Landmann vom Pfluge, den Geſetzeslehrer von
ſeinem heiligen Buche, den Prieſter vom Altar, den Frommen von

---

[1]) I. Makkabäerbuch 9. 18—21.

Dritter Zeitraum der jüdischen Geschichte.

Vom Untergange des jüdischen Staates bis auf die neueste Zeit. Von 70 bis 1850 nach der üblichen Zeitrechnung.

Einleitung.

Dieses ist der achtzehnhundertjährige Zeitraum der Zerstreuung, der beispiellosen Leiden, des ununterbrochenen Märtyrerthums, wie es einzig in der Weltgeschichte vorkommt, aber auch der geistigen Regsamkeit, der rastlosen Gedankenarbeit, der unermüdlichen For= schung. Wollte man von diesem Zeitraume ein deutliches ent= sprechendes Bild entwerfen, so könnte man ihn nur unter einem Doppelbilde darstellen. Von der einen Seite das geknechtete Ju= däa mit dem Wanderstabe in der Hand, dem Pilgerbündel auf dem Rücken, mit verdüsterten, zum Himmel gerichteten Zügen, um= geben von Kerkerwänden, Marterwerkzeugen und dem glühenden Eisen der Brandmarkung; auf der andern Seite dieselbe Figur mit dem Ernste des Denkers auf der lichten Stirn, mit der For= schermiene in den verklärten Gesichtszügen, in einer Studierstube,

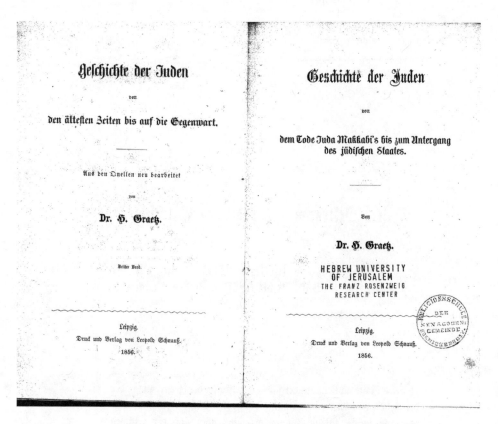

Pp. 70–1: Title pages of the first and third editions
of the third volume of Graetz's *Geschichte*. *Juden* became *Judäer*.

was also working on the third edition of vol. III, on the latter half of the Second Temple period. That third edition, which appeared in 1878, was not only "improved and greatly enlarged," as announced on its title page. It also included a very striking change in nomenclature: if the first two editions of vol. III had defined it as dealing with the history of the *Jews* (*Juden*) from the death of Judas Maccabaeus until the downfall of the *Jewish* state (*des jüdischen Staates*), the third edition offers the history of the *Judeans* (*Judäer*) until the downfall of the *Judean* state (*des judäischen Staates*). Correspondingly, throughout the entire volume this edition employs

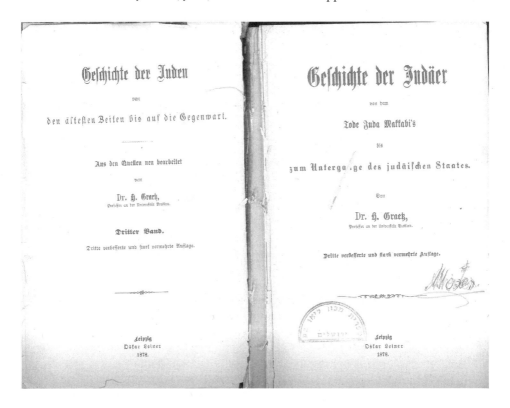

Judäer and *judäisch* instead of *Juden* and *jüdisch*. Contrary to all expectations, Graetz does not address the change or explain it in the preface to the volume, nor have I found anything of the kind anywhere else in his writings.

These six points all suggest that Graetz found it quite difficult to define the Second Temple period and its place in the full sweep of Jewish history. He dealt with this difficulty in two ways in which he departed from his plan as set forth in his programmatic *Structure of Jewish History*. On the negative side, he gave up on the distinction between the biblical era and the Second Temple era, instead attaching the first half of the Second Temple period to the biblical era and abstaining from identifying the second half of the Second Temple period as part of any era; he gave up on the attempt to number the Second Temple period in his general hierarchical scheme; and eventually he gave up on the attempt to provide the volume with an introduction characterizing the period it discusses. Positively, instead of *Juden*, upon which he had insisted in the *Structure*, he introduced two new names for the people described in vols. I–III: *Israeliten* in the first two volumes and *Judäer* in the third.

It is easy to understand the negative changes: they simply bespeak the fact that Graetz was no longer certain how to characterize the period and, accordingly, how to locate it in his grand scheme. But what about the positive changes? His adoption of *Israeliten* needs no special explanation, for basically it amounted to doing what was usual in scholarship of the biblical period (see n. 6). But what led him to move from *Juden* to *Judäer*?

As noted above, so far I have not discovered any published or archival source in which Graetz explained this change. Indeed, it seems not to have attracted much attention;[17] even Markus Brann, Graetz's disciple, bibliographer, and editor of the posthumous editions of his works, appears not to have noticed it.[18] However, the fact is that Graetz made the change, in the title of the volume and throughout its hundreds of pages, and so we must infer that he viewed it as important. Why?

II. Why the Change from *Jews* to *Judeans*?

I can think of four possible reasons that may have led Graetz, beginning with the 1878 edition of vol. III, to switch from *Juden* to *Judäer* in his account of the latter half of the Second Temple period:

1. *Response to accusation that the Jews had their own national aspirations.* A year after this edition appeared, Graetz was at the centre of what came to be known as the *Berliner Antisemitismusstreit* ("Berlin Anti-Semitism Controversy"): Prof. Heinrich von Treitschke's November 1879 attack on the Jews in general, and on Graetz in particular, set off a massive public debate that, given von Treitschke's prestige, made – as was recognized from the outset – a major contribution to legitimizing anti-Semitism.[19] This debate, best remembered for von Treitschke's complaint about the way Germany was being inundated by waves of young "trouser-selling" Polish Jews, and for the slogan popularized by von Treitschke, "Die Juden sind unser Unglück" ("The Jews are our misfortune"), which a half century later would grace the first page of every issue of *Der Stürmer*,

focused on the question whether the Jews – especially the *Juden* of Germany – should be understood as a nation (*Volk, Nation*) or, rather, as members of a religious community who were fully a part of the country in which they lived.[20] The debate engendered great sensitivity concerning Jewish statehood or striving for political sovereignty – and Graetz was at the eye of the storm and responded twice to von Treitschke.[21] It is quite easy to understand, in light of this debate, Graetz's avoidance of the use of *Juden* for those who, in the past, had a sovereign state of their own or strove for one. That was acceptable for the biblical *Israeliten*, or for ancient *Judäer*, but was problematic for *Juden*.

True, von Treitschke opened that debate only in 1879, a year after the publication of the third edition of Graetz's vol. III and a few years after the mid-decade appearance of vols. I–II. However, anti-Semitism was in the air much earlier in the decade, especially since the stock market crash of 1873, which was often blamed upon Jewish speculators.[22] Moreover, already in 1871, in the same month as the proclamation of the united Reich, an angry reviewer of vol. XI had attacked Graetz, in a prominent German journal, for expressing Jewish national hopes and interests. The reviewer argued, in a threatening tone, that German Jews should realize that if they have such hopes and interests they cannot expect the Germans to assume they will never conflict with those expected from German citizens.[23] And that reviewer was not alone.[24] Thus, it would be understandable if, by 1878, Graetz found it prudent, when describing Jews who once sought and achieved national sovereignty, to use nomenclature that distanced them from the *Juden* of Germany in his own day.

2. *Reaction to a new scholarly discipline.* As Graetz himself notes in his preface to the third edition of vol. III, the fifteen years that had passed since the second edition (1863) had seen the rise of a new discipline – the history of the New Testament period. Those were the years that witnessed the publication of the first and second editions (1868–1874 and 1873–1877) of Adolf Hausrath's *Neutestamentliche Zeitgeschichte*, of Emil Schürer's *Lehrbuch der neutestamentlichen Zeitgeschichte* (1874), as well as some lesser works – and, naturally, they tended to treat the Jews of antiquity with disdain, or worse, as background and foils for the heroes to whose history they were devoted.[25] Accordingly, it was natural for the authors of those works to use *Juden* for those ancient Jews – a term that in contemporary German frequently had a negative

valence, certainly when compared to *Israeliten*.[26] Graetz, who was
of course well aware of such derogatory usage,[27] and who was not
above expressing bitter hostility to the main practitioners of the
new discipline,[28] may have found it useful to distance himself from
them in his nomenclature concerning the subjects of his story. If
in 1846 he had proudly insisted on using *Juden* for the Jews of all
periods (see above, nn. 9–10), thirty years later he may have realized that he could not overcome centuries-old Christian hostility
towards the *Ioudaioi* of the New Testament period, and that a better
option, in writing about them, would be to distance himself and
his fellow *Juden* from those ancient villains (in Christian eyes) by
using another term to denote them: *Judäer*. Thus Graetz anticipated
by about a century the post-Holocaust scholars and clergy who
often recommend the use of "Judeans" rather than "Jews" when
translating "*Ioudaioi*" in ancient Christian texts, so as to prevent, as
far as possible, the translation of ancient hostility towards *Ioudaioi*
into modern hostility towards Jews.[29]

3. *Enhanced sensitivity to the geography of ancient Palestine?* Graetz visited
   Palestine in the spring of 1872, and, as we noted (see n. 4), he ascribed the visit great significance for the subsequent preparation of
   his two volumes on the biblical period. Indeed, perusal of Graetz's
   list of publications shows a very obvious jump in his interest in
   Palestinian geography in the wake of his trip.[30] Thus, it is likely that
   his first-hand acquaintance with the sites of Palestine and the lay of
   the land affected not only his new volumes on the biblical period
   but also his revision, for its third edition, of vol. III, for it too focused
   upon events that transpired in Palestine. Indeed, comparison of the
   first two editions of vol. III to the 1878 edition does reflect that. If, for
   example, in the first and second editions Graetz cited Josephus (*War*
   2.573; *Life* 188) for the statement that Meron and Achbara are both in
   Upper Galilee, and the Talmud (b. *Baba Meṣia* 84b) to show the two
   towns were indeed near one another, in the third edition he added
   that Meron is near Safed and did not bother to cite any source for the
   latter point;[31] Safed was and is a major site for Jewish tourists, and
   we know that Graetz travelled around the north.[32] Similarly, if in the
   first two editions he skips Josephus' reference to a place named Saab
   (or Saba) in *War* 3.229, and while mentioning a place named Ruma
   to which Josephus refers a few lines later (§233) he makes no effort
   to identify it, in the third edition he found it important or interesting
   both to mention Saab too and to add a note in which he informs his

readers that Saab is otherwise unknown but Ruma is to be identified as "Tell-Ruma between Sefurjeh and Kana- el G'elil."[33] More generally, if in the first two editions of vol. III Graetz wrote of the Galilee as part of *Judea*, in the third he more correctly termed it a part of *Palestine*.[34] This all indicates that he had become more aware of the specific limited geographic meaning of "Judea" (the southern part of Palestine around Jerusalem) and suggests that he chose to use the term because the Jewish states in the period under discussion were in fact centred upon Judea in that limited sense.

4. *Abandonment of the grand scheme.* However, the suggestion offered in the preceding paragraph only begs the real question: *should* the history of the Jews in this period be built around the Judean state(s)? After all, in his *Structure* Graetz had presented an impressively neat scheme, according to which Jewish history divided into three major eras, each with its own characterization, and if the first (the monarchy era) was state-oriented and the third (the exilic era, from 70 CE to the present) was clearly without a state, concerning the era between those two poles, the era of the Second Temple, Graetz had written that its "hallmark is that the religious element now achieves predominance and the social and political concerns assume a subordinate role ... religious interests gained exclusive control, to the point of negating all political independence; Judaism ceased to be the constitution for a state and became a religion in the usual sense of the word."[35] According to this scheme the Hasmonean and Herodian states of the Second Temple period were of only marginal importance, so the fact that they were Judea-centred states should not have so significantly affected the third volume of Graetz's *Geschichte*.

Moreover, note that Graetz had worked very hard, in his *Structure*, to characterize the second era both as one of a community in its land and as one having a basically religious orientation. Concerning the former point his procedure was quite clear: he simply ignored the Jews of the Graeco-Roman Diaspora, referring to them only once in his long account of the second era, in a passage (*Structure*, 88) that characterizes them generally and negatively as Hellenizing assimilationists who developed a "much distorted and impoverished spirit of Judaism" and produced the "bastard literature of the Apocrypha." As for the basically religious orientation of the Jews in this era – he made this claim time and again:

a. In referring to the first two eras, in which the people was in its own land, he emphasized that the second era, after the Babylonian exile, "is characterized by an overriding religious stamp, while the political-social tendency, which is only barely still visible, disappears entirely at the end of this era" (i.e., with the destruction of the Second Temple in 70 CE – DRS) (*Structure*, 72–3[36]).

b. Correspondingly, in listing the main "bearers" of the first two eras he contrasted the "political citizens, war heroes, and kings with only a touch of religious sentiment" of the first era to the "pious men, sages, teachers, students, and sectarians who manifest only a passing social interest" of the second (*Structure*, 73).

c. Graetz hardly alluded, in his *Structure*, to the fact that the Hasmoneans founded a state. The only Hasmonean ruler he mentioned is John Hyrcanus, emphasizing that he was a high priest, not a king, and asserting that "his wars have a religious rather than a political intent" (*Structure*, 89). While Graetz did offer some limited evidence for that assertion (pointing to the destruction of the Samaritans' temple and the forced circumcision of the Idumaeans, acts that he says "might be termed national religiosity"), he offered none whatsoever for his concluding statement in this section, a few lines later: "Political interests were pursued only secondarily, so that even the rulers themselves easily let the sceptre be pulled out of their hands." I can think of no evidence for that, and find it difficult to imagine any such ruler.[37]

d. With regard to the destruction of the Second Temple in 70 CE, Graetz wrote, in 1846, "It is noteworthy that the fall of the state, the burning of the Temple, did not make the same dreadful impression on contemporaries as did the demise of the first state" (*Structure*, 93). Thus, here too he contrasted the religion to the state and limits the importance of the latter in the Second Temple period.[38]

So much for Graetz's expectations, when giving a bird's-eye view of the Second Temple period in the course of his 1846 attempt to make neat sense of all of Jewish history. When he sat down to study and write up the nuts and bolts of the period, however, he was forced to discover that things were not so simple – and he drew the appropriate conclusions.[39] If at first, in the *Structure*, he had insisted that during the Second Temple period "religious interests gained exclusive control, to the point of negating all political independence" (*Structure*, 84), already in the introduction to the first edition of vol. III (1856) he opens his discussion by admitting that it *seems* that the period from the Hasmoneans until 70 CE was in fact characterized by political interests. True, he claims that such a view of the period is merely "external and superficial" ("*äus-serlich und oberflächlich betrachtet*"[40]), and within a page he establishes to his own satisfaction that "the basic character [*Grundcharakter*] of this era is therefore indisputably religious."[41] But his discussion seems artificial, readily recognized as an attempt to defend his preconceived scheme.

That this is so is shown by the fact that by the third (1878) edition of this volume, the one into which he introduced "Judeans" instead of "Jews," he rewrote that part of the introduction so as to hedge his ambiguous conclusion even further. He did that in two ways. First, he watered down the abovementioned statement in the first two editions, that the period's main character was indisputably religious, by adding the qualification "*vorherrschend*" ("predominantly").[42] Second, if towards the end of the introduction of the first two editions he had written that although he had proven ("*ist ... erwiesen*") that the basic character of the period was religious, it was still better, as a result of its external features, to characterize it as a "political-religious" period, in the third edition he replaced the claim to have "proven" that basic character with the assertion that one cannot fail to recognize it ("*ist ... unverkennbar*").[43] Although in and of itself there is not much difference between saying something has been proven and saying it cannot be overlooked, the fact that Graetz made the change shows that he was uncomfortable with the claim that he had satisfactorily characterized the period.

That change went hand in hand with two others made by Graetz in the introduction to vol. III in revising it for the third edition. One involves the change of a single word, the other the addition of two sentences. First, early in the introduction to the first edition, after offering some examples to flesh out his admission that, "externally and superficially," the period's character seems to be political, Graetz had declared,

Nevertheless, political striving was not the final purpose of this period of time. The people desired neither the fullness of power, nor influence upon foreign peoples; rather, what it desired was the undisturbed and unhindered observance of its religious laws with total strictness and consistency.[44]

That same text reappears in the introduction in both of the next two editions, but each time Graetz changed a single word: in 1863 he knocked "final purpose" (*Endzweck*) down to "main pathos" (*Hauptpathos*), and in

1878 he further knocked it down – to "main characteristic" (*Hauptzug*).[45]
That is, if in 1856 Graetz was still holding on to the teleological notion, which was perhaps of Hegelian inspiration, that historical periods have roles to play in grand processes that serve final purposes,[46] and
if in 1863, although backing away from that he was still holding on to the
claim that the period had a certain life ("pathos") of its own, by 1878 he
was settling for describing what he saw.

The second change that Graetz introduced into the introductory
statement about what he had "proven" or what one could not fail to
recognize consisted of two new sentences that declared that although
the religious orientation began to make its appearance early in the
Second Temple period "with Nehemiah's zeal for observing the Law,
became pervasive via the 'fencing about of the Law'[47] by the scribal
school, and received its lasting impetus from Simon the Just and his
successors," nevertheless, it was only the martyrdom (*Blutzeugenschaft*)
of the Maccabean period "that first endowed the religious orientation
with the irresistibility of a driving historical force."[48]

That is, in the same volume in which Graetz introduced "Judeans"
instead of "Jews," thus pulling the definition of his subjects in the political direction as is demanded by the external features of the period
beginning with the Hasmonean state (and continuing on through the
Herodian kingdom and to anti-Roman rebels who strove to restore the
Judean state), he also pulled in the other direction by underlining his
assessment that the religious nature of Jewish history underwent a
quantum leap, via martyrdom, in that very same Hasmonean period.
That means, however, that both elements, the religious and the political, saw a caesura with the Hasmonean period – and that explains why
a new volume of the *Geschichte* begins then.

This new presentation of just how different the Hasmonean period
was with regard to both elements made it difficult to characterize the
period one way or the other, for what characterized it was the very
tension between the enhanced political pole and the enhanced religious one. But it also made it more difficult, and self-contradictory, to
go on announcing, as Graetz blithely did in all the first three editions of
this volume, that "this era, if we let it begin with the return from the
Babylonian Exile, divides into three parts or periods," of which the second and third cover the years from 160 BCE until 70 CE. If Graetz some-
how allowed himself to get away with that in the first three editions of
the volume, his new emphasis on just how special the period addressed
in the volume was made it all the more ridiculous to go on pretending

that the period began almost four hundred years before the period in fact addressed in the volume. We can well understand that by the next edition, which appeared in 1888, Graetz simply omitted the introduction.

That recognition, of the mixed nature of the period dealt with in vol. III, together with the fact that it is quite short (only 230 years) – a point of which Graetz was especially aware in preparing the third edition[49] – should have led Graetz to the conclusion that, in fact, Jewish history has only two eras: a political era, focusing on events in the land of Israel, and a religious era, which was exilic. That would have left Graetz with a choice between two options: either associate the Second Temple period in its entirety (and not only its first half) with the first (biblical) period, or present it as a transitional period. Graetz, however, did neither, for at least three reasons:

1. He was stuck with his three-part scheme: he had committed himself to it in his 1846 *Structure* and had recommitted himself to it in 1853 by labelling vol. IV of his *Geschichte* (the first volume to be published) as the first volume on the *third* era; see above p. 69.
2. Reducing the eras to two would have amounted to accepting the widespread binary opposition between Israelite history and Jewish history, which he had so angrily rejected in his *Structure* (see above, n. 10). A three-part scheme allows for the notion of development along a continuum as opposed to polar options.
3. Graetz was fascinated by religious developments in the latter half of the Second Temple period, as is shown by his discussion of sects and the like in the *Structure*[50] and in the introduction to vol. III of the *Geschichte* (as long as it survived – until the third edition).[51] The same fascination is also demonstrated by the body of that third volume and its appendices: already the first edition included a twenty-page appendix on the three sects.[52] So Graetz did not want to give up on his characterization of the period as religious, however much he shortened the period and watered down the one-sidedness of the way he characterized it. But that religious characterization separated it from the state orientation of the first period.

If Graetz could not or would not reduce the three eras into two, but also could not really define the second era, what could he possibly do?

Here is where his introduction of *Judäer* instead of *Juden* came in, for the use of differential nomenclature can give the appearance of

differentiation even when analysis fails to justify it. Graetz's use of differential nomenclature stepped in to fill the gap created by his recognition that he was not able to define the period in any unitary way: use of
Judäer could distinguish the Jews of the latter half of the Second Temple
period even if Graetz could not pin down in prose, in any consistent
and satisfying way, the distinction between them and the *Israeliten*
who preceded them or the *Juden* who succeeded them. The use of such
differential nomenclature amounts, in other words, to a clever way to
define those 230 years as a transitional period between the Israelite
history that preceded them and the Jewish period that succeeded them,
for the use of the "Judeans" reminds us both of "Israelites" (insofar as
both are derived from the name of a country) and of "Jews" (insofar
as both are based upon Hebrew *Yehudim* and Greek *Ioudaioi*). The in-
between status of this period corresponds to Graetz's final verdict in his
introduction to vol. III, that the period should be characterized as one
that is hyphenated, "political-religious,"[53] and it stayed on to bespeak
that understanding even after Graetz despaired of trying to define it
out in any convincing way.

III. Conclusion

Graetz's move from *Juden* to *Judäer* is important in at least two contexts:
for our understanding of his development, and for our understanding
of our options in the use of those two terms. Concerning Graetz and his
development, we may note that his *Geschichte*, as it took shape by the
1878 edition of vol. III, avoids linking Jews to any state of their own.
Israelites once had a state, Judeans once had a state, but Jews do not;
they are not that type of collective. Whatever the basic reasons for the
switch, which we have attempted to tease out and present, that result
dovetails nicely with (1) changes Graetz authorized in vol. XI of his
Geschichte, the volume that angered reviewers and eventually aroused
von Treitschke's ire in the *Berliner Antisemitismusstreit* – changes that
amount to a move away from the nationalist and anti-German stance
he had adopted earlier;[54] (2) Graetz's 1885 resignation from the central
committee of Ḥovevei Zion, a Zionist organization devoted to the settlement of Palestine, as a protest against its provocative nationalism;[55]
and (3) his concomitant decision to devote his labours instead to the
Alliance Israélite Universelle, which was devoted to the welfare of
Jews and Jewish communities around the world. That move, from
"Zion" to the Diaspora and "universelle," is a practical application of

his new insistence that being a Jew (*Jude*), an adherent of Judaism (*Judentum*), does not imply an association with any particular state. Whether or not this is all part of an apologetic response to von Treitschke and others, the corresponding role played by the move from *Juden* to *Judäer* for the state-oriented part of the Second Temple period should be recognized.

As for the terms themselves, we saw that, for Graetz, *Judäer* served as a transitional term, poised between *Israelit*, which has a territorial sense, and *Juden*, which refers to members of a religious community. *Judäer*, which means something like the former but sounds something like the latter, served as a bridge between them. However, we have also seen that Graetz's insistence, in practice, upon using either *Juden* or *Judäer* but not both, reflected his basic assumption that the historical period in question had a certain *Grundcharakter*. That assumption, of course, was an integral part of the sweeping and philosophical approach he took to all of Jewish history in his *Structure*, and it was the same approach he took in his introduction to vol. III, in which he tried to define what that "basic character" was. However, we have also seen that Graetz gave it up; after doing all he could with hyphens and hedging, from one edition to the next, so as to leave room for a religious period being also political, or for a political period being also religious, he simply omitted the introduction (beginning with the fourth edition), even at the same time he went on working on the period and expanding the volume more and more.

My conclusion from Graetz's experience, therefore, is that, on the one hand, his attempt to impose unity upon the protagonists of Jewish history in the Second Temple period, a unity that presupposes that they shared a "basic character" and therefore could and should be denoted by a single term, was a failure. And that was more than a century ago. Since then the evidence for the variety of Jews and Judaism in the period has grown very substantially, as has also our awareness of the weight of a religious tradition that, in earlier times, kept scholars from realizing how much variety there had been. Today, therefore, it would be all the less warranted to try to impose a basic character on all of Jewish history of the period.

On the other hand, I would nonetheless retain, from Graetz, the challenge of making sense of the period as a whole. In particular, I would not recommend that we content ourselves with the unity of the Jewish people as lending unity to our histories of this period. That would be very banal, a counsel of despair; our wish to understand the world out of which both Christianity and rabbinic Judaism grew deserves more than that, and the evidence that survives allows more than that. So I suggest that we learn from Graetz's experience that our struggling with the application of "Jews" or "Judeans" to the protagonists of Jewish history of this period has everything to do with our struggle to define them, and that that is salutary, and that we depart from Graetz only insofar as we give up his assumption that we must decide to use only one or the other. Rather than assuming that they were all "basically" either Jews or Judeans, we should recognize that what united them (apart from their descent) was what divided them – a set of interrelated issues concerning which they took different positions. Our debates, about which ones we should call Judeans and which Jews, will, I believe, enhance our understanding of them all, as also of the issues that divided them.

Conclusion

Each of the first three chapters of this volume is dedicated to a different polarity: 1 Maccabees versus 2 Maccabees, priestly law versus rabbinic law, early Josephus versus later Josephus. Nevertheless, it seems that all three are, mutatis mutandis, different versions of the same basic dichotomy: one between the orientation and values of priestly Judea and those of diasporan Judaism – wherever the latter was found. The first chapter contrasted the values and orientation of a Jerusalemite spokesman of the high-priestly dynasty that ruled Judea with those of a Jewish author of the Hellenistic Diaspora. The second contrasted the values and legal approach characteristic of priests, who were defined by birth and whose world focused on Jerusalem, with those characteristic of the type of Judaism whose leaders were defined by choice and commitment, which I characterized as a diasporan type that, in this case, first appeared in Judea in competition to the priestly establishment but would survive the destruction of the Second Temple and flourish outside of Judea and, eventually, in the Diaspora. And the third contrasted the values of the work Josephus wrote when his main experience in life was as a priest and in Judea with those of his writings after more than two decades of life in the Diaspora and – as all other Jews – in a Jewish world bereft of its geographical centre in Judea: Jerusalem.

True, people are not ideal types, so the value of dichotomies is as a schematic tool that facilitates analysis rather than in capturing all the diversity that was really out there in history.[1] And there was substantial diversity. Thus, for some examples, (1) although Ben-Sira was a priestly Judean, quite capable of adulating priests and almost putting them on a divine pedestal (see esp. 7:29–31, also 45:20–6 and ch. 50),[2] he was also quite capable of delivering a universalist sermon that emphasizes that what is important is fear of God, not one's descent (10:19–24);[3] (2) even 1 Maccabees is capable of mentioning prayer now and then, just as even 2 Maccabees is proud that the Temple is world-renowned;[4] (3) although Qumran began as a priestly community, it was to see the development within it of universalist values more typical of Diaspora Judaism;[5] (4) although Philo was a Diasporan Jew through and through and thought, for example, that the only true temples are the world itself and the soul of a sage, he was nevertheless outraged when the Temple of Jerusalem was threatened;[6] (5) although by and large Pharisaic-rabbinic Judaism may be understood as an essentially diasporan opposition to priestly Judaism, it nevertheless had among its adherents those who tended towards the priestly pole,[7] and when it did not entail concessions to the competition was more generally willing to adopt positions that once typified priestly Judaism;[8] etc.

Cases like these, which could be multiplied at will, indicate that the real world was more variegated than a polarized scheme that contrasts Judeans and Jews might suggest. There is no good reason to expect this to have been otherwise. The point of the present volume is that, if so, our writing about the period should reflect that, and so if English offers us two terms, it is counterproductive to use only one, whether "Jews," as was once the rule, or "Judean," as is increasingly fashionable. Rather, we are better served by using both terms that English supplies us, each of which gives prominence to different criteria; they point to different poles of a continuum and invite us, in deciding which to use, to consider in each case which is more appropriate. That is a necessary move (for in writing in English we must use one or the other term, and indeed in translation we cannot even qualify it), but it is also a heuristic move, for it encourages us to consider in each case what creates the ambiguity. Thus, for example, once we recognize that although Ben-Sira represents priestly Judea, his home, he nevertheless betrays some views and expressions more typical of diasporan Judaism, it will encourage us to ask questions about the latter orientation, and that will bring us to ask to what extent it reflects Hellenization, a process that was stronger in the Diaspora but significant in Palestine as well, and will also ask us to wonder why Ben-Sira's situation allowed him to be comfortable in expressing such dichotomous views.[9]

Thus, this volume builds on the assumptions that it is impossible to write about the Second Temple period without using both "Jews" and "Judeans," and that it is useful to do so. It is impossible to do otherwise, because any use of "Judean," which is a rare term in English, demonstratively entails a loud statement about the usual term, "Jew" – namely, that it is not appropriate. But given the state of scholarship today, in which "Judean" has become so widespread, any use of "Jew" amounts to a demonstrative rejection of "Judean." Thus, one way or another, implicitly or explicitly, willy-nilly we use both terms, and this volume suggests that we should do that explicitly. Moreover, it suggests that it is useful – that is, it furthers our understanding – to use both terms in our discussions of antiquity. The first three chapters of this volume attempted to exemplify that, and the fourth illustrates just how misleading and impossible it is to attempt to use only one term. Namely, it seems that Graetz's repeated revisions of his introduction to vol. III, his eventual omission of it, his failure to assign the last centuries of the Second Temple to any historical era, and his switch from "Juden" to "Judäer," all show that he simply found it impossible to justify the use of one term for all of the *Ioudaioi* of the period. The present volume suggests that he would have been better off using two and that we learn from his experience.

True, the *Ioudaioi* of the ancient world, whatever their orientation and wherever they lived, shared (or thought they shared), for the most part (apart from proselytes), something very basic: the same ancestry. For the *Ioudaioi* of Judea, that fact paired very easily with the fact that they were born in and lived in a place called Judea; those two points paired just as easily as priests paired with the Temple of Jerusalem. Indeed, the two facts were parallel and part of the same world view, for the priests were understood to have the best descent among the *Ioudaioi*, just as the Temple of Jerusalem, which was their focus and the foundation of their status, was understood to be the centre of holiness of the country defined as its periphery. *Ioudaios* ancestry went together with Judea just as naturally as priestly ancestry went together with the Temple, and both were expressions of the same world view.

For the *Ioudaioi* of the Diaspora, in contrast, the natural fact that a baby was of *Ioudaios* ancestry conflicted with the natural fact of birth and residence not in Judea, and that discrepancy called for decisions. Without conscious and deliberate decisions, education, and commitments the natural course of events would make – leave – such a baby a non-*Ioudaios*. I have argued that this need for decision, as opposed to nature, which was required by diasporan life, was the hallmark of rabbinic religion as it developed in contrast to priestly religion. It also goes a long way towards explaining the difference between the authorities of rabbinic religion (sages by choice and recognition) as opposed to a hereditary priesthood defined by birth, as well as towards explaining their preference for nominalism versus realism in legal interpretation and their ability to survive the destruction of the Temple and exile from Judea.

Moreover, the Jews of the Diaspora in the period we study were not just in any Diaspora; they were in the *Hellenistic* Diaspora, which was a Diaspora within a Diaspora. They were living in a Greek world that was not in Greece: they were living among Greeks in the Orient who were Greeks by culture but not by descent, Greeks who in teaching and practice adopted – to whatever extent and with whatever variations – the notion that, in fact, it is not descent but rather education and accomplishment that make a person what he or she is. In such a world – in which (for some noted examples) Isocrates expressed pride that "Greek" had come to define a person by culture, not by any physical attribute, Erastothenes condemned those who urged Alexander the Great to distinguish between Greeks and barbarians and instead called for distinguishing between good people and bad people, and the Hellenized Jewish author of 2 Maccabees was happy to report that people of all nations mourned the murder of a Jew simply because he was a "man"[10] – Jewish descent would not go very far in defining Jews.

Thus, of the three ways of defining Jews – by being from Judea, by being of Jewish ancestry, and by being committed to the Jewish religion[11] – Diaspora conditions undercut the first by definition and Hellenistic culture, which, although not at all absent from Judea, was much more strongly felt in the Diaspora, tended to undercut the first two. That lent, for *Ioudaioi* of the Diaspora, much more importance to the third criterion, a focus that is squarely in the sphere that English usage denotes by "Jew." In Judea, in contrast, the land provided a basic definition of identity, and the people who had access to the Temple and officiated in it were defined by their ancestry, which demonstrated that ancestry was important; together, those two factors left less room, and less need, for the third criterion, religion. The typical result, in Judea, was either that religion fell by the wayside (ch. 1) or that it came to be united, as is typical of priestly religion, with the other two criteria. Hence "Judean" is a more appropriate term for the *Ioudaioi* of Judea, a point that also fits their frequent occupation, in our period, with affairs of state. To the extent we find non-priestly religion in Judea, I would classify it as tending towards diasporan Judaism, as is shown by the way Qumran was in exile during the Second Temple period and Pharisaic Judaism would be able to survive and flourish in exile.

Of course, we could abstain from using "Judean" as a noun altogether, and use it only as an adjective that distinguishes Judean Jews from diasporan Jews, using "Jews" to denote people by their descent, as is allowed by English usage. That was once the rule. However, putting such an emphasis upon pedigree does not touch anything essential, and it is, moreover, not at all without reason that scholarship has realized – perhaps due to the existence of the state of Israel – that there is much about the ancient *Ioudaioi* that has to do with land and state. It is therefore useful to use "Judean," the word English supplies for such contexts, when it is warranted: when the land- or state-oriented reference is salient and functional. Indeed, the use of such an unusual term, rather than the more familiar "Jew," will – like "chairperson" – call attention to the fact that students of antiquity must be prepared to imagine orientations and circumstances different from those current today.[12] But in contexts that usually point toward the people or the religion, rather than the state or the country, "Jew" seems to be more appropriate.

In sum, it used to be that historians of antiquity spoke regularly of Jews and Judaism. Lately, however, there has been such a move toward recognizing the territorial dimension of "Jewishness" that many doubt the legitimacy of using either term, preferring "Judean" instead of "Jews" and eschewing "Judaism" as anachronistic. To the extent this swing of the pendulum requires us to think about the issues, and to realize that indeed often Judea was at the heart of ancient phenomena we are discussing, it has been beneficial. However, as with most swings of pendulums, so too with this one: they can overcorrect. There is, in the evidence we have for antiquity, much that corresponds to what we expect when we hear "Judeans" but also much that corresponds to what we expect when we hear "Jews"; our use of such differential terminology, and of "Judaism" – even if many of the ancients did not have access to it – can allow us to be more accurate in our discussion, in our terms, in discussing the ancient phenomena; and the need to choose the appropriate term forces us to think about these issues, and thus brings us to ask questions that otherwise would not be asked and, thereby, to discover new perspectives that might otherwise be missed. This little volume has attempted to provide some examples of that.

To conclude with a glance beyond antiquity, at our own day, I would point out that this volume suggests that rabbinic Judaism, which began as an oppositional party outside of the Judean establishment during the Second Temple period and flourished after the destruction of the Second Temple, and whose central texts were produced in the Galilee and in Babylonia, is typically, perhaps essentially, a diasporan phenomenon. Life in a Jewish state, in contrast, leads – so this study suggests – either away from interest in God, given the way sovereignty allows and requires the Jews to take their fate into their own hands (ch. 1), or to a type of attitude towards God that I characterized as priestly religion, which is very different from rabbinic religion. Given the way priestly religion elevates the significance of a particular land and of a particular nation (and, in antiquity, accordingly elevated the prestige of the birth-defined priesthood that officiated at the central shrine of that land), that type of Judaism tended, as we saw, to limit God too to that particular place and to ascribe authority to nature (ch. 2) – an attitude that we normally think of as pagan and certainly as the opposite of rabbinic Judaism. For many Jews that is a troubling observation, but I think it is correct, and that it is also fair to say that no sensitive observer of the modern Jewish world could claim that there is nothing similar or analogous to point to today.

In brief, the contemporary phenomenon to which this volume reacts is the revival of priestly Judaism in Israel, where it is commonly called "religious-national" Judaism.[13] If the modern state of Israel was created by a non-religious Zionist movement, which revolted against the Jewish religion in the name of the Jewish people, thus creating a chasm between Israelis and Judaism,[14] and if Zionism succeeded in its goal of creating a state for the Jewish people – especially in the wake of the Holocaust, which was a massive catastrophe that many took to prove the non-existence or irrelevance of God and religion and that Jews must take their fate into their own hands – "religious-national" Judaism in Israel attempts to salvage Judaism for the Jews by reformulating Judaism in a way that can embrace Zionism. This is done by elevating the two foci of priestly Judaism – the land of Israel and Jewish descent – to a status that in rabbinic Judaism they only rarely enjoyed relative to the third pole of being Jewish: adherence to Jewish law. The results are easily seen. Two examples:

(1) Religious Zionism in Israel is – as a result of its commitment to the notion of "holy land" – almost always associated with settlement of the biblical land of Israel beyond the borders of the state of Israel, and with opposition to territorial concessions.

(2) Religious Zionism in Israel is – as a result of its commitment to
the notions of "holy seed" and "holy land" – almost always associated with the position that immigrants to Israel who are of
partial Jewish descent but are not Jewish according to religious
law, of whom there are hundreds of thousands (especially from
the former Soviet Union), should be allowed a relatively fast and
simplified process of conversion to Judaism. Such a process, which
demands and expects relatively little from these converts' commitment to the observance of Jewish law, is justified by reference
to their partial Jewish descent and to their commitment to living
in the Land of Israel, as if they were basically Jews already, so all
that is needed is formal ratification of that status. Here, then, is a
clear implication of the position that the priestly values of land and
descent are more important than religion. That position goes hand
in hand with a basic tendency of religious Zionists to emphasize
their commonalities with non-religious Israeli Jews, which too
entails a willingness to ascribe relatively little significance to their
non-observance of Jewish law, just as it goes hand in hand with a
tendency to deny or belittle the significance of commonality with
Israeli non-Jews.[15]

One can well understand the impetus to revise Judaism so as to allow
it to embrace Zionism. Nevertheless, apart from the fact that at times
the revisions entail positions that this or that observer or participant
might feel problematic or worse, I also note that too often the revision
of Judaism is not recognized or presented as such; too often the type of
religion it teaches is presented as if it were rabbinic Judaism.[16] Given
that rabbinic Judaism has a long history and a huge library, with appropriate picking and choosing of sources one can always present
things that way. This volume, which focuses on ancient history, reas-
serts that, nevertheless, there is a gulf between the two types of
Judaism, and that a stark recognition of the distance between them
can, if at the price of some schematization, be useful in fostering a better understanding of them.

Historians, certainly historians of antiquity, are not prophets. Nor do
the efforts they devote to analysing the past necessarily endow their
views about the present, much less the future, with any special weight.
But one may hope that their analyses of the past may at least clarify,
and perhaps also fructify, deliberation about the present and the future
as well.

Appendix: May We Speak of "Religion" and "Judaism" in the Second Temple Period?*

Having argued throughout this volume that the Second Temple period was witness to the rise of a religiously oriented Judaism, which (wherever it was found) was of essentially diasporan orientation, and that it is appropriate to use "Jews" to refer to those characterized by such an orientation, in contrast to those characterized by a land-, state-, and nature-centred orientation, for whom "Judeans" is more appropriate, I should relate to an original, erudite, and challenging study published in 2007, in which Steve Mason argued that "there was no category of 'Judaism' in the Graeco-Roman world, no 'religion' too."[1] As he explains at the outset of the article, this thesis is meant to justify his preference for "Judean," rather than "Jew," as the appropriate translation of *Ioudaios* in Josephus – as in the volumes that have so far appeared in the series that he edits, FJTC.

In the body of what follows, I will argue that the categories of both "religion" and "Judaism" did exist in the Graeco-Roman world, at least by Josephus' day. Before that, however, I would address two premises of Mason's study. The first is the apparent notion that if there was no "Judaism," it is not appropriate (or useful) for us to translate *Ioudaios* as "Jew"; in the absence of Judaism, the use of "Jew" is misleading. That assumes that "Jew" denotes an adherent of Judaism – an assumption found elsewhere as well.[2] Rather, Mason argues, we should use "Judean" because that term denotes an ethnos, and the *Ioudaioi* in antiquity were often assumed to be one ethnos among many ("Jews, Judaeans," 489–510). However, the fact is that (as we saw in the Introduction to this volume) in English "Jew" denotes people not only with regard to their religion, "Judaism," but also with regard to their ethnicity, insofar as the latter regards their pedigree. That is, when we

---

* This appendix is one of several products of a most fruitful period spent in the spring of 2008 in the congenial Netherlands Institute for Advanced Study.

say someone is "a Jew" we may refer both to his or her religion and ancestry or only to one of those. That means that even if "Judaism" did not exist in antiquity that would not entail, for those who use English, the conclusion that "Jews" did not exist.[3]

I should underline that that response of mine does not contradict Mason's argument, for his has to do with what *Ioudaioi* were thought to be in antiquity (an ethnos) and mine has to do with our modern English usage. That brings me to the next point.

Mason espouses an "emic" approach, which holds that our rendering of ancient texts should adhere as closely as possible to the notions and phrasing of the ancients who wrote them and read them. That leads easily to the conclusion that we should avoid speaking of "Judaism" with regard to the Second Temple period, for the term appears very rarely in texts of that period.[4] To this I would respond, first of all, that if the matter were to be decided only on the basis of the appearance of the word *Ioudaïsmos* in the ancient texts, I would agree with Mason, even if, as we shall see, I would not agree with all his attempts to show that *Ioudaïsmos* refers to something other than what we call "Judaism." However, my argument in this volume is that if the issues and values that defined or occupied ancient *Ioudaioi* related to what *we* call Judaism, we should call them "Jews" and may discuss their "Judaism."

The emic approach adopted by Mason is a legitimate one, and it has its place, but – in translation, as elsewhere[5] – it also has its price, no less than the "etic" approach. Thus, for the relevant example, in a series of translations that aspires, as the one Mason edits, to be a platform for the commentary, it perhaps makes sense to have the translation hew as closely as possible to the original and leave the work of interpretation to the commentary. That, however, entails a translation that is often difficult to read; when done most consistently, reflecting Greek pronunciation of names, Greek syntax, and the like, it is can be quite hard reading.[6] A particularly relevant aspect of this is that the closer a translation hews to the original, the more it will strive, as Mason's series does, to employ the same English word to render all occurrences of the same Greek word[7] – which has obvious disadvantages as well, because frequently the semantic ranges of the two words are not identical. The opposite approach, the "etic" one, strives to bring the text to the reader rather than bring the reader to the text,[8] making it easier to read at the price of missing the ancient nuances. Thus, for example, if we use different English words for different nuances of the same Greek word, our translations will be more understandable, but readers will not understand the dynamics of the original text, which may be playing with those different nuances. Choosing between these two approaches, in translation, is a challenge, often a thankless job; no one can ever make everyone happy.[9]

However, whatever translators do, the work of historians is not limited to translation. The genres in which we write allow us to mix, in our own text, both original texts and our own commentary upon them, as well as our own thoughts based on other evidence and models.[10] And if, as I have argued in this volume, for many *Ioudaioi* of the Second Temple period the issues and values that concerned them qua *Ioudaioi* were of the type that we, today, understand as pertaining to Judaism, then it is useful for us to use "Jews" and "Judaism" when discussing them. Therefore – and this is my second point – the move from translation policy, which was the point of departure of Mason's study, to history, is not a simple one. One might well admit that, historically, both "Jews" and "Judaism" existed, and therefore use those terms when helpful in historical analysis, but still, given an emic approach to translation, insist, in translations, on using "Judeans" throughout because Josephus uses the same term, *Ioudaios*, for both. Alternatively, one could use "Jews" throughout. The only question is what one leaves for the commentary or other forums, such as the present volume.

Apart from those two opening considerations, however, that regard the framework within which Mason couched the issue, it seems that, even from an emic point of view, it is difficult to deny the existence of "religion" and "Judaism" in Josephus' era, although both were somewhat new on the scene and, as we have seen, competed with the older and established territorially oriented way of being that typified "Judeans."

I. "Religion"

It is somewhat surprising to see such a round denial as that cited in the opening paragraph of this appendix, or Mason's fuller formulation at p. 480 of his study: "The concept of *religion*, which is fundamental to our outlook and our historical research, lacked a taxonomical counterpart in antiquity." Although it is true that translators of ancient texts sometimes use "religion" even when the Greek does not require it,[11] it is also the case that dictionaries, and scholars of ancient Greek, regularly render the Greek term *thrēskeia* as "religion." True, they agree that its original meaning was "worship" or "cult," that is, it referred to rituals performed to show reverence to a god. But they agree that, by the first century BCE or CE, i.e., by Josephus' day, it had also come to be used in a broader sense, "religion," which includes worship – *which I take to denote something that is actively done* – but also much more.[12] Thus, for example,

> LSJ, 806: "1. religious worship, cult, ritual; 2. religion, service of God."
> Spicq, *TLNT*, 2.200: *"thrēskeia*, worship, liturgy, ritual, religion; *thrēskos*, religious, reverent."
> E. Benveniste: "In Ionic Greek, in Herodotus, the term *thrēskeiē* properly refers to the observances of cult prescriptions. The term is unknown in Attic Greek and it does not appear until a late date (first century B.C.) to designate 'religion,' as a complex of beliefs and practices."[13]

If, then, already well before the time of Josephus *thrēskeia* had taken on, or was taking on, such a broader meaning,[14] it is somewhat surprising that the word figures, in Mason's study dedicated to justifying a point about the translation of Josephus, only as an item in a list of terms that relate to sacrificial worship: "An ancient *ethnos* normally had a national cult (*ta theia, ta hiera, thrēskeia, theōn therapeia, cura/cultus deorum, ritus, religio*), involving priests, temples, and animal sacrifice" ("Jews, Judaeans," 484). In fact, it seems that examination of Josephus' use of the term *thrēskeia*, which appears nearly a hundred times in his works, admirably illustrates the generalization cited above about the shift in the word's meaning by his era, and also our own characterization of Josephus, in ch. 3, as someone who turned, between his *War* and his *Antiquities*, from a Judean priest into a diasporan Jew.

In the *War*, most cases of *thrēskeia* are rendered suitably and sufficiently by "worship," "cult," "ceremony," or some other such term pertaining to rituals performed in service of God – as, for example, in 1.146, 148, discussed above (pp. 59–60). Some other examples: at 2.425 and 4.324 *thrēskeia* refers to ceremonies in the Temple, at 4.275 Jerusalem is said to be open for "worship," at 5.198–9 it appears in the context of sites of "worship" in the Temple, at 6.99–100 Josephus says that the denial of sacrifices to God amounts to denying him his eternal "worship," etc. In *Antiquities*, too, many instances of *thrēskeia* are best or at least sufficiently rendered that way. Thus, for example, at 5.101 Josephus reports that the construction of an altar led to a misunderstanding because people suspected it was intended to allow illicit *thrēskeia* (although in fact it had not been erected for *thrēskeia* – §112); at 5.339 he refers to women who came to the Tabernacle for *thrēskeia*; at 7.341 David says that those who help Solomon to build the Temple of Jerusalem will be devoting themselves to the *thrēskeia* of God; at 9.273 (and 11.182) priests and Levites, who work in the Temple, are said to receive tithes so they would not have to abandon the *thrēskeia* in order to support themselves; at 10.43–4 the restoration of the altar and sacrifices constitutes proper regulation of the *thrēskeia*; and 15.248 says that since Jews may not offer sacrifices outside of the Temple, if they lost access to the Temple they could not perform the customary *thrēskeia* to God; etc.

However, it seems that there are already some passages in the *War*, and there are definitely quite a few in the *Antiquities* and elsewhere in literature by and about *Ioudaioi* in the first century, in which "religion" is the appropriate translation of *thrēskeia*, while "worship" or the like, terms that (the way we use them) refer to only one part – an active part – of "religion," are virtually impossible. Thus, for some examples:

1. At *War* 2.456 Josephus underlines, so as to intensify his condemnation of a perfidious massacre perpetrated by Jewish rebels, the fact that it happened on the Sabbath, a day when the Jews' "because [*dia*] of the *thrēskeia*" abstain even *tōn hosiōn ergōn* ("from activities that are holy"). That seems to mean that their *thrēskeia* prohibits Jews from doing various activities – an apparent reference to the Fourth Commandment's prohibition of labour on the Sabbath (Exod 20:8–11; Deut 5:12–15). But worship is not the type of thing that forbids anyone from doing anything; it is itself a type of activity. In this passage *thrēskeia* does not seem to denote anything that is done, such as worship; rather, it is the authority that requires abstention from certain activities. Something like "religion" is required; so, for example, Thackeray (JLCL) offers "religious scruples."

2. True, one could contemplate another interpretation of *War* 2.456: that Josephus means that Jews abstain from other work on the Sabbath, even good works, not because of (a prohibition posited by the) *thrēskeia* but, rather, in order to keep their time free and available for doing something else, *thrēskeia* – which could then mean "worship." This, it seems, is the implication of Mason's FJTC translation of *War* 2.456: "for the sake of worship, they observe a moratorium." The same is possible at *War* 1.146 where Josephus uses the same formulation (*dia tēn thrēskeian*) to explain why Jews abstain from all labour on the Sabbath; there too both interpretations are

possible. However, even if one might be willing to accept "for the sake of" as a translation of *dia* + accusative, shifting the emphasis from what caused the abstinence to what it was meant to make possible,[15] comparison with *War* 2.391–3 clearly shows that Josephus' point is about the *violation* of *thrēskeia*, not about failure to perform it because of being too busy with other activities. There, *referring explicitly back to the episode in the days of Pompey described in 1.146–8*, Josephus has Agrippa II warn the Jews that if they indeed go to war they will find it impossible to maintain the *thrēskeia* in a state that is *akratos* – "unmixed, pure." Agrippa immediately goes on to illustrate his point with only one example: war will entail fighting on the Sabbath, and that will constitute "transgressing" (§393 – *parabainontes*[16]) the ancestral law. Agrippa makes no reference here to what the Jews will not be able to do, such as worship;[17] his concern is not that they will not be able to do something, such as worship, but that they will not be able to do nothing – that the necessity to fight, in violation of the law that forbids labour on the Sabbath, will in and of itself impair the totality ("unmixed" nature) of their maintenance of the *thrēskeia*. That is, in *War* 1.146 and 2.391 *thrēskeia* denotes an authoritative system that, in this case, forbids something, so "worship" will not do but "religion" (or, as Thackeray renders 2.391, "religious rules") will – and so it likely means the same at 2.456 as well, which is so similar.

3. According to *War* 2.198, Petronius was deeply impressed by the incomparable *thrēskeia* of the Jews, which led them to resign themselves even to die rather than accept the profanation of the Temple. Here too there is no way we could render *thrēskeia* as "worship," "cult," or the like. Rather, it must mean something like "religiosity" or – as Thackeray rendered it in LCL – "devotion to religion." In this case even Mason (ad loc.) translates "devotion," and elsewhere he goes even further and suggests "religiosity" for this passage.[18]

4. At *Ant.* 1.223, telling the story of the binding of Isaac (Gen 22), Josephus reports that God wanted to test Abraham's *thrēskeia* towards him. Therefore, according to §224, God asked Abraham to sacrifice his son, Isaac, so as to make manifest (*emphanisein*) (n.b. not to do) his *thrēskeia* towards him. Here we cannot say "worship" or "cult"; we must use something like "piety."[19]

5. At *Ant.* 6.88 Samuel admonishes the people that it was wrong to ask for a king, saying that it amounts to being impious (displaying

asebeia) towards God; then in §90 he restates that as being treason-ous vis-à-vis *thrēskeia* and *eusebeia* (piety). Thackeray renders the latter pair "worship" and "religion," but in a context where the topic is not how to worship God but, rather, whether it is right to ask for a human monarch, there is no particular allusion to "wor-ship" and so it seems that "religion and piety" is more appropriate.

6. At *Ant.* 8.279 Abijah says that illicit altars are not proof of *thrēskeia* but rather of impiety (*asebeia*). However, altars are not *proofs* of "worship"; they are *sites* of worship. Moreover, the opposite of "impiety" is not "worship" but, rather, "piety" (or "devoutness" or "devotion," offered by JLCL and FJTC, respectively, for this case of *thrēskeia*).

7. At *Ant.* 8.295–6 Azariah tells the Judeans that God had allowed them a victory because they had maintained themselves just and holy and had followed God's will in all ways, and then warns them that if they deviate from that path and instead turn away from his *thrēskeia* the opposite will be the result. Justice, holiness, and obedience to God are easily summarized by "religion," but not by "worship" (although, surprisingly, the latter appears here in JLCL and FJTC).

8. At *Ant.* 11.212 Josephus (paraphrasing Esth 3:8) has Haman com-plain that the Jews had neither the same *thrēskeia* nor the same laws as others. If that were all he said, *thrēskeia* could mean "rites" or "cult." But immediately thereafter Josephus has Haman go on in direct speech, saying that the Jews are hostile to the Persians in their customs and their customary practices, making no specific reference to worship. It seems evident that the latter is meant to repeat the former in Haman's own words, and that is probably why, in the JLCL translation, Marcus – although perfectly willing to use "cult" or "worship" for *thrēskeia* where the context requires it[20] – avoided that limited term here and used the broader term "religion."

9. At *Ant.* 12.269, when Mattathias and his sons declare they will never abandon their ancestral *thrēskeia*, it might mean only "wor-ship," for that was what they were being asked to violate in the scene described there (an attempt to coerce them to offer a pagan sacrifice). However, we should hesitate to limit *thrēskeia* that way, for Josephus is rendering, in indirect speech, Mattathias' declara-tion, according to Josephus' *Vorlage*, 1 Macc 2:20, that he and his sons and his brothers will continue "to walk in the covenant of our

fathers" – and that sounds like it is referring to the whole ancestral tradition, not just to worship. Similarly, two paragraphs later
(§271) Josephus follows 1 Macc 2:27 in reporting, in direct speech,
Mattathias' call upon Jews to join him in rebellion – but where the
original has Mattathias calling upon all those who were zealous
for the law and supported the *covenant*, Josephus again replaces
the latter with *thrēskeia*.[21] Thus, in these passages *thrēskeia* seems to
have a meaning more general than "cult" for Josephus, referring
to whatever the Jews' covenant with God entails – which is much
more than "worship." In English, "religion" is the general category
of which "worship" is an element.

10. At *Ant.* 16.2 Josephus complains that Herod's law that burglars
should be sold abroad was an offence against the *thrēskeia*, for
Jewish laws – he alludes to Exod 22:1 – mandated other punishments but forbade sale to non-Jews.[22] Here *thrēskeia* does not refer
to worship but rather to an authoritative system of laws set down
in the Bible, which constitutes the sacred scriptures of what we –
as Marcus here (JLCL) – call a religion.

11. At *Ant.* 19.283–4, in the course of a document he ascribes to
Claudius,[23] Josephus has the emperor insist that each nation abide
by its own customs and not be forced to transgress its ancestral
thrēskeia; Claudius also recalls that the Jews refused to call Gaius
Caligula a god because they were unwilling to transgress their
thrēskeia. "Transgress" (*parabainō*) is – as we saw in the second item
in this list, concerning *War* 2.393 – something one does or does not
do to an obligation (such as laws, customs, or treaties), not to worship; while according to English usage one can transgress the rules
of worship, one cannot transgress worship. Accordingly, Feldman
(JLCL) used "religion" in both cases.

12. At 4 Macc 5:7 (usually dated to the late first century CE, more or
less contemporary to Josephus[24]) we read that Eleazar refused to
save himself by eating pork, because he persevered in observing
the Jews' *thrēskeia*. Since, as noted with regard to abstinence from
labour on the Sabbath, abstinence (in this case, from eating pork) is
not a type of "worship" or "cult," we can understand why translators (such as RSV, NRSV, Hadas[25]) use "religion."

13. Turning to the New Testament, we read in James 1:26–7 that
anyone who wants to be thought *thrēskos* should bridle his tongue
and not deceive his heart, for pure *thrēskeia* consists of taking care
of orphans and widows and in keeping oneself untainted by the

world. There is nothing about those demands that pertain to ritual or worship, or demands metaphorical usage, and it is perfectly normal for English translations, from King James to the NRSV, to use "religious … religion."[26]

14. According to Luke (Acts 26:5), Paul insisted that he had lived as a Pharisee, that is, "according to the strictest sect of our *thrēskeia*." English translations, from King James until today, quite regularly and rightly offer "religion," for there is nothing here limiting its sense to cult or worship, and we know that the Pharisees had opinions and teachings concerning many topics and practices that could not be subsumed under such a narrow rubric as "worship."[27] Moreover, the way we use the word "sect" it often denotes a version or variety of a "religion," so it is easy to understand Pharisaism as a sect within the Jewish religion, Judaism. In contrast, although a sect might espouse a particular variety of worship, it makes no sense to say that a sect *is* a version of a "worship."

⁀

Mason's discussion of cult ("Jews, Judaeans," 484–6), which opens (as noted) by including *thrēskeia* in a short list of terms that denote a national cult, takes the meaning of "cult" for granted, glossing it as "involving priests, temples, and animal sacrifice" (484) and insisting, as he concludes this part of his study (486), that such cult does not conform to what we mean by "religion": "Paradoxically, whereas the sacrificial cult was the ancient category that most conspicuously involved 'religious' language, with respect to consecration, purity, and attendance upon the Gods, it is probably the one most alien to modern conceptions of religion."

There are three problems with this. First, as we have seen, frequently – and especially by the first century CE – ancient usage of *thrēskeia* included something of which cult is at most only a part; it was something broader, often best translated by "religion." Second, adherents of religions that exist in the modern world that practise sacrifice, or pray for its restoration, or use the term "sacrifice" as a metaphor or simile denoting something more spiritual (such as "offerings" on a church platter) – or scholars who take such religions into consideration – might well find it difficult to accept the assumption that sacrifice is very alien to modern conceptions of religion. Thus, the sweeping nature of Mason's statement seems to be overdone; minimally, it would be appropriate to

add "some" or "many" before the closing reference to "modern conceptions." Third, and most fundamentally, even if no modern religions
practised sacrifice, hoped to, or used sacrificial terminology metaphori-
cally for some non-sacrificial practice, it seems that it need not follow
that the fact that ancients preferred to deal with God via sacrificial worship while moderns prefer prayer, philosophy, or morality (for example) is reason to think that "religion" – a term that refers to how people
relate to God – cannot be used, helpfully, to describe both ways of doing so. All the more so if, as Mason put it (in the passage cited from
"Jews, Judaeans," 486), the ancients used "religious" language concerning it. Why should we use such quotation marks to hint that the
application of our modern terms to this ancient phenomenon is more
unacceptable than the use of other modern words for other ancient phenomena, although they too had their differences – which we may point
out?[28]

To illustrate this problem, let us examine Mason's general statement
about the lack of "religion" in antiquity (pp. 481–2). I have broken his
text into two parts, to facilitate discussion:

> 1. Modern westerners recognize a category of life called "religion." We
> know (because we constructed these categories) that Judaism, Islam, and
> Buddhism are religions, whose representatives may take turns appearing
> on the religious features of BBC Radio … Since at least the American and
> French revolutions, this category has been isolable from the rest of our
> lives: religious systems may be adopted or abandoned. Whereas questions
> such as "Are you religious?," "What is your religion?," or "What do you
> think of religion?" are easily intelligible to us, there was no way to frame
> such questions in the ancient world, which knew of no separate category
> of "religion." The various elements that constitute our religion [were] in-
> extricably bound up with other aspects of their lives.
> 2. Walter Burkert could write a magisterial treatise on *Greek Religion*, to be
> sure, but he had to concede in the introduction: "Ritual and myth are the
> two forms in which Greek religion presents itself to the historian of reli-
> gion."[29] That is: two categories that *are ancient* lend themselves to critical
> study, but we cannot study an ancient category called religion.

In my opinion, these considerations are somewhat less than convincing, at least insofar as they are meant to justify the practical conclusion
about translation. Let us take Mason's claims and assumptions in order.
His first argument has two parts: the main thesis is that "religion" must

be isolable from the rest of one's life, and it is supported by the point that we know of a plurality of religions, which may be adopted or abandoned – a point that underlines that they are not bound up inseparably with other parts of our lives. However, the notion that religion must be isolable from the rest of our lives will run up against objections from many who would insist that religion is especially meaningful insofar as it informs numerous parts of our lives. Certainly that would be the case for a religion that instructs its adherents "Know him in all your ways" (Prov 3:6) and whose most prominent apologist in the period we are studying, Josephus, thought that "the whole constitution [of the Jews] is organized like some rite of consecration" (*Ag. Ap.* 2.188).[30] And as for it being the plurality of religions that clarifies, for us, the existence of the category, that certainly helps. So it may well be that many ancients, who lived more local lives than we do, were not aware of the fact that others dealt with the gods differently, and were therefore not aware that they were devotees of a "religion." But does that mean that *we*, today, in our parlance, cannot discuss the way the people of any such time and place related to their gods, and use the term "religion" to facilitate our discussions? Does, or should, the fact that a baby is not aware of its own existence, or capable of calling another baby "baby," prevent us from calling any given baby by that name? So we're back to the emic/etic debate.

Moreover, many of the *Ioudaioi* who wrote ancient literature, or are discussed by such literature, lived in mixed settings where they would indeed have become aware of their own religion, since it contrasted to religions of others. This is shown, for example, by the fact that literature of the period upon which we focus, including Josephus, refers a few times to Jews who abandon Jewish ways (3 Macc 1:3; *Ant.* 20.100) and often to non-Jews who adopt them.[31] When we refer to such people, using our language, the words that bear the appropriate meaning are "apostasy from Judaism" and "conversion to Judaism."

Mason's other argument is an example from the study of Greek religion, but it is not at all clear that Burkert meant his statement to be taken as a "concession." Burkert's statement opens the final paragraph of a section of his introduction titled "The Scope of the Study," and just as the preceding paragraphs discuss the chronological limits of his study and in them Burkert explains why he thinks it is legitimate to speak of Greek religion in the singular despite local variations, the final paragraph is meant to explain why his book on Greek religion focuses upon ritual and myth. As the very next sentence explains, "There

are no founding figures and no documents of revelation, no organizations of priests and no monastic orders" – so those who wish to study
ancient Greek religion must focus upon ritual and myth. That in no
way hints that the latter do not witness to a religion, no more than a
statement that Judaism has no organizations of priests and no monastic orders, which means that those who would study Judaism must
study other things (beliefs, practices, sacred texts), amounts to an assertion that Judaism is not a religion merely because other religions do
have organizations of priests and monastic orders. There are many
items that characterize religions, and the assertion that a focus on
some or the absence of others precludes the use of the term "religion"
seems to assume a lack of breadth and variety that does not conform
to the way we in fact use the term.[32] Although Burkert might agree that
we cannot study a category *that the ancients called religion*, he obviously
found it meaningful to speak about ancient Greek religion – just as
much as he used a modern language to speak and to write about the
ancients, although they did not use that language. I believe that it is
useful and meaningful to do the same concerning the Jewish religion
– Judaism.

II. "Judaism"

As noted in the opening paragraph of this appendix, Mason's claim
that "there was no category of 'Judaism' in the Graeco-Roman world"
was presented in defence of his preference for "Judean," rather than
"Jew," as the appropriate translation of *Ioudaios* in Josephus. The latter
too is an involved issue.

Sometimes it is clear that Josephus thinks of the people he describes
as what we would call Judeans. At *Ag. Ap.* 1.179 he quotes (credibly or
not) a disciple of Aristotle, Clearchus of Soli, who reported that Aristotle
himself explained that the term *Ioudaios* derives from the name of the
country,[33] and elsewhere Josephus takes that for granted, not only in his
War where, in general "Judeans" is the best translation, but even in
Antiquities. Note, for two parallel examples, that at *Ant.* 18.2 "Judea" –
with no separate reference to *Ioudaioi* – is the only antecedent of "of
them" (αὐτῶν), while at 18.196 *Ioudaios* – with no separate reference to
"Judea" – is the only antecedent of "there" (ἐκείνῃ).[34] Both passages
make sense only on the assumption that those who heard *Ioudaios* were
expected to understand it the way we understand "Judean" – as referring to a person from a particular *place*, Judea.

But both of those passages deal with people from Judea or in Judea. Many of the *Ioudaioi* of antiquity were neither. The question therefore is whether, and when, it makes more sense to translate references to *Ioudaioi* in our texts as a rule, into our parlance, given the options our English language supplies, as "Judeans," or rather, as "Jews" – of whom some were Judeans and others were, for example, Alexandrians or Romans, just as today some Jews are New Yorkers and some are Parisians. Elsewhere I have set out my own views on this issue, both concerning the development of "being Jewish" in general, from a primarily territorial and ethnic category to a religious one,[35] and concerning the application of that development to the translation of Josephus in particular: as explained in ch. 3, I prefer "Judean" for the *War* and "Jew" for the *Antiquities*. That is because I understand Josephus as having become something of a diasporan Jew in the decades separating those two works, just as all *Ioudaioi* were becoming more diasporan, hence "Jews," as a result of the destruction of the Temple, which, as the most holy place, was the linchpin of the territorial notion of being Jewish.[36] Mason, in contrast, prefers "Judean" across the board – a preference that, given the modern link between "Jew" and "Judaism," he defends by arguing that "there was no category of 'Judaism' in the Graeco-Roman world." To that argument we now turn.

That argument is problematic for two reasons. One was noted above (at n. 3): since "Jew," in our English, may refer to a person's descent without any reference to his or her religion, it follows that even if we thought there were no Jewish religion ("Judaism") in antiquity we might think there were Jews then, defined by their descent. Second, Mason's argument is problematic because *"Ioudaïsmos"* appears already in the second century BCE, in the Second Book of Maccabees. Accordingly, Mason devotes a detailed discussion to that book (pp. 465–8), to which I shall now respond.

That book, which uses *Ioudaïsmos* four times (2:21; 8:1; and twice in 14:38), obviously presents a challenge – the central challenge – to the thesis that "there was no category of 'Judaism' in the Graeco-Roman world." True, it might have been possible to bracket this challenge out and say that the term is so rare – it recurs elsewhere in Jewish literature only in IV Maccabees (4:26), which is dependent upon 2 Maccabees – that whatever it indicates should not affect the big picture. Maybe, similarly, its occurrences in Paul's Epistle to the Galatians too (1:13–14) might be ignored, even if, as indicated in n. 27, I am not convinced by Mason's attempt to explain them away as meaning something else.

However, even if *Ioudaïsmos* did not appear in those ancient texts, one might still argue that it is legitimate for us to use "Judaism" in discussing the period, for it is quite possible that the concept of what we call Judaism existed even where and when the term was not used, just as we may legitimately speak, today, about ancient Jewish "culture," "ethics," "sovereignty," "nationalism" or the like, although ancient Jewish languages had no words for such concepts.[37] Indeed, frequently terms for phenomena come into vogue only after the phenomena have been around long enough for the language to recognize them. For example, given the stories in 2 Maccabees 6–7, would anyone seriously argue that "martyrdom" did not exist in the second century BCE, although the word only appears a few centuries later?[38] Rather, just as we use English to describe ancient phenomena although English was not used in antiquity, so too is it perfectly legitimate and meaningful for us to use "Judaism," as any other English term, to describe ancient phenomena that fit the bill.[39] That is, even if 2 Maccabees did not exist and it were true that no term existed in antiquity for Judaism as a religion, the move from that observation to the conclusion that "Judaism" did not exist then might be a difficult one. We would still want to examine the ancient phenomena to see if they correspond to what we term "Judaism."

Moreover, Mason did not bracket Second Maccabees out and attempt to marginalize it. Rather, he argues that where the term *Ioudaïsmos* appears in Second Maccabees it does not refer to a religion, "Judaism," but, rather, to an activity – "Judaizing," the attempt to bring others to observe Judean law and custom, or, as he explains, the "striving to bring back other Judeans and reinstate the ancestral laws" ("Jews, Judaeans," 467).[40] His arguments are from classical usage and from an examination of each passage in Second Maccabees. In what follows, I shall review his arguments in turn.

Classical Usage

Mason's point of departure in this context is in classical Greek usage of similar terms ("Jews, Judaeans," 461–5). Here he makes his major point: the verb ιουδαΐζειν ("to judaize") is demonstrably used here and there in the sense of "becoming a *Ioudaios*" or "acting like a *Ioudaios*"; so, for example, LXX Esth 8:17; Theodotus, apud Eusebius, *Praep. Ev.* 9.22.5; Plutarch, *Cicero* 7.6;[41] Gal 2:14; Josephus, *War* 2.454 and 463. That corresponds to other such verbs in ancient Greek, such as verbs for

Medizing, Atticizing, and the like. From this he infers that the noun *Ioudaïsmos* should denote the activity denoted by such verbs – the going over, or bringing over, to something, which we usually term Judaizing, or Judaization.[42]

Here we must make two observations. First, what is said about those who "Judaized" in the texts Mason cites is not that they supported another country in the context of some war or political conflict (which is what is said about Medizers, Atticizers, and the like). Rather, Theodotus talks about the Shechemites circumcising themselves; Plutarch's anecdote relates to an event said to have occurred in Rome, and although no details about the "Judaizing" are offered, there is nothing to link it to Judea; Josephus refers in *War* 2.454 to a Roman officer who "Judaized" by circumcision (just as at *Ant.* 11.285 he interprets the "Judaizers" of Esth 8:17 as having done the same); and Paul's statement in Galatians 2:14 pertains to Peter's observance of laws concerning the purity of food.[43] But circumcision and dietary restrictions are elements of what we call "Judaism." So if, in our English, we asked what these "Judaizers" undertook, or tended towards, we probably would not respond by reference to a place or state, Judea – in contrast to the way we think of Media and Athens when we hear of Medizers and Atticizers.[44] But neither would we say that they were undertaking or tending to "Judaizing." Rather, we would say that, via or as a result of their Judaizing, they were undertaking or tending to "Judaism."

Second, along the way to that argument Mason noted that, in general Greek usage of the classical period, such verbs had a "negative tinge" to them. "Inasmuch as fidelity to one's *ethnos* and ancestral customs was considered an axiomatic duty ..., such a change to other allegiances was normally to be deplored" ("Jews, Judaeans," 462). That is true. However, since no one would suggest that *Ioudaïsmos* in 2 Maccabees has such a negative tinge to it,[45] the apparent conclusion is that this aspect of classical usage will not be a conclusive guide to the use of our term in this book. Rather, we must review each of the four occurrences of *Ioudaïsmos* in Second Maccabees.

Ioudaïsmos in Second Maccabees

Concerning 2 Macc 2:21 Mason observes that this passage in the book's preface refers to those "who were assisted by heavenly interventions while they bravely vied for honour, which they did for the sake of *Ioudaïsmos* (*hyper tou Ioudaïsmou*), which activity consisted in *driving*

out the barbarian masses (ta barbara plēthē diōkein)." Then he remarks,
"Already here we have reason to think that *Ioudaïsmos* is not a general
term for 'Judaism,' but rather a certain kind of *activity* over against a
pull in another, foreign, direction" ("Jews, Judaeans," 465–6; original
emphasis). To judge from his use of italics for the last five words of his
rendition of 2:21, and from the fact that he also cites in full the Greek
text of those words, Mason's point is the apparent continuity and paral-
lelism between *Ioudaïsmos* and driving out barbarians, as if the latter
paraphrases the former, defining it or stating its practical meaning.

However, we should note, first of all, that in paraphrasing the verse
Mason skipped a clause that comes between "*Ioudaïsmos*" and "driving
out the barbarian masses": seven Greek words that report that Judas
and his brothers "plundered the entire country although they were few
in number." That creates quite a distance between the two items that
are apparently the focus of Mason's argument here, and, accordingly,
reason to doubt the assumption that one paraphrases the other. Rather,
we have here, in 2:21, the beginning of a list of a number of things Judas
and his brothers did – a list that goes on into v. 22 as well[46] – and there
is no particular reason to focus on any part of the list as indicating the
nature of *Ioudaïsmos*.

Moreover, note that even in Mason's paraphrase of 2:21 the words
"which activity" properly refer back not to *Ioudaïsmos* but, rather, to
"which they did," words that in turn point to "bravely vied." The only
way to make "which activity" refer to *Ioudaïsmos* is to beg the question
and assume that *Ioudaïsmos* refers to an activity done to others (transitive "Judaization"), not to a religion (or "a culture or system" – Mason,
466) practised by Jews – but that is the issue under debate. That is,
2 Macc 2:21 makes perfect sense if we assume, as is usual, that the author means that his heroes fought for Judaism by driving out the barbarian masses – whose presence, in one way or another, impeded the
Jews' ability to practise Judaism. There is no need to import the notion
that the presence of the barbarian masses impeded the efforts of heroic
Ioudaioi to make or encourage other *Ioudaioi* to do anything.

Mason supports his argument, that *Ioudaïsmos* in 2:21 refers to a pulling in a particular direction, by a discussion of 2 Maccabees' use of
Hellenismos at 4:10, which he translates: "There was such a pinnacle
of *Hellenizing* and an inroad of *foreignizing*." As he explains, "Here,
Hellenismos (like *allophylismos*) cannot indicate a culture or system; it
labels a *defection* that threatens the heart and soul of Judean tradition"
("Jews, Judaeans," 466, original emphasis). Then, *if* one assumes, as

Mason does on the next page, that the author of 2 Maccabees means for us to understand that "Judas' antidote to this *Hellenizing* was a counter-movement," it follows that we should understand it, as Mason puts it, as "a bringing back of those who had gone over to foreign ways: a 'Judaizing' or Judaization, which the author of 2 Maccabees programmatically labels *Ioudaïsmos*."

However, while Judas did field a counter-movement against Hellenizing, it is difficult to imagine that the author of 2 Maccabees called that movement *Ioudaïsmos*. Rather, according to 2 Macc 8:1 Judas built his movement by recruiting those *who had remained in Ioudaïsmos* – which seems to be something static, in which one could remain (on 8:1, see below). Moreover, while I agree with Mason that, in 2 Maccabees, *Hellenismos* (and *allophylismos*) should be understood as standing in contrast to *Ioudaïsmos*,[47] the author does not ever present *Ioudaïsmos* as bringing or inviting others to join ("defect to") anything or to do anything. Rather, *Ioudaïsmos* is presented as a legitimate status quo ante, a way of life followed by *Ioudaioi* that was threatened by Hellenizing and foreignizing. The author has no interest at all in claiming that he has a program that competes with another, no more than a Spartan would claim that, in Sparta, Medizing might compete with Spartanizing. Rather, Medizing threatened Sparta and the Spartan way of life, which were, or should have been, stable givens – not movements.[48] So too, for Second Maccabees, *Ioudaïsmos* is the legitimate *politeia* of Jerusalem, a stable system, like our "Judaism." It should not have needed to prove itself against any other system, and what was reprehensible about Jason's innovations, as later, of course, about Antiochus IV's decrees, was that they were an attempt to change and/or abrogate what was right and legitimate.

That this is so emerges clearly, I believe, from the author's usage in the other two passages in which *Ioudaïsmos* appears. With regard to 2 Macc 8:1 Mason opens his discussion of its characterization of Judas' supporters as those "who had remained in *Ioudaïsmos*" by admitting that it is tempting to translate "Judaism." That is quite correct, and other translators seem to be unanimous in rendering the words that way.[49] But given the needs of his thesis, Mason has to resist that natural reading, and instead took the verse to be referring "to those who 'had persisted in *the Judaizing* [program]' – that is, not simply clinging to their faith and *remaining Ioudaioi*, but striving to *bring back* other Judaeans and reinstate the ancestral law" ("Jews, Judaeans," 467; emphasis in the original). However, as noted, not a word in 2 Maccabees indicates that anyone tried to bring apostate Jews back to observance of the ancestral laws.

True, Mason offers an argument in favour of his interpretation of 2 Macc 8:1 ("Jews, Judaeans," 467): "Such a reading best explains how the group in question immediately behaves as an effective guerrilla organization (*systema*): burning towns, capturing strategic sites, and becoming invincible to foreigners (8:5 [+ 8:6 – DRS]). All along they have remained active in 'Judaizing' activities, and that is why they are ready for active service with Judas."

However, it is hardly warranted to say that activities such as "burning towns, capturing strategic sites, and becoming invincible to foreigners" fit the definition Mason proposes for *Ioudaïsmos* here: "striving to bring back other Judeans and reinstate the ancestral laws."[50] Nothing is said here about ancestral laws, no suggestion made that the kind of people who excelled in such military activity were also devoted to reinstating those laws; rather, they had "remained in Judaism." Moreover, while Mason is right that it is proper to use the author's characterization of the individuals involved (they had "remained in *Ioudaïsmos*") in order to explain what he says they did, *the author does not say they did any of the activities that Mason summarized on the basis of 8:5–6*. What the author says about them is that they joined Judas' movement (8:1) and prayed (8:2–4) – but they are not actors in vv. 5–6, as we shall now see.

Of course, if there were some question in readers' minds as to how Judas' group could have been successful, it might be natural to look at the reference to his followers' having previously "remained in *Ioudaïsmos*" to help us resolve the difficulty. However, there is no such question, for although Mason writes, summarizing 8:5–6, about what "the group in question did," that formulation in fact misses the point of the author of 2 Maccabees, who, in a typical case of "double causality,"[51] instead attributes the activities recounted in 8:6–7 to two other actors:

1. *Judas*: All the verbs in 8:5–7 are in the masculine singular, referring to Judas alone: he becomes invincible, he attacks by surprise, he burns, he captures, he causes his enemies to flee, he exploited the nights as his ally – and of course he did all that, successfully, thanks to "his valour," of which report spread everywhere. Accordingly, he is "the man" whose successes come to the attention of the Seleucid government (8:8).[52]
2. *God*: It is his move from wrath to mercy, reported in 8:5 – which is the turning point of the entire book – that allows for Judas' victories.

Given either one of these actors, and certainly both together, there is no need to assume that readers of 2 Maccabees will have felt a need to search for anything in the past of Judas' followers that might explain their current successes. Therefore, there is all the less reason for us to suspect that the statement in 8:1, that they had remained in *Ioudaïsmos*, is meant to explain anything more than what is reported there: that they had remained faithful to Judaism. That statement is illustrated immediately thereafter not by anything they did to others but, rather, by the fact that they did something we can only term religious – they prayed (vv. 2–4). Thus, although we may agree that readers should understand that those who remained in *Ioudaïsmos* became Judas' soldiers, there is no reason to think that we are meant to think that their military activities were understood as *Ioudaïsmos*.

That *Ioudaïsmos* in 2 Macc 8:1 means "Judaism" rather than transitive "Judaizing" derives, additionally, from the fact that 8:1 resumes the story begun in ch. 6, which opens with Antiochus' decrees against the observance of what it terms "laws of their fathers ... laws of God." The author presents those royal decrees as forbidding Jews not only to observe those laws, but even "simply to admit to being a Jew" (6:6). After describing those decrees, 2 Maccabees goes on to tell the stories of some who violated them. First we hear some brief reports about individuals who did so and unsuccessfully tried to keep it a secret; they were caught and punished (6:10–11). Then we hear at much greater length, in the remainder of ch. 6 and all of ch. 7, about some paradigmatic others who were arrested, who demonstratively refused to give in to the king's demands, and so were tortured and martyred.

Thus, those chapters describe people who were caught trying to observe the laws Antiochus had proscribed. They were, in the author's terms (6:6), people who insisted upon being *Ioudaioi*. Of such *Ioudaioi*, the stories of those who were apprehended and killed are told in chs. 6–7. But presumably others persisted and managed to escape detection – particularly if they were not in the capital but, rather, in scattered villages, further from the royal eye, *such as those mentioned in 8:1*: villagers who remained in *Ioudaïsmos*. In other words, it seems that responsible exegesis requires us to link those villagers who "remained in *Ioudaïsmos*" of 8:1 to those who persisted in doing what being a *Ioudaios* entailed, according to chs. 6–7.

But there, in chs. 6–7, nothing is said of "Judaizing," of anyone undertaking Jewish ways or encouraging others to do that or anything else. All that is reported is that there were *Ioudaioi* who insisted upon circumcising their sons (6:11), observing the Sabbath (6:12), and abstaining from meats forbidden to Jews either because they were from pagan sacrifices (6:7–8, 21) or simply because they were not kosher (6:18 and all of ch. 7). The *Ioudaioi* of chs. 6–7 call themselves *Ioudaioi* and do what *Ioudaioi* do, but there is nothing about them "Judaizing" themselves or others. That is, although *Ioudaïsmos* does not appear in chs. 6–7 it is appropriate, in our English – which, to reiterate, is what this is all about – to say that the heroes of chs. 6–7 died because they persisted in the observance of Judaism. It would, therefore, require some very compelling reason not to use that English term as the translation of *Ioudaïsmos* when it does appear in the same context, at the outset of ch. 8, which refers to others of the same orientation, who managed to survive.

Finally, Mason takes the last two appearances of *Ioudaïsmos* in 2 Maccabees, in the characterization of Razis at 2 Macc 14:38 as one who "was brought to trial on the charge of *Ioudaïsmos* – and indeed he had spent every ounce of energy, body and soul, for the sake of *Ioudaïsmos*," to mean that he had been charged with "striving to restore Judean law and custom against a powerful counter-current" ("Jews, Judaeans," 467–8). In support, Mason argues that "the charge of *Ioudaïsmos*, along with the gloss concerning Razis' extreme exertions in its behalf, cannot simply mean that he *remained a Jew* or 'within Judaism'; the high-priest Alcimus was also a prominent *Ioudaios*, and even our hostile author concedes that he presented himself as acting in the interests of his people" (14:6–10; original emphasis). That is, the case of Alcimus shows that simply *being* a *Ioudaios* was not enough to bring charges upon someone, so it must be that Razis was accused of doing more – and that more, according to Mason, was "judaizing" others. However:

1. Although the author of 2 Maccabees does not term Alcimus a *Ioudaios*, I assume, as does Mason, that readers should take that for granted. But that is not what the author wants to underline. Rather, what the author of 2 Maccabees explicitly says, at 14:3, is that Alcimus willingly polluted himself at the time of the persecutions – which, in terms of this book, means that he did what Antiochus' decrees demanded, in contrast to those heroes depicted in chs. 6–7 and 8:1. So although Mason is right that just being a *Ioudaios* was not enough to bring prosecution upon Razis, there is no need to import the notion of Judaizing others – what Mason here formulates as "striving to restore Judean law and custom," in order to explain the difference between Alcimus and Razis. Rather, we

should prefer to focus on the element the book itself addresses, and to conclude that Razis was accused of doing what Alcimus had not done: refusing to pollute himself, he had violated the royal decree against observing "the divine laws" (6:1). That is, the simplest reading of *Ioudaïsmos* in 14:38 is, in my opinion, that the author of 2 Maccabees is presenting Razis as another Jew who had himself "remained in Judaism," as those of chs. 6–7 and 8:1, as opposed to other Jews, such as Alcimus, who had not.

2. Similarly, when Mason ("Jews, Judaeans," 468) points to 14:6–10 as showing that "even our hostile author concedes that [Alcimus] presented himself as acting in the interests of his people," he apparently sees here additional support for his argument that merely *being* a *Ioudaios* was not enough to get one into trouble, which would indicate that if Razis did get into trouble he must have been Judaizing others. Beyond what I wrote about that argument in the preceding paragraph, here I would add that the author clearly guides his readers not to believe Alcimus, but rather to view him as a hypocrite. He does this in two ways:

    a. most obviously, by stating as the omniscient author at 14:3 that Alcimus' motive was purely self-serving, thus allowing us to recognize Alcimus' hypocrisy when, a few verses later, in the passage to which Mason alludes (14:6–10), he speaks in his own voice as if he had the interests of the king, and also of his people, at heart; and

    b. most artistically, by portraying Alcimus as a mirror image of the admirable Onias, whose mission to the Seleucid king portrayed in very similar terms in 4:5–6 was indeed on behalf of the national interest. Readers are clearly supposed to read Alcimus' speech ironically, as a hypocritical imitation of Onias'.[53]

This means that we cannot point to 2 Maccabees' account of Alcimus as if it demonstrated that, according to the author of this work, at this point of the story the Seleucids had no complaints about Jews who lived as Jews, and so struck out only against those who tried to Judaize others. If the Seleucids did not prosecute Alcimus, that did not prove they would not prosecute or persecute sincere Jews such as Razis simply for being sincere Jews.

In sum, there seems to be no weighty reason to move from the usual "Judaism" to "Judaizing" as the appropriate English translation of

Ioudaïsmos in 2 Maccabees. The heroes of that work are not at all portrayed
as having attempted to force or even encourage anyone to live as a
Jew;[54] rather, they themselves persevered in the observance of Jewish
law. Moreover, the laws they observe are "the laws of their fathers and
God" (6:1), featuring circumcision, Sabbath, and the laws of kosher
food. Although many died because they did so, refusing to desist from
declaring themselves to be *Ioudaioi* (6:6), others who so persisted managed – away from official eyes, perhaps especially in the countryside
(8:1) – to survive, and the author characterizes them as having "remained in *Ioudaïsmos*." But since circumcision, Sabbath observance, and
kashrut are, in our language, elements of the religion called "Judaism,"
those words – "religion" and "Judaism" – are the ones we should use in
telling this story. Indeed, it seems that the author of Second Maccabees
meant the same when he used – invented? – *Ioudaïsmos*.[55]

     As noted at the outset of this appendix, *Ioudaios* in ancient texts is at
times best rendered by "Judean," at times by "Jew." *Ioudaïsmos*, however, is a much rarer term, and what I have suggested is that we should
leave it where we found it: associated with usage of *Ioudaios* of the
latter type. The fact that it is rare means, apparently, that it witnesses
to a process that began in the period that saw the word appear – the
Hellenistic period – but was far from complete: the move from being
"Judeans" to being "Jews." That process, however, although not so
far along in Judea (which explains how Jews there, even a couple of
centuries after the composition of Second Maccabees, were capable of
starting something that is appropriately termed a "Judean" war against
Rome), was most natural and to be expected and understood among
Ioudaioi such as the author of Second Maccabees, who were Jews of the
Hellenistic Diaspora.[56] For such *Ioudaioi*, despite whatever memories
they maintained of a past elsewhere, and despite whatever hopes they
may or may not have held for a future elsewhere, were not "Judeans"
in the only sense the English language, according to its most respectable authorities, ascribes to that term: natives or inhabitants of Judea.
Rather, they were "Jews" – what those authorities and common usage
define as a matter of descent and/or religion.

Notes

Preface

1 See below, ch. 4, n. 23.

2 In fact, a similar issue would arise for "Greeks" if the term "Grecian" were more popular. That noun was used a few times (Acts 6:1, 9:29, and, it seems, 11:20) by the King James version of the Bible in order to render *Hellēnistēs* ("Hellenist"), as opposed to its use of "Greek" for *Hellēn*. However, "Grecian" is extremely rare in English and, moreover, when used it is almost exclusively as an adjective and as a synonym of "Greek" or "ancient Greek." Accordingly, those who choose to use it, for example when referring to "Grecian architecture," are not making a demonstrative statement about which term is appropriate and which is not.

3 Compare the way New Testament translators typically render *Hellēn* by "Greek" and *Rhomaios* by "Roman" and let commentators and readers debate, in some cases incessantly, whether the former means "Greek" or, more generally, "Gentile," and whether the latter means "Roman" or, more specifically, "Roman citizen." When they do opt for interpretive translation, such as with the KJV's "Gentiles" at Romans 2:9–10 and the RSV's "Roman citizens" at Acts 16:37–8 (contrast the RSV's "Greeks" in the former case and KJV's "Romans" in the latter [that is, the RSV moved once in one direction, once in the other]), they do something very different from merely choosing another translation, as in the case of "Judean" and "Jew."

4 W. D. Davies, *Paul and Rabbinic Judaism* (4th ed.; Philadelphia: Fortress, 1980), xxiii (preface, dated 1981). Over the next few pages Davies discusses the "eclipse" of such earlier dichotomies as those between Palestinian and Hellenistic Judaism (which mixes geography and culture) and between

Pharisaism and apocalypticism. The present volume offers a new version of the former. For a recent attempt to reassess the latter, thirty years after Davies, see R. Boustan, "Rabbinization and the Making of Early Jewish Mysticism," *JQR* 101 (2010/2011): 482–501.

5 S. J. D. Cohen, "The Modern Study of Ancient Judaism," in *The State of Jewish Studies* (ed. S. J. D. Cohen and E. L. Greenstein; Detroit: Wayne State University Press, 1990), 55–73.

6 On "the rule of the Martian," see below, ch. 2, n. 16. Similarly, for analysis and criticism of the tendency to speak of "Judaisms" rather than of varieties of Judaism, see S. Schwartz's study cited in n. 1 to the Appendix.

7 Davies, as above, n. 4.

Introduction

1 *The Oxford English Dictionary* (ed. J. A. Simpson and E. S. C. Weiner; Oxford: Clarendon, 1989), 7.291.

2 Ibid., 228.

3 *Webster's Third New International Dictionary of the English Language, Unabridged* (ed. P. B. Gove; Springfield, Mass.: Merriam, 1976), 1222–3.

4 Ibid., 1215.

5 *The Random House Dictionary of the English Language* (ed. J. Stein; New York: Random House, 1971), 772.

6 Ibid., 767.

7 Other non-cognate terms, such as Greek transliterations of "Hebrew" and "Israel(ite)," were also used now and then; see G. Harvey, *The True Israel: Uses of the Names Jew, Hebrew and Israel in Ancient Jewish and Early Christian Literature* (AGJU 35; Leiden: Brill, 1996). However, *Ioudaios* was by far the most common term used for the people in question, and also the one that raises the problems upon which this volume shall focus. For a hint at how problems like these continue to occupy Greek-speaking Jews today, see the frontispiece of the present volume.

8 On the definition of "religion," see below, Appendix, n. 32.

9 This is common to much of recent scholarship on Jewish identity in antiquity. Among the most central works: S. J. D. Cohen, *The Beginnings of Jewishness: Boundaries, Varieties, Uncertainties* (HCS 31; Berkeley: University of California Press, 1999); S. Schwartz, *Imperialism and Jewish Society, 200 B.C.E. to 640 C.E.* (Princeton: Princeton University Press, 2001); D. Boyarin, *Border Lines: The Partition of Judaeo-Christianity* (Philadelphia: University of Pennsylvania Press, 2004); D. M. Goodblatt, *Elements of Ancient Jewish Nationalism* (New York: Cambridge University Press, 2006); J. Frey, S.

Gripentrog, and D. R. Schwartz, eds., *Jewish Identity in the Greco-Roman World: Jüdische Identität in der griechisch-römischen Welt* (AJEC 71; Leiden: Brill, 2007); L. I. Levine and D. R. Schwartz, eds., *Jewish Identities in Antiquity: Studies in Memory of Menahem Stern* (TSAJ 130; Tübingen: Mohr Siebeck, 2009). For a survey and analysis, see D. M. Miller, "The Meaning of *Ioudaios* and Its Relationship to Other Group Labels in Ancient 'Judaism,'" *Currents in Biblical Research* 9/1 (2010): 98–126.

10 See Josephus, *Ag. Ap.* 1.179 (quoting Aristotle via one of his disciples) and *Ant.* 18.196. For these texts, see below, 102.

11 Including C. R. Holladay, ed., *Fragments from Hellenistic Jewish Authors* (4 vols.; SBLTT 20, 30, 39, 40; Chico, Calif.: Scholars, 1983–1996); D. Noy, ed., *Jewish Inscriptions of Western Europe* (2 vols.; Cambridge: Cambridge University Press, 1993–1995); M. S. Cowey and K. Maresch, *Urkunden des Politeuma der Juden von Herakleopolis (144/3 – 133/2 v.Chr.) (P. Polit. Iud.)* (Papyrologica Coloniensia 29; Wiesbaden: Westdeutscher, 2001); D. Noy et al., eds., *Inscriptiones Judaicae Orientis* (3 vols.; TSAJ 99, 101, 102; Tübingen: Mohr Siebeck, 2004); and numerous annotated translations of diasporan works, including those in such series as FJTC, JSHRZ, CEJL, and the Philo of Alexandria Commentary Series.

12 Such as P. R. Trebilco, *Jewish Communities in Asia Minor* (SNTSMS 69; Cambridge: Cambridge University Press, 1991); W. C. van Unnik, *Das Selbstverständnis der jüdischen Diaspora in der hellenistisch-römischer Zeit* (ed. P. W. van der Horst; AGJU 17; Leiden: Brill, 1993); B. Halpern-Amaru, *Rewriting the Bible: Land and Covenant in Post-Biblical Jewish Literature* (Valley Forge, Penn.: Trinity, 1994); J. Mélèze Modrzejewski, *The Jews of Egypt from Rameses II to Emperor Hadrian* (Philadelphia and Jerusalem: Jewish Publication Society, 1995); L. V. Rutgers, *The Jews in Late Ancient Rome: Evidence of Cultural Interaction in the Roman Diaspora* (Religions in the Greco-Roman World 126; Leiden: Brill, 1995); G. Bohak, *Joseph and Asenath and the Jewish Temple in Heliopolis* (SBLEJL 10; Atlanta: Scholars, 1996); B. Bar-Kochva, *Pseudo-Hecataeus, On the Jews: Legitimizing the Jewish Diaspora* (HCS 21; Berkeley: University of California Press, 1996); M. Pucci Ben Zeev, *Jewish Rights in the Roman World: The Greek and Roman Documents Quoted by Josephus Flavius* (TSAJ 74; Tübingen: Mohr Siebeck, 1998); E. Leigh Gibson, *The Jewish Manumission Inscriptions of the Bosphorus Kingdom* (TSAJ 75; Tübingen: Mohr Siebeck, 1999); L. Roth-Gerson, *The Jews of Syria as Reflected in Greek Inscriptions* (Jerusalem: Shazar Center, 2001 [in Hebrew]); M. Pucci Ben Zeev, *Diaspora Judaism in Turmoil, 116/117 CE: Ancient Sources and Modern Insights* (Interdisciplinary Studies in Ancient Culture and Religion 6; Leuven: Peeters, 2005); L. Capponi, *Il tempio di*

*Leontopoli in Egitto: Identità politica e religiosa dei Guidei di Onia (c. 150 a. C. –
73 d. C.)* (Pubblicazioni della Facoltà di lettere e filosofia dell'Università di
Pavia 118; Pisa: ETS, 2007); A. Edrei and D. Mendels, "A Split Jewish
Diaspora: Its Dramatic Consequences," *JSP* 16 (2007): 91–137 and 17
(2008): 163–87.

13 Including S. J. D. Cohen and E. S. Frerichs, eds., *Diasporas in Antiquity* (BJS
288; Atlanta: Scholars, 1993); A. Oppenheimer and B. Isaac, eds., *Studies on
the Jewish Diaspora in the Hellenistic and Roman Periods* (Te'udah 12; Tel-
Aviv: Ramot, 1996); J. M. Scott, ed., *Exile: Old Testament, Jewish, and
Christian Conceptions* (JSJSup 56; Leiden: Brill, 1997); I. M. Gafni, *Land,
Center and Diaspora: Jewish Constructs in Late Antiquity* (JSPSup 21;
Sheffield: Sheffield Academic, 1997); L. V. Rutgers, *The Hidden Heritage of
Diaspora Judaism* (2nd ed.; CBET 20; Leuven: Peeters, 1998); K. P. Donfried
and P. Richardson, eds., *Judaism and Christianity in First-Century Rome*
(Grand Rapids, Mich.: Eerdmans, 1998); M. Goodman, ed., *Jews in a
Graeco-Roman World* (Oxford: Oxford University Press, 1998); I. M. Gafni,
ed., *Center and Diaspora: The Land of Israel and the Diaspora in the Second
Temple, Mishna and Talmud Periods* (Jerusalem: Shazar Center, 2004 [in
Hebrew]); J. M. G. Barclay, ed., *Negotiating Diaspora: Jewish Strategies in the
Roman Empire* (Library of Second Temple Studies 45; London: Clark, 2004);
several studies grouped under the rubric "Mapping Diaspora Identities"
in *Heavenly Tablets: Interpretation, Identity and Tradition in Ancient Judaism*
(ed. L. LiDonnici and A. Lieber; JSJSup 119; Leiden: Brill, 2007), 111–210.

14 J. M. G. Barclay, *Jews in the Mediterranean Diaspora from Alexander to Hadrian
(323 BCE – 117 CE)* (Edinburgh: Clark, 1996); E. S. Gruen, *Heritage and
Hellenism: The Reinvention of Jewish Tradition* (HCS 30; Berkeley: University
of California Press, 1998); Gruen, *Diaspora: Jews amidst Greeks and Romans*
(Cambridge, Mass.: Harvard University Press, 2002).

15 In his commentary on *War* 2.487 (FJTC 1b, 351, n. 2988), S. Mason – who
indeed uses "Judeans" here, as throughout – suggests that we takes
Josephus' use of the verb *metoikeō*, of the Jews' residence in Alexandria, as
if it refers to something second-class: "'living alongside' – as a foreign or
alien resident"; he refers to his n. 783 on *War* 2.124, where he adds the
comparison to "metics" in Greek cities. That could allow more room for
reference to another, more permanent homeland, Judea. However,
Josephus goes on, in the same line of *War*, as also in *Ant.* 19.281, to stress
that the *Ioudaioi* enjoyed equal rights in Alexandria (unlike metics in
Athens) and in *Ant.* 19.281 he uses a verb that clearly points in the direction of sharing and parity: centuries ago both the *Ioudaioi* and "the

Alexandrians" settled *together* (*sygkatoikizō*) in the city. It is, therefore, unlikely that he would be happy if we took his wording in *War* to mean that the *Ioudaioi* of Alexandria were comparable to metics.

16 Cohen, *Beginnings of Jewishness*, 71–2.

17 S. Mason, "Jews, Judaeans, Judaizing, Judaism: Problems of Categorization in Ancient History," *JSJ* 38 (2007): 503–4 (original emphases).

18 On this phenomenon, see S. McKnight, *A Light among the Gentiles: Jewish Missionary Activity in the Second Temple Period* (Minneapolis: Fortress, 1991); M. Goodman, *Mission and Conversion: Proselytizing in the Religious History of the Roman Empire* (Oxford: Clarendon, 1994); M. E. Bird, *Crossing over Sea and Land: Jewish Missionary Activity in the Second Temple Period* (Peabody, Mass.: Hendrickson, 2010).

19 See, for example, I. Malkin, ed., *Ancient Perceptions of Greek Ethnicity* (Center for Hellenic Studies Colloquia 5; Cambridge, Mass.: Harvard University Press, 2001).

20 Many English dictionaries have no entry for "Judean" or "Judaean."

21 Compare, for example, our reactions when someone is referred to by the neologism "chairperson" instead of the traditional "chairman."

22 On Hellenism in Judea, see, inter alia: M. Hengel, *Judaism and Hellenism: Studies in Their Encounter in Palestine during the Early Hellenistic Period* (2 vols.; London: SCM, 1974); L. I. Levine, *Judaism and Hellenism in Antiquity: Conflict or Confluence?* (Seattle: University of Washington Press, 1998); J. J. Collins, ed., *Hellenism in the Land of Israel* (Christianity and Judaism in Antiquity 13; Notre Dame, Ind.: University of Notre Dame Press, 2001); O. Tal, *The Archaeology of Hellenistic Palestine: Between Tradition and Renewal* (Jerusalem: Bialik Institute, 2006 [in Hebrew]).

23 On the Jewish community of Rome, which was already of significant size in the days of Cicero (see his *Pro Flacco* 28 – *GLAJJ* I, no. 68) and Augustus (see Josephus, *Ant.* 17.330 and Philo, *Embassy to Gaius* 155) and becoming quite large by the days of Tiberius and Claudius (Cassius Dio 57.18.5a and 60.6.6 – *GLAJJ* I, nos. 419, 422), see Rutgers, *Jews in Late Ancient Rome*; Rutgers, *Hidden Heritage of Diaspora Judaism*; Donfried and Richardson, *Judaism and Christianity*; and H. J. Leon, *The Jews of Ancient Rome* (updated ed.; Peabody, Mass.: Hendrickson, 1995).

Chapter 1

1 For a succinct comparison of the two books, see G. W. E. Nickelsburg, "1 and 2 Maccabees: Same Story, Different Meaning," in *George W. E.*

Nickelsburg in Perspective: An Ongoing Dialogue of Learning (vol. 2; ed. J. Neusner and A. J. Avery-Peck; JSJSup 80; Leiden: Brill, 2003), 659–84 (originally in *CTM* 42 [1971]: 515–26).

2 In 1 Maccabees: the first nine verses of ch. 1, which survey the century-and-a-half from Alexander the Great to Antiochus IV. In 2 Maccabees: the introductory letters and author's preface in chs. 1–2. The narrative begins in 2 Macc 3, with events that transpired in the days of Seleucus IV, but that chapter is basically a prologue that shows how God protected Jerusalem and the Temple before the Jews became sinful. Thus, the real story begins in ch. 4, with the concomitant appearance of the Jews' sins and their nemesis (Seleucus' brother): Antiochus IV Epiphanes.

3 See, for example, the literal Greek rendering of such Hebrew phrases as "by the mouth of a sword" (= "by the blade of a sword," 5:28, 51; e.g., Josh 6:21, 8:24; Judg 20:37) and "each man to his neighbour" (= "to one another," 2:40; 3:43; e.g., Judg 6:29; 2 Kgs 7:3, 9). As for Hebrew style underlying the Greek of 1 Maccabees, see the details and references about "Translation Profile of the Greek" in G. T. Zervos, "1 Makkabees," in *New English Translation of the Septuagint* (ed. A. Pietersma and B. G. Wright; New York and Oxford: Oxford University Press, 2007), 478–9; and the numerous examples in H. W. Ettelson, *The Integrity of I Maccabees* (Transactions of the Connecticut Academy of Arts and Sciences 27; New Haven: Connecticut Academy of Arts and Sciences, 1925), 307–41.

4 On pathetic (or "tragic") historiography in 2 Maccabees, see R. Doran, *Temple Propaganda: The Purpose and Character of 2 Maccabees* (CBQMS 12; Washington, D.C.: Catholic Biblical Association of America, 1981), 77–109; B. Bar-Kochva, *Judas Maccabaeus: The Jewish Struggle against the Seleucids* (Cambridge: Cambridge University Press, 1989), 172–8. For some florid examples, see 2 Macc 3:14b–21; 5:11b–14; 6:9b–11; 9:5–10; 14:39–46.

5 Note, for example, the explicit comparison of the enmity between Jews and their neighbours to that between Jacob and Esau (5:2–3) and the description of Simon's days with the help of biblical prophecies concerning the messianic age (1 Macc 14:8//Zech 8:12; 1 Macc 14:9//Zech 8:4; 1 Macc 14:12//Micah 4:4). See, in general, U. Rappaport, "A Note on the Use of the Bible in 1 Maccabees," in *Biblical Perspectives: Early Use and Interpretation of the Bible in Light of the Dead Sea Scrolls* (ed. M. E. Stone and E. G. Chazon; STDJ 28; Leiden: Brill, 1998), 175–9.

6 Indeed, although 2 Maccabees quotes the Bible explicitly only twice (7:6; 10:26), it seems that it alludes to it somewhat more often than is generally recognized (see Schwartz, *2 Maccabees*, 62–3), and that a very historical

chapter of the Torah (Deut 32) in fact underlies its basic understanding of its story (see Schwartz, *2 Maccabees*, 21–2).

7 See, for example, the references to Scythians as the embodiment of barbarity (4:47; 7:4) and the implicit comparisons (5:21; 9:8) of Antiochus' hubris and arrogance to those of Herodotus' Xerxes (Herodotus 7.22–4, 33–6) – an episode so popular in Greek antiquity that already Isocrates (*Panegyricus* 89) commented about how often it was cited. In general, on Hellenism in 2 Maccabees, see M. Himmelfarb, "Judaism and Hellenism in 2 Maccabees," *Poetics Today* 19 (1998): 19–40.

8 For 2 Maccabees as a diasporan work, see my *2 Maccabees*, 45–55. As is noted there (45, n. 100), we do not know where the author was when he wrote it, but what is clear and of importance, in the present context, is that he was, culturally, a Jew of the Hellenistic Diaspora.

9 Note especially the way 1 Macc 2:65 has Mattathias designate Simon as his successor, although already 3:1 ignores that, and the rest of the story reflects no knowledge of such a testament. See my "Mattathias' Deathbed Speech: From Religious Zeal to Simonide Propaganda," in *"Go Out and Study the Land" (Judges 18:2): Archaeological, Historical and Textual Studies in Honor of Hanan Eshel* (ed. A. M. Maeir, J. Magness, and L. H. Schiffman; JSJSup 148; Leiden: Brill, 2012), 213–23.

10 See, in general, J. Sievers, *The Hasmoneans and Their Supporters from Mattathias to the Death of John Hyrcanus I* (South Florida Studies in the History of Judaism 6; Atlanta: Scholars, 1990).

11 Thus, at 15:37 the author announces the end of the story: "Because the affairs concerning Nicanor turned out this way, and ever since the city was taken over by the Hebrews it has been in their hands, here I too will conclude this account."

12 For a study that shows just how thoroughly the polis influenced Hellenistic Jewish self-understanding, see C. Carlier, *La cité de Moïse: Le peuple juif chez Philon d'Alexandrie* (Monothéismes et philosophie; Turnhout, Belgium: Brepols, 2008).

13 For the mutual hostility of Jews and Gentiles in 1 Maccabees, see S. Schwartz, "Israel and the Nations Roundabout: 1 Maccabees and the Hasmonean Expansion," *JJS* 42 (1991), esp. 21–9. The only major exceptions are the Romans and the Spartans, who are far away (ch. 8; 12:1–23; 14:16–24, 40; 15:15–24).

14 See above, n. 2.

15 The formulation here recalls the pointed way in which, in the New Testament, Acts 10:1 introduces Cornelius as a "man" – thus guaranteeing

that the question raised frontally in that chapter, whether a Gentile can have access to salvation, will be answered in the affirmative.

16 For the diasporan preference/need for God to be God of heaven, accessible to prayers that may be offered anywhere and not only to sacrifices that may be offered only in Jerusalem, note that the very term "God of Heaven" is typically diasporan. See D. R. Schwartz, *Studies in the Jewish Background of Christianity* (WUNT 60; Tübingen: Mohr [Siebeck], 1992), 7; A. Rofé, "An Enquiry into the Betrothal of Rebekah," in *Die Hebräische Bibel und ihre zweifache Nachgeschichte: Festschrift für Rolf Rendtdorf zum 65. Geburtstag* (ed. E. Blum, C. Macholz, and E. W. Stegemann; Neukirchen-Vluyn: Neukirchener, 1990), 28. For a corresponding preference for the Tabernacle, which moved about, as opposed to the Temple, which was anchored to Jerusalem – a preference that would be expressed quite polemically in Stephen's speech (Acts 7) – see already Philo's *Life of Moses* 2.72, along with my "Humbly Second-Rate in the Diaspora? Philo and Stephen on the Tabernacle and the Temple," in *Envisioning Judaism: Studies in Honor of Peter Schäfer on the Occasion of His Seventieth Birthday* (ed. R. Boustan et al.; Tübingen: Mohr Siebeck, 2013) 1.81–9.

17 For a Judean, such stories would require practical responses, which, as the example of Qumran shows, amount either to an attempt to purify and reconstruct the Temple or to reason to develop a diasporan religion in exile within Judea itself – on which see ch. 2, n. 10. For another, more restrained diasporan way of expressing a lack of dependence upon the Jerusalem priesthood, note that 3 Maccabees, another work of the Alexandrian Diaspora, allows the prayer of one of the provincial Jewish priests of Egypt (6:1–15), seconded by the prayers of other Jews of Egypt (5:51 and 6:17), to be more effective than that of the high priest in the Temple of Jerusalem (2:1–20); see N. Hacham, "Sanctity and the Attitude towards the Temple in Hellenistic Judaism," in *Was 70 CE a Watershed in Jewish History?* (ed. D. R. Schwartz and Z. Weiss, with R. A. Clements; AJEC 78; Leiden: Brill, 2012), 155–79. See also M. Tuval, "Doing without the Temple: Paradigms in Judaic Literature of the Diaspora," ibid., 181–239, esp. 206–8, on a more elegant approach to the same problem: the Wisdom of Solomon 18:20–5 presents Aaron as a righteous man and focuses on his efficacious prayers, thus totally rewriting – and making functional for a diasporan community – the original story of Numbers 16:41–9, where Aaron is a priest and offers up incense alone, without any prayer.

18 And note especially 7:37–8, where the last of the seven sons to be martyred adumbrates the turning point at 8:5 by declaring that, just as his brothers before him, so too he dies willingly for the ancestral laws in the

hope that God will soon become merciful, "and that, with me and my brothers, shall be stayed the anger of the All-Ruler which was justly loosed against our entire nation." On the crucial and pivotal role of martyrs in 2 Maccabees, see especially J. W. van Henten, *The Maccabean Martyrs as Saviours of the Jewish People: A Study of 2 and 4 Maccabees* (JSJSup 57; Leiden: Brill, 1997).

19 For a similar point elsewhere in Jewish Hellenistic literature, note Philo's *In Flaccum* 115: the wicked Flaccus, "who had made myriad homes of totally innocent people heartless," was arrested at his own hearth. See also ibid., 171–4 and esp. 189 – the very end of the book: "Justice" saw to it that the number of Flaccus' wounds, in being executed, corresponded precisely to the number of his victims. "Such were the sufferings of Flaccus, too, who thus became an indubitable proof that the Jewish people had not been deprived of the help of God" (trans. van der Horst). See also below, n. 23.

20 Here the author uses paronomasia to underline the irony: *apoksenōsas epi ksenēs apōleto.*

21 Prayers or references to prayer in 1 Maccabees after ch. 4: 5:33; 7:36–7, 40–2; 9:46 (a call to prayer); 11:71; 12:11 (mention of prayer in a diplomatic missive); 13:47, 51 (psalms in the wake of military success), 16:3 (a banal expression of hope for help from heaven). Note especially the contrast between the news of invasion in 3:42, which engenders twelve verses of prayer, and the prayer-less reception of similar news at 5:16, 6:28, 9:6, 10:74, 12:24, and 13:1; the closest we get to prayer in such contexts is the banal "may help from heaven be with you" in 16:3. Similarly, contrast the post-victory prayer at 4:24 with its absence at 7:47 (contrast the prayers on the same occasion according to 2 Macc 15:34!), 10:87, 11:74, 12:33–5, and 16:10. As for why things change, beginning with ch. 5 (although note the sacrifices at 5:54), see below, n. 26.

22 Prayers or references to prayer in 2 Maccabees 3–15 (the body of the story): 3:14–15, 18–21, 29; 5:4; 7:37; 8:2–4; 10:16, 25–6, 38; 11:6; 12:6, 28, 41, 44; 13:10–12; 14:15, 34–5, 46; 15:21–4, 26–7, 29, 34.

23 Suffice it to say that the great power of God, and his providential care for the Jews, is the lesson learned by all those who attacked the Jews: 3:36–9; 8:36; 9:11–17; 11:13. For another dramatic presentation of the same point in another Hellenistic Jewish work, see Philo's *In Flaccum* 170, where Flaccus proclaims, "All who deny that the Jews have you [God] for a champion and defender go astray from sound opinion. I am a clear proof of this, for all the mad acts that I have committed against the Jews I have now suffered myself" (trans. van der Horst).

24 On the senses of *kairos* in the Septuagint, see G. Delling, *"kairos," TDNT*
   3.458–9. For usage similar to that in 1 Maccabees, A. Finkelstein pointed
   (in his *"Kairos* in I Maccabees: A Non-Biblical Concept in a Biblically
   Styled Book" [unpublished M.A. thesis, Hebrew University of Jerusalem,
   2004]) especially to another historiographical work of the second century
   BCE, Polybius's *Histories*, where *kairos* appears in the sense of "fate";
   see esp. 3.30.4 (where the formulation is quite similar to that in 1 Macc
   15:33–4), also 18.22.8.

25 For the centrality, in 2 Maccabees, of the Deuteronomic notion that God
   "hides his face" in response to the Jews' sins, but is reconciled with
   them after atonement has been achieved by the spilling of blood, see
   my *2 Maccabees*, 21–2.

26 Although the copyists of some manuscripts (just as various modern translators), who were usually religious people, could not withstand the tempta-
   tion to rectify what they saw as a problem, according to Kappler's edition
   of 1 Maccabees neither *Kyrios* ("Lord") nor *theos* ("God") ever appears with
   regard to God, and even "Heaven" is mentioned only four times after ch. 4
   – at 5:31, 9:46, 12:15, and 16:3. The difference between the first four chapters
   of the book, which culminate with the dedication of the Temple, on the one
   hand, and the story of the wars thereafter (chs. 5–16), which we have noticed above (n. 21) with regard to prayers and now with regard to reference
   to God, on the other, seems to indicate a difference in sources. Whoever edited the book, in the last third of the second century BCE, perforce used
   earlier materials in preparing the first part of his story, and, as we see, in
   those pre-state years the religious elements were more salient.

27 That is, the old way of understanding what makes things happen in light
   of beliefs about God.

28 C. L. W. Grimm, *Das erste Buch der Maccabäer* (Kurzgefasstes exegetisches
   Handbuch zu den Apokryphen des Alten Testamentes 3; Leipzig: Hirzel,
   1853), xvii–xviii (my translation).

29 See Y. Z. Eliav, "Abraham Kahana (1874–1946): A Self-Trained Scholar and
   Publisher in Jewish Studies," in *Kiryat Sefer: Collected Essays* (ed. Y.
   Rosenberg; supplement to *Kiryat Sefer* 68; Jerusalem: Jewish National and
   University Library, 1998 [in Hebrew]), 7–19.

30 A. Kahana, *HaSepharim HaHitzonim* (Tel-Aviv: Meqorot, 1936/1937), 2.84
   (in Hebrew; my translation, original emphasis).

31 See I. L. Seeligmann, "Menschliches Heldentum und göttliche Hilfe: Die
   doppelte Kausalität im alttestamentlichen Geschichtsdenken," *TZ* 19
   (1963): 385–411; Y. Amit, "The Dual Causality Principle and Its Effects on

Biblical Literature," *VT* 37 (1987): 385–400. However, Amit does not discuss 1–2 Maccabees, and Seeligmann says nothing of 2 Maccabees and – at pp. 400–1 – only a little about 1 Maccabees; see the next note.

32 For the distinction between the first four chapters and the rest of the book, see above, n. 26. According to Seeligmann ("Menschliches Heldentum," 400), "The idea of a saving God is expressed quite unambiguously in passages such as 3:18 and 4:8–11; cf. 16:3" (my translation – DRS) – but as his use of "cf." for 16:3 indicates, it is indeed difficult to find anything of this sort past ch. 4. The situation is similar regarding one of the more amusing passages in German literature: K.-D. Schunck's statement, "In line with what was usual at the time, the author of 1 Maccabees avoids the use of the divine name 'Jahweh,' as also any other direct reference to God, and uses instead the term 'Heaven' (3:18f., 50, 60; 4:10, 40 and often)" (*1. Makabäerbuch* [JSHRZ 1; Gütersloh: Mohn, 1980], 293), which gives readers the impression that the term reappears several times per chapter, rather than only four more times in the last twelve chapters of the book. While some ancient Jewish texts avoid God's name out of reverence, 1 Maccabees is not among them.

Chapter 2

1 D. R. Schwartz, "Law and Truth: On Qumran-Sadducean and Rabbinic Views of Law," in *The Dead Sea Scrolls: Forty Years of Research* (ed. D. Dimant and U. Rappaport; STDJ 10; Leiden: Brill, and Jerusalem: Magnes, 1992), 229–40; Schwartz, "Between Priests and Sages in the Second Temple Period," in *Variety of Opinions and Views in Jewish Culture* (ed. Dror Kerem; n.p.: Israeli Ministry of Education and Culture, 1992 [in Hebrew]), 2.63–79.

2 See, for example, J. W. Bennett and M. M. Tumin, *Social Life: Structure and Function* (New York: Knopf, 1948), 93–6. For the application of the distinction to ancient priests and rabbis, see S. N. Eisenstadt, *Explorations in Jewish Historical Experience: The Civilizational Dimension* (Jewish Identities in a Changing World 3; Leiden: Brill, 2004), 28–30, and especially M. Himmelfarb, *A Kingdom of Priests: Ancestry and Merit in Ancient Judaism* (Philadelphia: University of Pennsylvania Press, 2006).

3 In this chapter I assume, as is usual, not only the basic identity of "Pharisees" and "sages" of the Second Temple period but also the basic continuity from them to the "rabbis" of the post-70 period – however much necessarily changed. True, the last generation has seen much consideration given to both assumptions, which used to be accepted much more

sweepingly – a remnant of traditional assumptions about an unchanging
and unitary tradition. Sweeps of a scholarly pendulum, however, can often go too far, and it is good to remember the basic points that underlie the
old consensus: the equation of "the sages" and "Pharisees" is explicit in
such texts as the old story in b. *Qidd.* 66a and in the fact that at times "the
sages" function vis-à-vis the Sadducees the way "the Pharisees" do in other texts; the continuity from the Pharisees/sages to the rabbis is shown by
the fact that R. Gamaliel and his son, who are identified as "Pharisees" in
Acts 5:34 and Josephus' *Life* 191, respectively, figure in the rabbinic chain
of tradition offered in m. *Avot* 1; the same continuity is indicated by the
fact that rabbinic literature virtually always portrays the Pharisees (or "the
sages") as defeating the Sadducees (or "the priests" or "the Boethusians")
in their disputes; and it is also borne out by the fact that rabbinic literature
preaches, concerning the theological issues that Josephus says distinguished Pharisees from Sadducees (free will vs. determinism, life after
death, authority of oral tradition), more or less the same views that
Josephus attributes to the Pharisees. See, for discussions of this issue,
J. Neusner, "'Pharisaic-Rabbinic' Judaism: A Clarification," *HR* 12
(1972/1973), 250–70; S. J. D. Cohen, "The Significance of Yavneh: Pharisees,
Rabbis, and the End of Jewish Sectarianism," *HUCA* 55 (1984), esp. 36–42;
G. Stemberger, *Jewish Contemporaries of Jesus: Pharisees, Sadducees, Essenes*
(Minneapolis: Fortress, 1995), 140–7; and C. Hezser, *The Social Structure
of the Rabbinic Movement in Roman Palestine* (TSAJ 66; Tübingen: Mohr
Siebeck, 1997), 69. Note that Hezser's summary of Cohen's position
("some of the first-generation tannaim may have been Pharisees … some
but not all rabbis were [the descendants of] Pharisees") is understated.
What Cohen actually concluded was that although the rabbis of Yavneh
were not interested in trumpeting their sectarian past, for they were seeking to form a grand coalition, nevertheless evidence such as that summarized above indicates that "we must conclude that the rabbis were
latter-day Pharisees who had no desire to publicize the connection"
(Cohen, "Significance," 40–1). In a recent reprinting of this essay, however,
he carefully added "or at least some of them" after "the rabbis" (S. J. D.
Cohen, *The Significance of Yavneh and Other Essays in Jewish Hellenism* [TSAJ
136; Tübingen: Mohr Siebeck, 2010], 58).

4 *War* 2.119; *Ant.* 13.171–3, 298; 18.11; *Life* 10.

5 Such discussions are numerous; for two examples, see Ch. Guignebert, *The
   Jewish World in the Time of Jesus* (London: Kegan Paul, Trench, Trubner,
   1939), 161–210 ("Book III: The Real Nature of Jewish Religious Life in
   Palestine," with chapters titled "The Main Currents of Orthodox Religion:

The Sadducees, the Pharisees, the Zealots"; "The Essenes"; and "The Sects, The People"), and Stemberger, *Jewish Contemporaries of Jesus*.

6 Matt 22:34; Acts 23:6–8; m. *Yad.* 4:6–7; t. *Ḥag.* 3:35 (ed. Lieberman, 394); *'Abot R. Nat.* A, ch. 5 (ed. Schechter, 26). This list would be much longer if we included texts that pit "the sages" against the Sadducees, or the sages or Pharisees against the Boethusians. "Boethus" was the name of a high-priestly family of the Herodian period (see *Ant.* 15.320–2; 19.297–8) and, as Lightstone put it, the name of this group (whatever details may specifically have distinguished it from the Sadducees; see M. D. Herr, "Who Were the Baethusians?" in *Proceedings of the Seventh World Congress of Jewish Studies* [Jerusalem: World Union of Jewish Studies, 1981], 3.1–20 [in Hebrew]; A. J. Saldarini, *Pharisees Scribes and Sadducees in Palestinian Society* [Edinburgh: Clark, 1989], 227–8) functions in rabbinic literature as a "lexical equivalent" of "Sadducees"; see J. N. Lightstone, "The Pharisees and the Sadducees in the Earliest Rabbinic Documents," in *In Quest of the Historical Pharisees* (ed. J. Neusner and B. D. Chilton; Waco, Texas: Baylor University Press, 2007), 266 (referring to the way t. *Yad.* 2:20 [ed. Zuckermandel, 684] uses "Boethusians" in reporting an argument other sources ascribe to the Sadducees; see below, n. 109). Similarly, in connection with the equivalence of "Boethusian" in t. *Suk.* 3:16 (ed. Lieberman, 270) and "Sadducee" in b. *Suk* 48b, J. Rubenstein noted and documented that "this interchange occurs often between the Tosefta and parallel sources: the Tosefta consistently reads 'Boethusian' while the Mishnah, Talmuds, and halakhic Midrashim read 'Sadducee'" ("The Sadducees and the Water Libation," *JQR* 84 [1993/1994]: 422). Indeed, in the passage from *'Abot de R. Natan* quoted at the outset of this note, the Sadducees and the Boethusians are said to have originated with the same heresy and to have lived the same way, and the passage exemplifies their views by citing a statement of the Sadducees, implying that it represented the Boethusians too.

7 Other cases: at *Life* 123–4 Josephus reports that of the three largest cities of the Galilee one rejected the overtures of John of Gischala, one refused to revolt but did agree to befriend John, and one went over to John; at *War* 2.271–7 Josephus pointedly presents the last three Roman governors prior to the outbreak of the rebellion as having been, respectively, wonderful, bad, and horrible (to such an extent that the third made the second seem very positive in comparison); and at *War* 6.236–43 he reports that while some Roman generals wanted to destroy the Temple of Jerusalem at all costs and others wanted to preserve it at all costs, there were also those in the middle who favoured destroying it if the Jews persisted in using it as a fortress, but would preserve it if they desisted.

8 See, for example, such classic discussions as A. Geiger, "Sadducäer und Pharisäer,"*Jüdische Zeitschrift für Wissenschaft und Leben* 2 (1863), 11–54; J. Wellhausen, *Die Pharisäer und die Sadducäer: Eine Untersuchung zur inneren jüdischen Geschichte* (Greifswald: Bamberg, 1874; in English: *The Pharisees and the Sadducees* [Macon, Ga.: Mercer University Press, 2001]); and E. Schürer, *A History of the Jewish People in the Time of Jesus Christ*, II/2 (Edinburgh: Clark, 1885), where §26 (pp. 4–43) is titled "Pharisees and Sadducees" and – 140 pages later – §30 (pp. 188–218) is "The Essenes." So too Baeck's "Die Pharisäer" (1927) deals only with the Pharisees (the "men of the synagogue"), as contrasted with the Sadducees ("men of the Temple"); for an English version, see his *The Pharisees and Other Essays* (New York: Schocken, 1966), 3–50. For the modern history of the study of the Pharisees, see R. Deines, *Die Pharisäer: Ihr Verständnis im Spiegel der christlichen und jüdischen Forschung seit Wellhausen und Graetz* (WUNT 101; Tübingen: Mohr Siebeck, 1997); for that of the Essenes, see S. Wagner, *Die Essener in der wissenschaftlichen Diskussion, vom Ausgang des 18. bis zum Beginn des 20. Jahrhunderts: Eine wissenschaftsgeschichtliche Studie* (BZAW 79; Berlin: Töpelmann, 1960).

9 For a review of this topic, and of scholarship's move, in the wake of publication of halakhic material from Qumran, from an identification of Qumran halakhah as specifically Sadducean to a more general identification of both sects as "priestly," see E. Regev, "Were the Priests All the Same? Qumranic Halakhah in Comparison with Sadducean Halakhah," *DSD* 12 (2005): 158–88. For another broad application of the "priestly" category to the study of Judaism in the Second Temple period, see Himmelfarb, *Kingdom of Priests*.

10 Note especially that, competing with what I have termed the "basically priestly nature" of the Qumran sect, there were factors that pulled it in another, universalist, and indeed diasporan direction, which would lead it to think universally about "Sons of Light" and to view their own community as something of a surrogate Temple; see my *Studies* (ch. 1, n. 16), 19–24; and N. Hacham, "Exile and Self-Identity in the Qumran Sect and in Hellenistic Judaism," in *New Perspectives on Old Texts* (ed. E. G. Chazon and B. Halpern-Amaru; STDJ 88; Leiden: Brill, 2010), 3–21. In the present chapter, which deals with law, I have focused on the basic priestly nature.

11 See T. S. Beall, *Josephus' Description of the Essenes Illustrated by the Dead Sea Scrolls* (SNTSMS 58; Cambridge: Cambridge University Press, 1988); J. Magness, *The Archaeology of Qumran and the Dead Sea Scrolls* (Grand Rapids: Eerdmans, 2002), 39–43; and J. E. Taylor, "The Classical Sources on the Essenes and the Scrolls Communities," in *Oxford Handbook of the Dead*

Sea Scrolls (ed. T. H. Lim and J. J. Collins; Oxford: Oxford University Press, 2010), 173–99. For my own survey of this issue, see "The Dead Sea Sect and the Essenes," in *The Qumran Scrolls and Their World* (ed. M. Kister; Jerusalem: Yad Ben-Zvi, 2009 [in Hebrew]), 2.601–12.

12 Which does not impugn our ability to associate these movements at the level of generalization at which our thesis is suggested. That is, I view the notion that the Qumran sect was not Essene, and that Essenes were even hostile to the Qumran sect, as similar to the established fact that two varieties of Protestants, or of Hasidim, are different from each other and might even be hostile to one another, but may nevertheless be meaningfully characterized as Protestant or Hasidic; see below, n. 16.

13 See S. Mason, "Essenes and Lurking Spartans in Josephus' *Judean War*: From Story to History," in *Making History: Josephus and Historical Method* (ed. Z. Rodgers; JSJSup 110; Leiden: Brill, 2007), 219–61, also idem, FJTC 2b.84–95, and R. Elior, *Memory and Oblivion: The Secret of the Dead Sea Scrolls* (Tel-Aviv: Van Leer Jerusalem Institute and HaKibbutz HaMeuchad, 2009 [in Hebrew]). Although various popular or even scholarly discussions have portrayed these studies as if they deny the Essenes ever existed, in fact they do not. They merely insist that Greek and Latin evidence for the Essenes (supplied mainly by Josephus, Philo, and Pliny) should not be mixed with that of the Scrolls. Namely, Mason urges that we should not allow the Scrolls to govern our interpretation of Josephus' accounts of the Essenes, for Josephus had his own interests and agendas (see FJTC 2b, xiii, and 95–7 ["The Historical Essenes"]). Elior similarly urges that we should not allow first-century accounts of the Essenes, by outsiders, to govern our interpretation of the Qumran sect, for which the Scrolls provide evidence that is by insiders and centuries earlier; see especially her summary of the issue on p. 52.

14 Such as *Manual of Discipline* 5:2 (all members of the community must "answer in accordance with [the instructions of] the Sons of Zadok, the priests who keep the covenant") and 9:7 ("Only the Sons of Aaron shall rule in matters of law and property"), also *Damascus Document* 14:3–6, which insists that at the sect's meetings the priests sit in the first rank, and all the others sit separately after them, in descending order according to their descent: Levites, Israelites, and proselytes.

15 M. P. Horgan, *Pesharim: Qumran Interpretations of Biblical Books* (CBQMS 8; Washington, D.C.: Catholic Biblical Association of America, 1979), 17–20, 40–55.

16 This is a case of what A. I. Baumgarten has called "the rule of the Martian": "Hostility is likely to be greatest between two groups between

which a Martian would have the most difficult distinguishing" ("The Rule of the Martian as Applied to Qumran," *IOS* 14 [1994]: 121). That is, the differences that are hardest for an observer from afar to discern are the ones that might be most salient in the eyes of the participant. Thus, for example, two types of Protestants might take the differences between them more seriously than the differences between them and Catholics, because the latter are really simply beyond the pale; so too, among Jews, two types of Hasidim might be more exercised about the differences between them than about those between both of them, on the one hand, and Reform Jews on the other. But observers from afar would be justified in justifying the former as Protestants and the latter as Hasidim. See also above, n. 12.

17 This point was essential to the analysis of the Pharisees and Sadducees in A. Geiger, *Urschrift und Übersetzungen der Bibel in ihrer Abhängigkeit von der innern Entwicklung des Judentums* (Breslau: Hainauer, 1857), 101–58 – the study that is basically the beginning of the modern study of these sects. For a "Panorama de la recherche depuis Abraham Geiger (1857)," see J. Le Moyne, *Les Sadducéens* (EBib; Paris: Gabalda, 1972), 11–26.

18 On this psalm, which is probably a secondary addition to Ben-Sira but perhaps not much later than the original book, see J. Liver, "The 'Sons of Zadok the Priests' in the Dead Sea Sect," *RevQ* 6/1 (no. 21, Feb. 1967): 22–4; and A. Hunt, *Missing Priests: The Zadokites in History and Tradition* (Library of Bible / Old Testament Studies 452; New York: Clark, 2006), 155–7.

19 This is so even if the Sadducees later made their peace with the Hasmoneans, as may probably be inferred from the Hasmoneans' break with the Pharisees (*Ant.* 13.296–7, 402) and other evidence; certainly the rabbis, referring to the same period, thought the Hasmoneans became Sadducees (b. *Berakhot* 29a).

20 True, M. Goodman has argued that Acts 5:17 suggests only "that those who accompanied the high priest *on this occasion* were Sadducees" (his emphasis), just as concerning Acts 4:1 he emphasizes that the fact that Luke names the actors separately indicates they are not identical ("it appears that in this drama Sadducees were just one group alongside the priests"); see his *Judaism in the Roman World* (AJEC 66; Leiden: Brill, 2007), 129–30. However, the fact is that in both cases they work together and the author assumed that readers would not think that requires any explanation. Moreover, at 4:1–2 what "the priests, the captain of the Temple, and the Sadducees" oppose is the belief in resurrection of the dead, and Luke could assume that readers of his Gospel (20:27) and Acts (23:8) would know that rejection of that belief characterized the Sadducees. So although Luke uses different terms to describe the antagonists, referring to some as

office-holders (priests, captain of Temple, high priests) and others as members of a sect or party, these texts retain their value as indicating the basic priest-Sadducee nexus.

21 Such as b. *Yoma* 19b, where a high priest tells his son that "Although we are Sadducees…," and the scholion to *Megillat Ta'anit* for 27 Marḥeshvan (ed. Noam, 250), where, in an obvious parody, a Sadducee is made to defend the view that "Moses loved Aaron" and therefore made the law congenial to the priests' interests.

22 So, for some examples, Joazar (Josephus, *Life* 197); Jose b. Joezer (see m. *Ḥag.* 2:7, along with m. *Avot* 1:4); R. Tarphon (see ch. 3, n. 22); and R. Eliezer b. Hyrcanus (see below, n. 69). This point is emphasized by R. L. Kohn and R. Moore, "Rethinking Sectarian Judaism: The Centrality of the Priesthood in the Second Temple Period," in *Sacred History, Sacred Literature: Essays on Ancient Israel, the Bible, and Religion in Honor of R. E. Friedman* (ed. S. Dolansky; Winona Lake, Ind.: Eisenbrauns, 2008), 208, in the context of their general argument that sectarianism in the Second Temple period often amounted to competition with the priesthood.

23 Several of these texts will be cited below.

24 P. Schäfer, "Rabbis and Priests, or: How to Do Away with the Glorious Past of the Sons of Aaron," in *Antiquity in Antiquity: Jewish and Christian Pasts in the Greco-Roman World* (ed. G. Gardner and K. L. Osterloh; TSAJ 123; Tübingen: Mohr Siebeck, 2008), 155–72.

25 On this particular comparison, see especially S. D. Fraade, "Shifting from Priestly to Non-Priestly Legal Authority: A Comparison of the Damascus Document and the Midrash Sifra," *DSD* 6 (1999): 109–25.

26 See, especially, in connection with Qumran, chs. 5–10 of the *Aramaic Levi Document* (ed. J. C. Greenfield, M. E. Stone, and E. Eshel; SVTP 19; Leiden: Brill, 2004); also H. Drawnel, "Priestly Education in the *Aramaic Levi Document (Visions of Levi)* and *Aramaic Astronomical Book* (4Q208–211)," *RevQ* 22 (2005/2006): 547–74.

27 Translation by J. M. Baumgarten in "Damascus Document (CD)," in *The Dead Sea Scrolls: Hebrew, Aramaic, and Greek Texts with English Translations*, II (ed. J. H. Charlesworth; Tübingen: Mohr [Siebeck] and Louisville: John Knox, 1995), 53–5.

28 The priest. So too the next "he."

29 The person being examined.

30 Translation by H. Danby, *The Mishnah* (Oxford: Oxford University Press, 1933), 678.

31 On the latter as a site of prayer, see S. B. Hoenig, "Historical Inquiries: I. *Heber Ir*. II. City-Square," *JQR* 48 (1957/1958), esp. 132–9.

32 See above, n. 8.

33 For some scraps of post-70 evidence for priestly sects, which hardly change the picture, see Goodman, *Judaism in the Roman World*, 153–62; idem, "Religious Variety and the Temple in the Late Second Temple Period and Its Aftermath," *Sects and Sectarianism in Jewish History* (ed. S. Stern; IJS Studies in Judaica 12; Leiden: Brill, 2011), 33–5. I ignore the question of a new *revival* of interest in ancient Jewish priesthood in the Byzantine period, which is beyond the period addressed by this book. On it see, lately, D. Stökl Ben Ezra, "Templisierung: Die Rückkehr des Tempels in die jüdische und christliche Liturgie der Spätantike," in *Rites et croyances dans les religions du monde romain* (ed. J. Scheid; Entretiens sur l'antiquité classique 53; Vandœvres, Geneva: Fondation Hardt, 2007); 231–87; also Z. Weiss, "Were Priests Communal Leaders in Late Antique Palestine? The Archaeological Evidence," and M. D. Swartz, "Liturgy, Poetry, and the Persistence of Sacrifice," in *Was 70 CE a Watershed?* (ed. Schwartz and Weiss, with Clements), 91–111 and 393–412, respectively.

34 See H. Birenboim, "'A Kingdom of Priests': Did the Pharisees Try to Live like Priests?" ibid., 59–68; also my *Studies*, 57–80 (on ancient and modern interpretation of "kingdom of priests" in Exod 19:6).

35 For this kind of material, see below, n. 114. Of course, this kind of polemic would be all the more likely in an age in which others were voicing it as well; see this volume's conclusion, n. 3.

36 On the ancient Jewish calendar, see M. D. Herr, "The Calendar," in *The Jewish People in the First Century* (ed. S. Safrai and M. Stern; CRINT I; Assen: Van Gorcum, 1976), 2.834–64; and S. Stern, *Calendar and Community: A History of the Jewish Calendar, Second Century BCE – Tenth Century CE* (Oxford: Oxford University Press, 2001).

37 See t. *Sanhedrin*, ch. 2 (ed. Zuckermandel, 416–18); along with Herr, "Calendar," 852–7; and Stern, *Calendar and Community*, 47–98 and 161–2.

38 See the programmatic story in m. *Rosh Hashanah* 2:8–9; along with C. Hayes, "Rabbinic Contestations of Authority," *Cardozo Law Review* 28 (2006): 132–3.

39 For an example from the days of Rabban Gamaliel (probably the first of that name, pre-70 CE), see t. *Sanhedrin* 2:6 (ed. Zuckermandel, 416–17); Herr, "Calendar," 856–7; and Stern, *Calendar and Community*, 237–8.

40 Translation according to E. Qimron and J. H. Charlesworth, "Rule of the Community (1QS)," in *The Dead Sea Scrolls: Hebrew, Aramaic, and Greek Texts with English Translations*, I (ed. J. H. Charlesworth; Tübingen: Mohr [Siebeck] and Louisville: John Knox, 1994), 7. I capitalized all the occurrences of "his" in this citation, for clarity.

41 See A. Shemesh, *Halakhah in the Making: The Development of Jewish Law from Qumran to the Rabbis* (Taubman Lectures in Jewish Studies 7; Berkeley: University of California Press, 2009), 46–9.

42 As Shemesh shows, ibid., this same Qumran attitude is bespoken by the *Temple Scroll* (56:1–11), which, while paraphrasing the same law in Deut 17, insists in l. 4 that to be valid the court's decision must also be (1) "according to the Torah" and (2) "true." Similarly, l. 3 has "and you shall do according to the Torah that they tell you" instead of Deut 17:10's "and you shall do according to the *word* that they tell you," for, as the rabbis noted, the Torah's use of "word" here, and its repeated emphasis upon what the judges *say*, seem to endow the judges' words with authority even when they are not based on the Torah – and that is rejected by the Qumran paraphrase.

43 On the Qumran calendar(s), see Herr, "Calendar," 839–43; Stern, *Calendar and Community*, 11–18.

44 For the early (priestly) Josephus' use of *athemitos* in the same sense, see below, 56.

45 For both law and practice see T. Ilan, *Jewish Women in Greco-Roman Palestine: An Inquiry into Image and Status* (TSAJ 44; Mohr [Siebeck], 1995), 85–8; and A. Schremer, "How Much Jewish Polygyny in Roman Palestine?" *PAAJR* 63 (1997/2001): 181–223.

46 Translation by C. Rabin, *The Zadokite Documents* (2nd ed.; Oxford: Clarendon, 1958), 16. Immediately below we shall discuss the second snare in which sinners are entrapped. For a review of scholarship on this text and related material, see T. Ilan, "Women in Qumran and the Dead Sea Scrolls," in *The Oxford Handbook of the Dead Sea Scrolls* (ed. T. H. Lim and J. J. Collins; Oxford: Oxford University Press, 2010), 133–5.

47 For a similar phrase and law in *Damascus Document* 12:14–15, see below, at n. 66. Note that although, according to Mark 10:6, Jesus too cited Gen 1:27, in a somewhat similar context, it is applied in a very different sense: if in the *Damascus Document* it is cited to show that one man should marry only one woman, for Jesus it shows that originally man and woman were separate one from the other. That is the point that Jesus needs in order to set up his claim in the next verse that, according to Gen 2:24, marriage makes them into one ("so they are no longer two [as they first were], but rather one flesh, and what God has joined together man should not divide"). That is, for Jesus, Gen 1:27 is not a source of law, as it is for the *Damascus Document*. Nor is Gen 2:24 a source of law, for Jesus, since he admits that Mosaic law admits divorce (Deut 24:1, cited in Mark 12:4). Jesus' point here is that one should not follow that law, for it is a concession to human

hardness of hearts; rather, one should adhere to what God established. Such a demand to adhere to a norm that is beyond what the law requires or allows is a moral attitude that is outside the realm of the debate that divided legalists in the two camps we are discussing.

48 For a list of cases of such marriages documented in Josephus and in rabbinic literature (e.g., *Ant.* 12.186–9 and b. *Yev.* 15a), see A. Schremer, "Qumran Polemic on Marital Law: CD 4:30–5:11 and Its Social Background," in *The Damascus Document: A Centennial of Discovery* (ed. J. M. Baumgarten, E. G. Chazon, and A. Pinnick; STDJ 34; Leiden: Brill, 2000), 155–6.

49 See t. *Qidd.* 1:4 (ed. Lieberman, 276): "A man should not marry until his sister's daughter grows up"; b. *Yebam.* 62b–63a: "He who loves his neighbours, brings his relations close to one another, marries his sister's daughter, or gives a poor man a *sela* [coin] when he is in need – of him Scripture says: 'Then you shall call out and God will answer, you shall cry for help and He shall say "I am here"'" (Isa 58:9; ibid. v. 7 warns against ignoring one's own kin). As A. Schremer has shown, references to "sister's daughter" are not meant to exclude daughters of brothers, but, rather, to recommend *even* the sister's daughter, within the context of a general recommendation of marriage within the family, despite the fact that the sister, by her marriage, might have been thought to have left her original family; see his "Kinship Terminology and Endogamous Marriage in the Mishnaic and Talmudic Periods," *Zion* 60 (1994/1995): 13–21 (in Hebrew).

50 My translation ("Damascus Document" [above, n. 27], 21). For the same prohibition, although without a statement of the reasoning, see *Temple Scroll* 66:15–17: "A man shall not take [in marriage] the daughter of his brother or of his sister, for it is an abomination." For a review of scholarship concerning this law, and of related texts, see Ilan, "Women in Qumran," 135–7.

51 Against this interpretation Rubenstein ("Nominalism and Realism," 165–8) has argued that (1) the rabbis too, in other cases, extended marital prohibitions by analogy, and (2) it is not self-evident that what is "really" forbidden (by nature) to men is also "really" forbidden to women. See his "Nominalism and Realism in Qumranic and Rabbinic Law: A Reassessment," *DSD* 6 (1999): 165–8. For the first objection, see below, section III of this chapter, where I distinguish between what the rabbis did in the face of priestly competition and what they did when freed from that situation. As for the second: whether or not the natural analogy is self-evident, the facts that no explanation is given, and that the immediately preceding case is

explicitly explained by reference to the "principle of nature," seem to show that the analogy is indeed assumed by the Qumran legislator.

52 See J. M. Baumgarten, "The Pharisaic-Sadducean Controversies about Purity and the Qumran Texts," *JJS* 31 (1980): 161–3; and – about the buried bones – L. H. Schiffman, *Reclaiming the Dead Sea Scrolls* (Philadelphia: Jewish Publication Society, 1994), 337–8. Schiffman focuses on the risk that dogs or other animals might scatter the bones, but that is an aspect of the basic issue: preventing pure people from coming into contact with the bones.

53 For an explanation of the Mishnah's rhetoric and who says what, see Baumgarten, "Pharisaic-Sadducean Controversies," 162–3.

54 Rubenstein ("Nominalism and Realism," 168–70) argues (1) that it is not clear that a realist would assume that the nature of human bones and animal bones is the same, and that (2) the fact that Qumran law explicitly limited the impurity of human bones to those of a dead person indicates that they did not hold that bones were really impure. (Concerning the latter point, his argument follows that of Y. Elman, "Some Remarks on 4QMMT and the Rabbinic Tradition, or: When Is a Parallel Not a Parallel?" in *Reading 4QMMT* [ed. J. Kampen and M. J. Bernstein; SBLSymS 2; Atlanta: Scholars, 1996], 100–2). However, necessary or not, the Qumran legislator did assume that animal bones, as human bones, are impure, and the most obvious and economical explanation for that seems to be the assumption that bones are bones. As for the second point, *if* the fact that the Temple Scroll (50:4–7), in paraphrasing Num 19:16, adds a word (*met*) that clarifies that the human bone that defiles is of a dead person "points to a concern on the part of the drafter to exclude amputated ('living') limbs from this law" (Elman, 101), then we should probably conclude that what generated that exclusion was the assumption that bones of live people are pure; even realists must hold that, for otherwise all live people would be impure. The fact that rabbinic law includes the view that bones amputated from live people are impure (Elman, 101, n. 8; Rubenstein, 169, n. 37) must, accordingly, be understood as a nominalistic view: the law calls such bones impure so as to endow them with the same protection that it grants to those of dead people, and the rabbis who held that position would not readily consent to Elman's parenthetical characterization of amputated bones as "living." But perhaps the whole discussion is superfluous, and we should take the addition of *met* merely as a clarification concerning what is usual, just like the adjacent reference in Num 19:16 to a "sword," which no one (I suppose) would take restrictively, as if the bones of people killed some other way do not defile.

55 I borrowed that terminology (which has its own long history) and its application to Jewish law from the work of Y. Silman; see especially his
"Halakhic Determinations of a Nominalistic and Realistic Nature: Legal
and Philosophical Considerations," *Diné Israel* 12 (1984/1985): 249–66 (in
Hebrew); in English, see his "Introduction to the Philosophical Analysis of
the Normative-Ontological Tension in the Halakha," *Daat* 31 (Summer
1993): v–xx. In Silman's terms (ibid., xix–xx), "The realistic tendency is
connected with the opinion that the origin of halakhic determination is
rooted and exists in a general order which was permanently established
during creation" (and he goes on to make God's function only "heuristic,"
comparing commandments to medicine, which is like Highway
Department signs), while "the nominalistic tendency is connected system-
atically with the opinion that the sole origin of halakhic determination is
the free-will decision of God himself, applied to human beings through
the making of a concrete demand" (and he goes on to say that, on this
view, God's commandments have not only a "heuristic" function, but also
an "obligatory" one, for without them there is no obligation). I use "realistic" the same way but broaden "nominalistic" to include the tendency to
ascribe halakhic authority not only to God's decisions, but also to those of
people, in fields in which it is relevant – for example, an individual who
defines the transfer of money as a loan or the court that fixes the beginning of a month. On Silman's work, see also below, n. 75.

56 See, inter alia, C. Werman, "The Rules of Consuming and Covering the
Blood in Priestly and Rabbinic Law," *RevQ* 16 (1993/1995), esp. 633–4;
Shemesh, *Halakhah in the Making*, 107–28; C. Hayes, "Legal Realism and
the Fashioning of Sectarians in Jewish Antiquity," *Sects and Sectarianism in
Jewish History* (ed. S. Stern; IJS Studies in Judaica 12; Leiden: Brill, 2011),
119–46; and K. P. Donfried, "Paul the Jew and the Dead Sea Scrolls," in *The
Dead Sea Scrolls in Context: Integrating the Dead Sea Scrolls in the Study of
Ancient Texts, Languages, and Cultures* (ed. A. Lange, E. Tov, and M.
Weigold; VTSup 140; Leiden: Brill, 2011), 2.721–33.

57 See Rubenstein, "Nominalism and Realism," 157–83; and V. Noam,
"Ritual Impurity in Tannaitic Literature: Two Opposing Perspectives,"
Journal of Ancient Judaism 1 (2010): 65–103. For my response to Noam in
particular, see below, 39–40. As for Rubenstein, he offered four main arguments: (1) that I ignored rabbinic realism (to which the present section of
this chapter is now dedicated); (2) that alternative explanations could be
offered for several of the disagreements I analyzed (for my responses, see
my nn. 51, 54, 92, 99), (3) that rabbinic law tended to nominalism because
of its age, and (4) that I did not relate seriously to the possibility that laws

derive from biblical exegesis. Indeed, I do not find the latter two points very problematic, because they sidestep the historical question that interests us: why do some people differ in typical ways from others? If all legal systems tend to nominalism, why did priestly law do so much less than rabbinic law? And as for derivation of laws from the Bible, the question remains: why do some people, such as priests, interpret the Bible one way and some others, such as rabbis, interpret it another way? Moreover, even an exegetically derived law held by a community will help shape its world view.

58 Rubenstein, "Nominalism and Realism," 179–83.

59 Noam, "Ritual Impurity," 103.

60 Rubenstein, "Nominalism and Realism," 165–6. See above, 29–31.

61 Summarizing the rabbinic approach, H. H. Cohn wrote ("Incest in Jewish Law," *EncJud* 8.1316), "This list [of incestuous relations prohibited in the Torah – Lev 18 and 20] is exhaustive and may not be added to by analogies (*Sifra, AḤarei-Mot* 13:15 [ed. Weiss, 86b]), since creation of any criminal offence requires the express pronouncement of the conduct prohibited and the resulting punishment (… cf. Ker. 3a; Sanh. 74a)." On the rule stated in those two passages of the Babylonian Talmud, see below, at n. 100. The *locus classicus* for the notion of "fences" around the law, that prohibit things that are allowed so as to prevent people from even getting close to doing something the law forbids, is m. *Avot* 1:1.

62 So, for example, b. *Sanh.* 46a: "R. Eliezer b. Jacob says: 'I have heard that a court may whip and punish without any basis in the Torah – not in order to violate the words of the Torah but, rather, to make a fence for the Torah. And it once happened, in the days of the Greeks, that someone rode on a horse on the Sabbath, and he was brought to the court and stoned – not that he deserved it, but because the situation (lit.: "hour") required it.'"

63 Rubenstein, "Nominalism and Realism," 166.

64 Here I allude to yet another difference between the two legal systems. The rabbis insisted, even demonstratively, that if only one witness saw a murder, there was no way to try or punish him (although they were happy to report that God has extra-systemic snakes available to handle such criminals; see t. *Sanh.* 8:3 [ed. Zuckermandel, 427]//b. *Sanh.* 37b). According to the *Damascus Document* 9:16–23, in contrast, even single testimony could be recorded, and if other single witnesses to other instances of the same crime appeared, they could be accumulated and serve as basis for trial and punishment. On this passage, see the studies by B. A. Levine, J. Neusner, and L. H. Schiffman in *RevQ* 8 (1973): 195–6, 197–217, and 603–12 (respectively).

65 See Rubenstein, "Nominalism and Realism," 170–1; and especially Noam, "Ritual Impurity," esp. 73–86.

66 The formulation of this law is, of course, similar to that of *Damascus Document* 4:21 with regard to monogamy; see above, at n. 46.

67 Rubenstein, "Nominalism and Realism," 164.

68 A. Oppenheimer, *Galilee in the Mishnaic Period* (Jerusalem: Shazar Center, 1991 [in Hebrew]), 119.

69 V. Noam, "Polemic and Dispute: Why Rabbi Eliezer Was Excommunicated," *Massekhet* 5 (Spring 2006), esp. 140–1 (in Hebrew). Noam does not raise the point, but it seems likely that R. Eliezer b. Hyrcanus was a priest, as was surmised by David Fraenkel (d. 1762) in his commentary (*Qorban Ha'Edah*) on y. *Soṭah* 3:4, 19a, from the fact that his son refers to the tithes the family was accustomed to receive (see also *Tarbiz* 74 [2004/2005]: 31, n. 30 [in Hebrew]).

70 On the way Dosa's name functions in the Mishnah as a marker that calls attention to the natural-priestly stance, see my "On Pharisees and Sadducees in the Mishnah: From Composition Criticism to History," in *Judaistik und neutestamentliche Wissenschaft* (ed. L. Doering, H.-G. Waubke, and F. Wilk; FRLANT 226; Göttingen: Vandenhoeck und Ruprecht, 2008), 140–3.

71 Explanation: since Rosh Hashanah is on the first of the month of Tishri, but in antiquity Jews could not be sure, in advance, whether the preceding month would have twenty-nine or thirty days and the determination would be made only retroactively, at the beginning of Tishri, the practice was adopted of observing both the thirtieth and the thirty-first days of the preceding month as Rosh Hashanah in order to cover both possibilities. See Herr, "Calendar," 860–1.

72 That is, Dosa insists that if each raisin has 0 impurity, the aggregate impurity of many raisins is 0, whereas the rabbis say that the common name, "raisins," unites them into a larger unit, one susceptible to impurity.

73 See above, n. 65.

74 See B. Bar-Kochva, *Pseudo-Hecataeus*, On the Jews: *Legitimizing the Jewish Diaspora* (HCS 21; Berkeley: University of California Press, 1996), 271–88.

75 M. Silberg, "The Order *Qodashim* as a Legal Work," *Sinai* 52 (1962/1963): 8–18 (in Hebrew; reprinted in *The Writings of Moshe Silberg* [Jerusalem: Magnes, 1998]: 160–73 [in Hebrew]. On case (c) below, see also ibid., 444–5). To place the present discussion in its context, note that Silberg imputed a "naturalistic" approach to the halakhah; Silman (in his studies cited in n. 55, although citing Silberg only in the Hebrew one) agreed with him

that halakhic writings do bespeak that approach, termed it "realistic," but added that Silberg ignored a large part of halakhic thought since it often conforms to a contrary approach, which he termed "nominalistic"; in my studies (above, n. 1) I adopted Silman's terminology and argued that the two views were, respectively, typical of priests and rabbis; and Rubenstein ("Nominalism and Realism," 159) complained that I "seized upon Silman's nominalist examples but ignored or rejected his claims of a tension between the two tendencies." The present discussion is my response to that criticism. Note that although Silberg's and Silman's studies are avowedly ahistorical, and so had no need to focus on the question as to which approach was more characteristic of whom, Silman ("Introduction to the Philosophical Analysis," vii) did note that "it is possible to classify different sages and even different periods according to their tendency towards one or the other of the two poles of this tension." My work on priests and rabbis is offered as a case in point.

76 For example, although the Torah specifically forbids marital relations between a man and his mother-in-law and imposes death by fire as the punishment (Lev 20:14), if at the time of the relations the woman was still married to his wife's father, the case is treated only as one of adultery (for which the punishment is considered to be lighter: strangulation), because the woman was prohibited to him as a married woman before she became his mother-in-law (b. *Yebam.* 32a). In general, on the rule that a prohibition cannot apply to something that is already forbidden, and its ramifications and logic, see *Encyclopedia Talmudica*, vol. 1 (Jerusalem: Talmudic Encyclopedia Institute, 1969), cols. 715–27.

77 As was noted by S. Wozner, "Ontological and Naturalistic Thinking in Talmudic Law and in Lithuanian Yeshivot," *Diné Israel* 25 (2008): 53 (in Hebrew).

78 See, for example, the argument in m. *Ḥul.* 7:6 as to whether someone who eats the hip-sinew of an impure animal is guilty of one sin or two. The majority view, that only one sin has been committed, is based on the logic that the prohibition of the hip-sinew (Gen 32:32) applies only to animals that are otherwise allowed.

79 Noam, "Ritual Impurity," 85.

80 As, for example, Danby notes on 3:6, "The principle implied is stated more fully in 7³" (Danby, *Mishnah*, 654, n. 2).

81 Noam, "Ritual Impurity," 84–5.

82 As does Danby (above, n. 80): "Not only what is within the room suffers corpse-uncleanness but even what is outside a shut door becomes unclean if it is beneath the lintel of the entrance … unless it has been specifically

determined through which of the entrances the uncleanness shall be taken out. This 'protects' the other openings."

83 See y. *Sanh.* 1.2 (19a) where, in the context of the presumption that a girl who was raped below the age of three regains her virginity, the question is posed: what about a girl who was raped a day after her third birthday and then the court intercalated the year, thus making her less than three years old? In response, one of the rabbis, quoting Ps 57:2 in the sense that God makes things conform to our will, asserts that in such a case the girl's virginity restores itself. Whether or not the question reflects any real case, and whether or not the assertion is meant literally or rather only that *the law is as if* her virginity restores itself, this response sharpens the nominalistic principle involved. For this and other cases in which the halakhah posits that calendrical changes affect nature, see Silman, "Halakhic Determinations," 261–6 (more briefly in English: Silman, "Introduction to the Philosophical Analysis," xvii–xix).

84 Rather, their recognition of the second marriage's validity led them to require a divorce to dissolve it. See S. Friedman, "The Case of the Woman with Two Husbands in Talmudic and Ancient Near Eastern Law," *Israel Law Review* 15 (1980), esp. 544–58. As Friedman shows, the rabbis required that both marriages be sundered, by divorce, precisely because they recognized both as valid – a recognition that meant that each marriage rendered her relation with the other man adulterous. (Friedman also shows, with reference to b. *Yebam.* 88a–b, y. *Yebam.* 10:7 [11a], and other sources, that although some rabbis would allow such a woman to remain with the second husband, that was only via recourse to the pretence that the identity of the returned first husband was in fact in doubt.)

85 For an earlier statement of this revision of my original argument, see my "*Qal vaHomer* Arguments as Sadducean Realism," *Massekhet* 5 (2006): 145–56 (in Hebrew).

86 Concerning other possible explanations, see above, n. 57.

87 On the human need, and need of groups, not to make any concessions to their close competitors, see G. Simmel, *Conflict and the Web of Group-Affiliations* (Glencoe, Ill.: Free Press, 1955), esp. 42–5. On p. 43 Simmel notes that "some of the strongest examples of such hatred are church relations[;] because of dogmatic fixation, the minutest divergence here at once comes to have logical irreconcilability." Ibid. 28 Simmel speaks of this as contrariness (*Widerspruchsgeist*), which basically corresponds to what M. Goodman meant by the "bloodymindedness" that characterized relations among ancient Jewish sects; see his *Mission and Conversion*, 170–3, where he assembles several ancient Jewish cases in which, when one group held

something was allowed and another forbade it, the former not only allowed it but actually insisted, demonstratively, that it must be done. For similar dynamics in another context, see R. Y. Hazan, *Centre Parties: Polarization and Competition in European Parliamentary Democracies* (London: Pinter, 1997). In contrast, when there is no competition there is no such need for consistency.

88 For another simple illustration of this dynamic, note that Ben-Sira, writing in Jerusalem a decade or two before the days of Antiochus Epiphanes, had no problem with expressing universalist views, although they smacked of Hellenism and were fundamentally contrary to his own basically priestly orientation. This would have been impossible once Antiochus' decrees against Judaism made Jews choose one way or the other. See D. R. Schwartz, "From the Return to Zion until the Hasmonean Revolt," *Israel: People, Land, State – A Nation and Its Homeland* (ed. A. Shinan; Jerusalem: Yad Izhak Ben-Zvi, 2005), 52–5. (For the argument, that Ben-Sira actually wrote in Alexandria, see P. McKechnie, "The Career of Joshua Ben Sira," *JTS* 51 [2000]: 3–26. But even McKechnie assumes that Ben-Sira was a Jerusalemite, so although the issue has various implications, in the present context it is more or less like the case of 2 Maccabees – above, ch. 1, n. 8.)

89 For another analysis of this text, but focusing on issues of literature and rhetoric, see Lightstone, "Pharisees and the Sadducees in the Earliest Rabbinic Documents," 263–79. In his concluding discussion of the *substance* of the debates, Lightstone notes that he does not discern any "grand or overarching legal or theological programs" in them. That makes it all the likelier that the point is elsewhere – the mode of argumentation.

90 Although various editions read "Sadducee" here, thus levelling out the text (and perhaps also avoiding censorship), the manuscripts agree that the antagonist in §8 is a "Galilean heretic (*min*)." See Le Moyne, *Sadducéens*, 99, who cites S. Lieberman, "Light on the Cave Scrolls from Rabbinic Sources," *PAAJR* 20 (1951): 401–2. On pejorative use of "Galilean," see also above, at nn. 67–8.

91 This argument well illustrates the point that the Mishnaic account is a partisan rabbinic account, for – as we have seen (above, 31–2) – the Sadducees indeed held that animal bones are impure. As for the impurity incurred by hands that touch biblical scrolls – it is usually assumed that it was a measure taken to prevent people from eating while reading such scrolls, thus protecting the scrolls from crumbs and ensuing damage. Naturally, the rabbis did not think that texts of Homer required such protection.

92 In this case the Sadducees' position seems to be the same as that bespoken, polemically, by a Qumran text; see Baumgarten, "Pharisaic-Sadducean

Controversies," 163–4. Concerning this argument, I suggested ("Law and Truth," 232) that the rabbis' position was that the water in the pitcher was not affected by the impurity in the pail because a "pitcher" is distinct from the "pail," despite the fact that they are connected by the stream of water, just as a tanker insured for damage by oil spillage in the Caribbean would not be covered for damage done in the Atlantic, despite the fact that nature does not care about such names and oil spilled in the Caribbean might flow into the Atlantic. Rubenstein ("Nominalism and Realism" 170–1), in response, suggests that the rabbis' position was realist, as that of Qumran: the rabbis, he suggests, simply disagreed with Qumran as to whether the nature of impurity allows it to move upstream. However, the fact is that the Qumran text cited at the beginning of this note explains its point quite clearly, emphasizing that the impurity spreads through the connecting stream because it is all one body of water: "for the liquid which is poured and the liquid which is in the vessels that receive it are like it – one liquid" (4QMMT B, 57–8, ed. E. Qimron and J. Strugnell; DJD 10, p. 52).

93 This case is "heavier" than that of the pitcher for several reasons: (1) an aqueduct is much larger than a pitcher; (2) it refers to a permanent situation, not just a one-time incident; and (3) the water that flowed through the aqueduct will have carried the impurity with it downstream, which is natural, whereas in the case of the pitcher even a realist might think (as Rubenstein noted; see n. 92) that the water in the stream and the pitcher remained pure because the impurity in the pit cannot travel upstream.

94 Indeed, it seems that the aqueduct has been identified, and that it brought water to the Temple itself! See J. Patrich, "A Sadducean Halakha and the Jerusalem Aqueduct," *The Jerusalem Cathedra* 2 (ed. L. I. Levine; Jerusalem: Yad Izḥak Ben-Zvi; Detroit: Wayne University Press, 1982), 25–39.

95 Namely, slaves, who as opposed to animals can understand the legal situation, might deliberately damage other people's property in order to hurt their owners.

96 That such a sensitivity is not at all far-fetched is shown by the way ancient Jews interpreted Exod 22:28, which prohibits, in parallel, cursing *'elohim* and cursing "princes of your people." Although usually *'elohim* means "God," ancient Jews resisted that translation here, preferring either to take it as referring to human judges (so the rabbinic tradition, e.g., *Mek. ad loc.* [ed. Horovitz-Rabin, 317]; b. *Sanh.* 66a) or to pagan gods (so the Septuagint and Hellenistic Jews who quote it; see Josephus, *Ag. Ap.* 2.237 and J. Barclay's note *ad loc.* in FJTC 10.306, n. 958).

97 The Mishnah reports that the Sadducees point to "life for life" (Deut 19:21) as if it meant that a life had been taken and not merely threatened, and that "the sages" responded by citing "had planned to do to *his brother*" (v. 19) as if it implies the intended victim is still alive. In context, neither argument has any weight at all, and especially the Pharisees' cannot be serious, for, as we shall see, the Pharisees were willing, in another legal context (inheritance), to consider a dead son as if he were still alive; see below, n. 109. It is important to note that the Mishnah does not say (as later commentators will) that the argument is based on "had planned," as if that excluded the case in which the false witnesses had been fully successful. That argument would become possible only in the wake of Beribbi's innovative position, to be discussed below. On the history of these laws, see S. Friedman, "The 'Plotting Witness' and Beyond: A Continuum in Ancient Near Eastern, Biblical, and Talmudic Law," in Birkat Shalom: *Studies in the Bible, Ancient Near Eastern Literature, and Postbiblical Judaism Presented to Shalom M. Paul on the Occasion of His Seventieth Birthday* (ed. C. Cohen et al.; Winona Lake, Ind.: Eisenbrauns, 2008), 2.801–29.

98 Note that this is a clear case in which Sadducean law deviates from the plain sense of Scripture – which is often thought to be their guide. That notion derives to some extent from a traditional Jewish conflation of Sadducees with the medieval Karaites – on which see, inter alia, Y. Erder, "The Karaites' Sadducee Dilemma," *IOS* 14 (1994), esp. 215–21. For another clear case of such Sadducean deviation from the Bible, due to "realism," see t. *Kippurim* 1:8 (ed. Lieberman, 222–3), y. *Yoma* 1:5, 39a–b, and b. *Yoma* 19a–b, 53a: the Sadducees insisted that, in the most sacred rite of the Jewish year, the high priest put incense on the coals in his censer not after entering the Holy of Holies on the Day of Atonement, as is demanded by Lev 16:12–13, but rather prior to entry, contrary to the order of those two verses. As J. Z. Lauterbach, who collected and studied the various sources regarding this dispute, realized, this reflected the Sadducean assumption that the Holy of Holies was – I would add: *really* – a dangerous place; see his *Rabbinic Essays* (Cincinnati: Hebrew Union College, 1951), 51–83. The cloud of incense was meant, in their view, to protect the high priest, and so, like a gas mask, should be in place prior to entry. The Pharisees, in contrast, held that the law was created not by any real danger, but, rather, by the biblical legislation itself.

99 The suggestion offered here for the Sadducean position was already offered by L. Finkelstein, *The Pharisees: The Sociological Background of Their Faith* (3rd ed.; Philadelphia: Jewish Publication Society, 1966), 1.143.

However, for the Pharisees he suggests that their position was not that the witnesses were treated as if they had killed the victim, but, rather, that they understood the witness's crime as one against the state, not against the individual, and the former had been committed even if it did not entail the death of the victim. A similar argument was offered by Rubenstein ("Nominalism and Realism," 174), who argues that "it is a stretch" to think that the Pharisees' position bespeaks the notion that the witness's victim is dead. Rather, he argues, "a more plausible interpretation of the dispute relates to the issue of whether attempted murderers should receive the death penalty." However, (1) it would be quite difficult to find, in rabbinic literature, support for the imposition of such a penalty for attempted murder ("It seems that, just as under other systems of law in antiquity, so also under Talmudic Law, an *unsuccessful attempt* to commit a crime was not considered a crime in itself" [J. Bazak, "An Unsuccessful Attempt to Commit a Crime," *Jewish Law Association Studies* 18 (2008): 11 (original emphasis)]), and (2) if the issue were, nevertheless, whether attempted murderers should be executed, we would be hard pressed to explain why it comes up only in connection with this type of attempted murder, via false testimony in court. For other rabbinic treatment of condemned people as if they are dead, note the rulings that if such a man, on the way to his execution, makes a vow donating his value (see Lev 27) to the Temple, "he has said nothing" (b. '*Arak.* 6b), and that if anyone murders him or maims him he will be exempt from punishment (*Sifre Num.* 160 [ed. Horovitz, 221]; t. *Sanh.* 9:15 [ed. Lieberman, 45]).

100 This is not at all a surprising position for legalists. Note the English common law rule that penal statutes are to be construed strictly, that is, in favour of the accused, so something that logically should have been punishable, but the law did not mention it, is not punishable; see R. Cross, *Statutory Interpretation* (ed. J. Bell and G. Engle; 3rd ed.; London: Butterworths, 1995), 172–5.

101 See *Encyclopedia Talmudica*, vol. 2 (Jerusalem: Yad Harav Herzog, 1974), cols. 111–18. To illustrate how common it became to assume that rabbis used arguments a fortiori, note the report in an extra-Talmudic treatise (*Tosephta Derekh 'Erez* 3:6 – *The Treatises Derek Erez* [ed. M. Higger; New York: Debe Rabanan, 1935], 96–7) about a troublemaker who mocked rabbinic argumentation by concocting the following: given the fact that a man is not allowed to have sexual relations with his wife's daughter although he is allowed to do so with her mother (i.e., with his own wife), it follows a fortiori, from the fact that he is not allowed such relations with another man's wife, that he is certainly not allowed such with her

daughter. That argument is ridiculous because it amounts to forbidding marriage altogether, and, according to the report, R. Gamaliel excommunicated the mocker.

102 So, for example, "ox or ass" (Exod 21:33) means "any animal," for "Scripture simply gave usual examples" (m. *B. Qam.* 5:7); see L. Moscovitz, *Talmudic Reasoning: From Casuistics to Conceptualization* (TSAJ 89; Tübingen: Mohr Siebeck, 2002), 161–2.

103 See Geiger, *Urschrift*, 200–30. For a more recent restatement of the argument that 1 Maccabees is Sadducean, see D. Gera, "The Battle of Beth Zachariah and Greek Literature," in *The Jews in the Hellenistic-Roman World: Studies in Memory of Menahem Stern* (ed. I. M. Gafni, A. Oppenheimer, and D. R. Schwartz; Jerusalem: Zalman Shazar Center, 1996), 49–51 (in Hebrew).

104 Apart from the polemic hyperbole in Matt 23:15, which complains that the Pharisees are willing to cross the land and the sea to make a single convert.

105 Given the Galilee's origins as "Galilee of the Gentiles" (Isa 8:23//1 Macc 5:15/Matt 4:15) and the fact that it was separated from Judea by Samaria, the Galilee might be said to have been Diaspora during the Second Temple period. The point need not be pursued here.

106 See *Ant.* 13.171–3; 18.13; *War* 2.162–3; also S. Mason, "Scholarly Interpretations of Josephus on Fate and Free Will," in his *Flavius Josephus on the Pharisees: A Composition-Critical Study* (StPB 39; Leiden: Brill, 1991), 384–98; and, more recently, J. Klawans, "Josephus on Fate, Free Will, and Ancient Jewish Types of Compatibilism," *Numen* 56 (2009): 44–90.

107 See E. E. Urbach, *The Sages: Their Concepts and Beliefs* (2nd ed.; Jerusalem: Magnes, 1979), 1.255–85.

108 See especially the pedantic explanation in 2 Macc 12:43–6, also 7:9, 11, 14, 23, 29; and 14:46.

109 Josephus, *War* 2.165; *Ant.* 18.16; Luke 20:27–40; Acts 4:1–2 and 23:6–8; m. *Sanhedrin* 10:1; Le Moyne, *Les Sadducéens*, 167–75. On Josephus, see the next note. I would add that this argument between Pharisees and Sadducees was probably also to be at the bottom of the dispute between the Pharisees and Sadducees (or "Boethusians," their "lexical equivalent" [above, n. 6]) concerning the disposition of the estate of a man who died leaving only a daughter and the daughter of a predeceased son: the Pharisees held that the granddaughter inherits all, contrary to the Sadducees, who held that the estate should be split between the two women (t. *Yad.* 2:20 [ed. Zuckermandel, 684]; *Megillat Ta'anit*, 24 Av [ed. Noam, 223–5]; y. *B. Bat.* 8:1 (16a); b. *B. Bat.* 115b–16a; Le Moyne, *Les*

Sadducéens, 299–306). Although other explanations have been offered (see Le Moyne, ibid.), the simplest seems to be that the Pharisees held that the dead son is to be treated as if he were still alive, so Num 27:8 ("if a man dies and has no son, you shall pass his estate to his daughter") does not apply. Rather, according to the Pharisees, the son, although in his grave, is thought to inherit the entire estate, as a live son would, and then immediately bequeath it to his daughter. The Sadducees, in contrast, held that the man has no son, and – in the absence of any specific directive in the Torah concerning the case of a man who once *had* a son and has a daughter – recommended what seems to be an equitable solution. The fact that this argument about inheritance, which could have been a benign one about exegesis and a rare case, was recorded as one between the Pharisees and the Sadducees, suggests that its origin in this basic difference about life after death was understood.

110 For another version of this belief, note that Josephus, in the passages mentioned in the preceding note, ascribes to the Pharisees belief not in resurrection but, rather, in the immortality of the soul; although different from the belief in resurrection, it agrees that souls can exist outside of bodies.

111 Note, for example, Philo's plaint in *In Flaccum* 123, that the Alexandrian "pogrom" of 38 CE made the Jews "city-less," also above, ch. 1, n. 12.

112 For a programmatic statement of that position, via the contrast between the beginning and the end of the first chapter of m. *Avot*, see below, ch. 3, after n. 23. For another example note the rabbinic prayer for Hanukkah (*'Al Hanissim*): it opens with the general statement that the Greek persecutors wanted to cause the Jews to forget God's Torah and cause them to violate his laws, making no mention of the attack on the Temple – which is reflected only toward the end of the prayer when its restoration is mentioned. That is, the general attack was on our religion, which is a matter of law; it had a particular implication, concerning the Temple. However, since it seems that that prayer cannot be traced much earlier than seventh or eighth century (S. C. Reif, *Problems with Prayers: Studies in the Textual History of Early Rabbinic Liturgy* [SJ 37; Berlin: De Gruyter, 2006], 291–313), citation of it here is only as an illustration of the point of view I am underlining, not to document it for the earlier period that is our focus.

113 For Antigonus and Hillel, see m. *Avot* 1:3, 12. For Hillel's Babylonian origins, see, e.g., t. *Neg.* 1:16 (ed. Zuckermandel, 619); J. Neusner, *A History of the Jews in Babylonia, I: The Parthian Period* (BJS 62; Chico, Cal.: Scholars, 1984), 39–41. For his centrality in early rabbinic Judaism, see *Hillel and Jesus: Comparative Studies of Two Major Religious Leaders* (ed. J. H. Charlesworth and L. L. Johns; Minneapolis: Fortress, 1997).

114 Namely, at m. *Avot* 1:12 Hillel urges us to "be of the disciples of Aaron, loving peace and pursuing peace, loving people and bringing them near to the Torah." In the Second Temple period "sons of Aaron" was a common phrase used to define priests, while "disciples of Aaron" are never mentioned, so Hillel's statement, which posits the moral qualities of the latter, had a polemic edge. This is illustrated quite well by a Talmudic story that reports that when an arrogant high priest snubbed Hillel's teachers due to their foreign ancestry, they responded that it is better to be of foreign ancestry but do "the works of Aaron" (as Hillel defined them) than to be sons of Aaron and not do them (b. *Yoma* 71b). This is a rabbinic version of the kind of polemic attributed to John the Baptist at Matt 3:9 // Luke 3:8.

115 For a large collection of rabbinic materials about them, see M. Guttmann, *Clavis Talmudis*, II (Budapest: Kohn, 1917 [in Hebrew]), 74–96.

116 See R. T. Herford, *The Ethics of the Talmud: Sayings of the Fathers* (New York: Schocken, 1962), 74, 116.

117 I tend to think the rabbinic attitude toward martyrdom was more positive than is sometime assumed. See S. Shepkaru, *Jewish Martyrs in the Pagan and Christian Worlds* (Cambridge: Cambridge University Press, 2006), my review of it in the *Review of Biblical Literature* 2/2007 (online); and my "Martyrdom, the Middle Way, and Mediocrity (*Genesis Rabbah* 82:8)," in *"Follow the Wise": Studies in Jewish History and Culture in Honor of Lee I. Levine* (ed. Z. Weiss et al.; Winona Lake, Ind.: Eisenbrauns, 2010), 343–53.

Chapter 3

1 S. Mason, "Series Preface," FJTC 3.xi–xii.

2 He indicates the year clearly in his *Life* 5 and *Ant.* 20.267. For an introduction to Josephus, see P. Bilde, *Flavius Josephus between Jerusalem and Rome: His Life, His Works, and Their Importance* (JSPSup 2; Sheffield: Sheffield Academic, 1988).

3 Pliny, *Naturalis Historia* 5.70 (*GLAJJ* I, no. 204).

4 See esp. *War* 1.3 and *Life* 7, 198.

5 See especially *Life* 1–6, 198; *Ag. Ap.* 1.54; and *War* 1.3; 3.352. Indeed, at *Life* 2 Josephus claims that one of his ancestors married into the Hasmonean high-priestly dynasty, and at *Ant.* 16.187 he roundly presents himself as a descendant of the Hasmoneans.

6 Similarly, a few paragraphs earlier (*Ant.* 6.79) Josephus reports the priests carried the ark, although the biblical text (2 Sam 6:3 // 1 Chr 13:7) has

only an undefined "they." On priesthood in Josephus, see S. N. Mason, "Priesthood in Josephus and the 'Pharisaic Revolution,'" *JBL* 107 (1988): 657–61; O. Gussmann, *Das Priesterverständnis des Flavius Josephus* (TSAJ 124; Tübingen: Mohr Siebeck, 2008); and M. Tuval, *From Jerusalem Priest to Roman Jew: On Josephus and Paradigms of Ancient Judaism* (WUNT II 357; Tübingen: Mohr Siebeck, 2013).

7 Although we Jews may frequently and justifiably suspect that we exaggerate the importance of Jews in world history, in this case it seems that it is in fact difficult to exaggerate. For a recent Italian point of view, see F. Coarelli, ed., *Divus Vespasianus: Il bimillenario dei Flavi* (Milan: Electa, 2009); four of the first six essays are on the role of the Judean war and Josephus in the Flavians' rise to power. On the way that war was the most important item in the Flavians' curriculum vitae, and their concomitant need to play it up, see F. Millar, "Last Year in Jerusalem: Monuments of the Jewish War in Rome," in *Flavius Josephus and Flavian Rome* (ed. J. Edmondson, S. Mason, and J. Rives; Oxford: Oxford University Press, 2005), 101. Of course, this need not entail the view that Josephus was merely the Flavians' abject or venal lackey, serving their interests alone or even unambiguously. Thus, for example, in this chapter we shall see that even in the *War* he serves Jewish interests too, as he understood them, by condemning as exceptional troublemakers, unrepresentative of the Jews at large, the rebels who engendered the clash with Rome and, in its suite, the catastrophe. See, in general, T. Rajak, "Flavian Patronage and Jewish Patriotism," in *Josephus: The Historian and His Society* (2nd ed.; London: Duckworth, 2002), 185–222; the studies by P. Spilsbury ("Reading the Bible in Rome: Josephus and the Constraints of Empire") and J. S. McLaren ("Josephus on Titus: The Vanquished Writing about the Victor") in *Josephus and Jewish History in Flavian Rome and Beyond* (ed. J. Sievers and G. Lembi; JSJSup 104; Leiden: Brill, 2005), 209–27 and 279–95 respectively; and now W. den Hollander, *Josephus, the Emperors, and the City of Rome: From Hostage to Historian* (AJEC 86; Leiden: Brill, 2014).

8 Virtually all of the little we know about Josephus' post-70 life comes from the direct testimony in the last two chapters of his *Life* (§§414–30), along with indirect and speculative inferences from his writings. See Rajak, "Epilogue: The Later Josephus," in *Josephus*, 223–9; and den Hollander, *Josephus, the Emperors, and the City of Rome*. That Josephus died no earlier than the mid-nineties derives from the date of his *Antiquities* together with the fact that his two smaller works are later than it; see the next footnote.

9 That the *Antiquities* was completed in 93/94 CE is stated at 20.267; *Against Apion* opens with a reference to the *Antiquities* as an earlier work; and the

Life presents itself as an appendix to the *Antiquities* (see esp. *Life* 430, also the transition from *Ant.* 20.266 to *Life* 1) and, correspondingly, refers (at §360) to at least twenty years having passed since the rebellion of 66–73 CE. That the *War* (or at least most of it), in contrast, was completed in the seventies, derives from Josephus' statement in *Ag. Ap.* 51 (similar in *Life* 361) that he presented a copy of the *War* to Vespasian – who died in 79 CE. For details, see Mason in FJTC 9, 148–9, n. 1493; C. P. Jones, "Towards a Chronology of Josephus," *Scripta Classica Israelica* 21 (2002): 113–21; and my article cited in n. 21, below. As for what "publication" meant, see L. Huitink and J. W. van Henten, "The Publication of Flavius Josephus' Works and Their Audiences," *Zutot* 6 (2009): 49–60; and S. Mason, "Josephus, Publication, and Audiences: A Response," *Zutot* 8 (2011): 81–94.

10 On Sicarii and other anti-Roman rebels, see M. Hengel, *The Zealots: Investigations into the Jewish Freedom Movement in the Period from Herod I until 70 A.D.* (Edinburgh: Clark, 1989), esp. 46–53 and 380–404; M. A. Brighton, *Sicarii in Josephus' Judean War: Rhetorical Analysis and Historical Observations* (SBLEJL 27; Atlanta: Society of Biblical Literature, 2009).

11 Here as elsewhere, I added subdivisions (a, b, c), bold type, and some bracketed explanations or alternate translations.

12 On scholarship concerning "Jesus and the Zealots" see my *Studies*, 128–46.

13 On this passage see G. Haaland, "What Difference Does Philosophy Make? The Three Schools as a Rhetorical Device in Josephus," in *Making History*, 264–70.

14 On this episode, and Josephus' attempt to hide the theological legitimacy of the rebels' argument, see my *Studies*, 102–16.

15 Thackeray offers "pleaded that they were forbidden"; but nothing in the Greek links the prohibition to anyone in particular.

16 See J. W. van Henten, "Ruler or God? The Demolition of Herod's Eagle," in *The New Testament and Early Christian Literature in Greco-Roman Context: Studies in Honor of David E. Aune* (ed. J. Fotopoulos; NovTSup 122; Leiden: Brill, 2006), 257–86; A. I. Baumgarten, "Herod's Eagle," in *"Go Out and Study the Land,"* 7–21.

17 BDAG, 24. Compare above, 29.

18 For the notion that *Antiquities* and its contrasts with *War* show that Josephus became a Pharisee in the post-70 decades, see especially M. Smith, "Palestinian Judaism in the First Century," in *Israel: Its Role in Civilization* (ed. M. Davis; New York: Harper and Brothers, 1956), 74–8 (= Smith, *Studies in the Cult of Yahweh* [ed. S. J. D. Cohen; Religions in the Graeco-Roman World 130; Leiden: Brill, 1996], 1.109–13); and S. J. D. Cohen, *Josephus in Galilee and Rome: His Vita and Development as a Historian*

(Columbia Studies in the Classical Tradition 8; Leiden: Brill, 1979), 144–51. My present contribution is to link that with his becoming a Jew of the Diaspora. See my "Josephus on the Pharisees as Diaspora Jews," in *Josephus und das Neue Testament: Wechselseitige Wahrnehmungen* (ed. C. Böttrich and J. Herzer; WUNT 209; Tübingen: Mohr Siebeck, 2007), 137–46.

19 "On the whole, one who would wish to read through it [*Antiquities*] would especially learn from this history that those who comply with the will of God and do not venture to transgress laws that have been well enacted succeed in all things beyond belief and that happiness lies before them as a reward from God. But to the extent that they dissociate themselves from the scrupulous observance of these laws, the practicable things become impracticable, and whatever seemingly good thing they pursue with zeal turns into irremediable misfortunes" ... "God, who is the Father and Lord of all and who looks upon all things, grants a happy life to those who follow Him and surrounds with great misfortunes those who transgress virtue" (*Ant.* 1.14, 20, trans. Feldman, FJTC).

20 H. W. Attridge, *The Interpretation of Biblical History in the* Antiquitates Judaicae *of Flavius Josephus* (HDR 7; Missoula, Mont.: Scholars, 1976). For Josephus' emphasis upon divine providence at some turning points in *Antiquities*, note his extended comments at 10.277–81; 13.163 (Jonathan renews treaty with Rome when God's providence made him successful [contrast Josephus' source – 1 Macc 12:1 – above, 18!]); 17.354 and 18.127 (the history of the Herodian line demonstrates divine providence); 18.309 (Petronius marvelled at God's providential timing of Gaius' death); 20.91 (God's providence protects Izates); etc.

21 See S. Schwartz, "The Composition and Publication of Josephus's *Bellum Iudaicum* Book 7," *HTR* 79 (1986): 373–86; and my "Josephus, Catullus, Divine Providence, and the Date of the *Judean War*," in *Flavius Josephus: Interpretation and History* (ed. J. Pastor, P. Stern, and M. Mor; JSJSup 146; Leiden: Brill, 2011), 331–52.

22 The Hebrew noun *'avodah* literally means "labour," but in biblical and rabbinic Hebrew had the specific sense of "sacrificial service." Note, for example, the amusing story about R. Tarphon in *Sifre Num.* §116 (ed. Horovitz, 133)//b. *PesaH* 72b and the text of the seventeenth of the Eighteen Benedictions: "and restore the *'avodah* to the sanctuary of Your house." See the discussion in C. Taylor, *Sayings of the Jewish Fathers* (Cambridge: Cambridge University Press, 1897), 12–13, n. 5.

23 There is some doubt about his precise identity, because Josephus ascribes the epithet "the Just" to Simon I, who was high priest ca. 300 BCE (*Ant.* 12.43), but a few other sources, including the list in m. *Avot* 1, point rather to Simon II, who was high priest about a century later. See J. C.

VanderKam, *From Joshua to Caiaphas: High Priests after the Exile*
(Minneapolis: Fortress, and Assen, the Netherlands: Van Gorcum, 2004),
137–57, 181–8; also A. Tropper, *Simeon the Righteous in Rabbinic Literature:
A Legend Reinvented* (AJEC 84; Leiden: Brill, 2013).

24 Some witnesses read *'omed* ("stands"), as in 1:2, but others read *qayyām*
("exists"); modern editions differ. The latter reading has been defended by
a recent scholar, who explains, "It stands to reason that 1:2 influenced 1:18
and generated the change from *qayyām* to *'omed*" (A. Tropper, *Wisdom,
Politics, and Historiography: Tractate Avot in the Context of the Graeco-Roman
Near East* [Oxford Oriental Monographs; Oxford: Oxford University Press,
2004]) 26, n. 29). However, it seems at least as likely that scribes introduced *qayyām* instead of *'omed* in order to eliminate the obvious contradic-
tion (and to allow such harmonizing interpretations as those offered by
standard traditional commentators: 1:2 explains why the world was created and 1:18 explains why it continues to exist, or 1:2 sets forth the ideal
values and 1:18 – the minimum necessary). Be that as it may, whatever the
verb, it is clear that 1:18 functions as a response to 1:2.

25 On the question whether the Simon b. Gamaliel cited in 1:18 is the first of
the sages of that name, who was an important figure in Jerusalem during
the rebellion of 66–70 (Josephus, *Life* 190–1), or rather his grandson of the
mid-second century, and for the assumption, followed above, that he is the
former, see the chart and discussion in Herford, *Ethics of the Talmud*, 36–8.
For the present purpose, the point does not matter.

26 Somewhat revised by the author.

27 On the use of *nomima* for something of a lesser status than laws (*nomoi*),
hence my "ordinances," see *Ant.* 13.296–7 and especially the way that text
is echoed at *Ant.* 13.408: the former says that Hyrcanus abrogated the
Pharisees' *nomima* and the latter says that "if there was anything, even (!)
of the *nomima*," that the Pharisees had introduced and Hyrcanus had abrogated, Salome restored it. Note also Plato, *Laws* 7.793a–d and Philo's very
explicit statement in *Hypothetica* 7.6, where he distinguishes between un-
written *ethē* (customs), *nomima*, and "the *nomoi* themselves." Thus, by using *nomima* here Josephus is praising the priests for their perseverance in
fulfilling even the least of their obligations.

28 On the translation of *thrēskeia* see below, 93–9.

29 The exception is in §148, where *tōn … nomimōn eis tēn thrēskeian*"
(Thackeray: "the religious rites") is, more literally, "the things done regularly according to law [or: ordinance or custom] for the cult."

30 The same new construction of the Temple cult as a part of Jewish law rather than (as for Simon the Just of *Avot* and Josephus of *War*) an independent
institution, parallel to the Law, may, of course, be observed elsewhere in

the *Antiquities* as well, not only where it contrasts with a parallel narrative in Josephus' *War*. Note, for example, *Ant.* 8.276–81, where Josephus has King Abijah contrast the northern kingdom's lawlessness (*paranomia*) and violation of the *nomoi* to the southerners' observance of the *nomima*, and has him call upon the northerners to respect ancestral practices (*patria*); in contrast, his source for this speech, 2 Chr 13:4–12, refers in detail to cultic institutions and makes no reference to law. Similarly, in *Ant.* 12 Josephus inserts several legal formulations not found in his source, 1 Maccabees: at 12.251 Antiochus suspends the daily sacrifice offered according to the Law (contrast 1 Macc 1:44–6); at 12.253 Antiochus introduces a cult that was neither lawful nor ancestral (contrast 1 Macc 1:47); and at 12.267 Mattathias, lamenting Antiochus' attack upon Jerusalem and the Temple, says it is better to die for the ancestral laws than to live without glory (contrast 1 Macc 2:7–13). On this theme, see I. M. Gafni, "Josephus and I Maccabees," in *Josephus, the Bible, and History* (ed. L. H. Feldman and G. Hata; Leiden: Brill, 1989), 121–3. Note too, similarly, the comparison between *War* 1 and *Ant.* 17 concerning Herod's eagle (above, 55).

31 In passing, note yet another consideration that may have reinforced the shift in Josephus' orientation: the Roman respect for law (to some extent in contrast to Greek predilection for philosophy) may have made it all the more desirable for Josephus to picture the Jews as especially devoted to their own laws. See M. Goodman, "Josephus as a Roman Citizen," in *Josephus and the History of the Greco-Roman Period: Essays in Memory of Morton Smith* (ed. F. Parente and J. Sievers; StPB 41; Leiden: Brill, 1994), 335; also G. Haaland, "Beyond Philosophy: Studies in Josephus and His *Contra Apionem*" (Dr. theol. diss.; MF Norwegian School of Theology, 2006), 47–53.

32 For two cases in *Antiquities* 18 that imply that *Ioudaios* means "Judean," see the Appendix, at n. 34. As for *Ioudaios* being better rendered "Jew" in *War*, when used of *Ioudaioi* in the Diaspora, see n. 15 to the Introduction.

Chapter 4

1 This chapter is largely based upon my "Jews, Judaeans and the Epoch That Disappeared: H. Graetz's Changing View of the Second Temple Period," *Zion* 70 (2004/2005): 293–309 (in Hebrew). I am grateful to the publisher of *Zion*, the Historical Society of Israel, for permission to publish this version here. There is an extensive literature about Graetz. Among recent works, see R. Michael, *Hirsch (Heinrich) Graetz: The Historian of the Jewish People* (Jerusalem: Bialik Institute and Leo Baeck Institute, 2003 [in

Hebrew]); N. H. Roemer, *Jewish Scholarship and Culture in Nineteenth-Century Germany: Between History and Faith* (Studies in German Jewish Cultural History and Literature; Madison: University of Wisconsin Press, 2005); M. Pyka, *Jüdische Identität bei Heinrich Graetz* (Jüdische Religion, Geschichte und Kultur 5; Göttingen: Vandenhoeck und Ruprecht, 2009); and M. Brenner, *Prophets of the Past: Interpreters of Jewish History* (Princeton: Princeton University Press, 2010), 53–91.

2 *"... ist die Geschichte dieser Zeit die interessanteste und anziehendste, aber auch die reichste der ganzen jüdischen Geschichte"* (Graetz, *Geschichte* III, 1st ed., 1; basically the same in III, 2nd ed., 1; slightly toned down in III, 3rd ed., xiii).

3 By way of contrast, note that although vol. VIII/2 too appeared in a *"verbesserte und stark vermehrte"* third edition in Graetz's lifetime, that 1890 volume was only ten pages longer than the original edition of 1864. For a list of Graetz's writings, see M. Brann, "Verzeichnis von H. Graetzens Schriften und Abhandlungen," *MGWJ* n.F. 25 (1917): 444–91.

4 As he explained in the 1870 preface to *Geschichte* XI, vi–vii (also reprinted in its second edition), and retrospectively in *Geschichte* I, 1st ed., viii–ix.

5 The two volumes split the biblical period at the death of Solomon: *Geschichte der Israeliten von ihren Uranfängen (um 1500) bis zum Tode des Königs Salomo (um 977 vorchr. Zeit)* (Leipzig: Leiner, 1874); *Geschichte der Israeliten vom Tode des König's Salomo (um 977 vorchr. Zeit) bis zum Tode des Juda Makkabi (160)* (2 parts; Leipzig: Leiner, 1875–6).

6 J. Wellhausen, *Prolegomena to the History of Israel* (Edinburgh: Black, 1885), 1. Part III of this volume is titled "Israel and Judaism."

7 *Cambridge History of Judaism, I: Introduction – The Persian Period* (ed. W. D. Davies and L. Finkelstein; Cambridge: Cambridge University Press, 1984). According to the opening of the preface of this volume (p. v), "Critical study of Judaism, by which is meant the form which the religion of Israel assumed in and after the Babylonian exile, is of comparatively recent origin ..."

8 I will cite that essay according to its English translation: H. Graetz, *The Structure of Jewish History and Other Essays* (trans. and ed. I. Schorsch; New York: Jewish Theological Seminary of America, 1975). The German original of the essay, "Die Construktion der jüdischen Geschichte," appeared in four instalments in *Zeitschrift für die religiösen Interessen des Judenthums* 3 (1846); in 1936 the Schocken Verlag (Berlin) republished the essay as a separate volume with the same title (apart from updating the spelling of the second word: *Konstruktion*).

9 See Graetz, *Structure*, 75 (referring to "the Jewish judge" in the period of the biblical Judges).

10 Ibid., 73. For a longer statement of Graetz's complaint about Jost's split of our history between *Israeliten* and *Juden*, see Graetz, *Geschichte*, XI (1st ed.; Leipzig: Leiner, 1870), 456 = 2nd ed. (1900), 427. For a much more recent and more articulated version of the same Jewish complaint, see M. Brettler, "Judaism in the Hebrew Bible? The Transition from Ancient Israelite Religion to Judaism," *CBQ* 61 (1999), 429–47.

11 As noted, in the *Structure* Graetz referred not to the exile but, rather, to the return from it as the beginning of the second era. But if that were the only discrepancy, we would accept this somewhat earlier caesura as appropriate for understanding the background of the Return.

12 Which appears in both editions of vol. II.

13 Graetz, *Geschichte* III/1, 4th ed., 1 = III/1, 5th ed., 1.

14 So *Geschichte* III, 3rd ed., xiii ("*von etwa zwei Jahrhunderten*"). The first two editions say the period discussed is one *von kaum drei Jahrhunderten* (of barely three centuries); that misstatement is tantalizing, but so far I have discovered no explanation for it, other than carelessness.

15 *Geschichte* III, 1st ed., 4 = 2nd ed., 3 = 3rd ed., xvi.

16 *Geschichte* III: 1st ed., 457 = 2nd ed., 414 = 3rd ed., 596.

17 Although B. Dinur pointed out the fact that Graetz used *Israeliten* and *Judäer* for the early periods, and explained that *Judäer* meant "'the people of the Jews,' [i.e.,] the residents of the land of the Jews," he did not notice that Graetz introduced the latter only in the third edition of vol. III; see Dinur, "The Problem of Dividing Jewish History into Periods in Jewish Historiography," in *Fourth World Congress of Jewish Studies: Papers* (Jerusalem: World Union of Jewish Studies, 1967), 1.55 (= Dinur, *Dorot uReshumot* [Jerusalem: Bialik Institute, 1978] 46 [both in Hebrew]). I have noticed only one scholar who noted that Graetz changed his nomenclature (although he erroneously wrote that the change came in the second edition): R. Deines, *Die Pharisäer: Ihr Verständnis im Spiegel der christlichen und jüdischen Forschung seit Wellhausen und Graetz* (WUNT 101; Tübingen: Mohr Siebeck, 1997), 162, n. 84. Deines suggests no explanation for the change.

18 See Brann, "Verzeichnis." The editions of vol. III, of which the fourth and fifth appeared in two volumes each, are nos. 58, 87, 249, 355, and 391–2 in that list – and Brann used *Juden* and *jüdischen* in the titles of all of them.

19 See K. Krieger, ed., *Der "Berliner Antisemitismusstreit" 1879–1881: Eine Kontroverse um die Zugehörigkeit der deutschen Juden zur Nation – Kommentierte Quellenedition* (2 vols.; Münich: Saur, 2003); M. Stoetzler, *The State, the Nation, and the Jews: Liberalism and the Antisemitism Dispute in Bismarck's Germany* (Lincoln: University of Nebraska Press, 2008). Other

literature is cited in nn. 22–3. For von Treitschke's essay that started the debate off, see Krieger, 1.6–16 (against Graetz, p. 12); for an English translation of it, see Stoetzler, 309–16.

20 As formulated in the subtitle of Krieger's anthology cited in the preceding note, it was a "controversy about the belonging of the German Jews to the [German] nation."

21 For Graetz's responses, see Krieger, ibid., 1.96–101, 186–92. Note also Graetz's December 1880 lettter to J. Bernays, ibid., II, 754–5 (= H. Graetz, *Tagebuch und Briefe* [ed. R. Michael; Schriftenreihe wissenschaftlicher Abhandlungen des Leo-Baeck-Instituts 34; Tübingen: Mohr (Siebeck), 1977], 367–8) and his obiter dictum in *Geschichte*, III/1, 4th ed., 228, n. 5 (= 5th ed., 227, n. 4). In that note, which cites the Ionians' complaint, in the days of Herod, that if the Jews wanted to be accepted as their fellows they ought to worship their gods (*Ant.* 12.126 and 16.59), Graetz comments that it is remarkable (*beachtenswert*) that the very same argument for the exclusion (*Ausschließung*) of the Jews used in his own day was already being offered then. There is no such remark in the parallel sections of the first three editions of *Geschichte* III (1st ed., 223; 2nd ed., 185–6; 3rd ed., 239–40).

22 For anti-Semitism earlier in the decade, see J. Katz, "The Preparatory Stage of the Modern Antisemitic Movement (1873–1879)," in *Antisemitism through the Ages* (ed. S. Almog; Oxford: Pergamon, 1988), 279–89; and N. Kampe, "Von der 'Gründerkrise' zum 'Berliner Antisemitismusstreit': Die Entstehung des modernen Antisemitismus in Berlin, 1875–1881," in *Jüdische Geschichte in Berlin* (ed. R. Rürup; Berlin: Hentrich, 1995), 85–100.

23 For the review, see *Literarisches Centralblatt für Deutschland*, 14 January 1871, cols. 29–31. The review, signed M.L., was written by Max Lehmann (1845–1929), soon to be a friend of von Treitschke's and eventually a professor in Göttingen; it is the point of departure for my study: "From Feuding Medievalists to the Berlin Antisemitismusstreit of 1879–1881," *Jahrbuch für Antisemitismusforschung* 21 (2012): 239–67.

24 As Graetz noted in a letter of July 1871, the press and university circles attacked him severely for that volume. See Graetz, *Tagebuch und Briefe*, 310; also J. Meisl, *Heinrich Graetz: Eine Würdigung des Historikers und Juden zu seinem 100. Geburtstage 31. Oktober 1917 (21. Cheschwan)* (Berlin: Lamm, 1917), 127–8, n. 51.

25 See, e.g., G. F. Moore, "Christian Writers on Judaism," *HTR* 14 (1921): 197–254; K. Hoheisel, *Das antike Judentum in christlicher Sicht* (StOR 2; Wiesbaden: Harrasowitz, 1978).

26 See I. Schorsch, *Jewish Reactions to German Anti-Semitism, 1870–1914* (New York: Columbia University Press, 1972), 157–8.

27 See, for example, his complaints in *Geschichte* I (1874), viii, x, about those who would disparage the biblical period by terming it merely *Judengeschichte*.

28 See Graetz's angry complaint in *Geschichte* III/2 (4th ed., 1888) 629, n. 1 (= 5th ed., 631, n. 1) that members of Schürer's clique dote on each other's words but ignore the work of outsiders like him.

29 See, for a prominent example, BDAG, 478: "Since the term 'Judaism' suggests a monolithic entity that fails to take account of the many varieties of thought and social expression associated with such adherents, the calque or loanword 'Judean' is used in this and other entries where *I[oudaios]* is treated ... Incalculable harm has been caused by simply glossing *I[oudaios]* with 'Jew,' for many readers or auditors of Bible translations do not practice the historical judgment necessary to distinguish between circumstances and events of an ancient time and contemporary ethnic-religious realities, with the result that anti-Judaism in the modern sense is needlessly fostered through biblical texts." For some responses pro and con, see Miller, "Meaning of *Ioudaios*," 98–9.

30 See, in Brann's "Verzeichnis," the following items published between 1876 and 1884: nos. 220, 225, 247, 248, 253, 255, 256, 278, 294, and 312. There is nothing comparable to this in the years prior to his trip.

31 Contrast *Geschichte* III, 1st ed., 394, n. 1 (= 2nd ed., 361, n. 4) with 3rd ed., 507, n. 5.

32 See Michael, *Hirsch (Heinrich) Graetz*, 127: Graetz visited Sepphoris, the Sea of Galilee, Acco, and Haifa. For his first-hand impressions of Safed, see his 1872 memoir reproduced in Meisl, *Heinrich Graetz*, 148–9.

33 Contrast *Geschichte* III, 1st ed., 414 (= 2nd ed., 377) with 3rd ed., 529–30 (with 530, n. 1).

34 Contrast *Geschichte* III, 1st ed., 392 (= 2nd ed., 360) with 3rd ed., 506.

35 *Structure*, 84. As for the question of what then distinguishes between the second era and the third, if they were both were religiously oriented, Graetz located the difference both in the difference between being in the land and being in exile and in the realm of self-consciousness concerning religion: "In the former [Second Temple – DRS] era religion was cultivated in reflectionless immediacy; it followed an entirely external, naive course. In contrast, in the later era religion immersed itself in the inwardness of reflection; it pursued the study of its own being and significance" (*Structure*, 95). For the sake of clarity, in this English translation I twice used "era" instead of the more nebulous "period" used in *Structure*, 95 (as in Graetz, *Konstruktion*, 51 – "Periode").

36 Here too, for the sake of clarity, I used "era" at this end of this passage, instead of "period" (*Structure*, 73). In the German original of the essay

(*Konstruktion*, 20) Graetz uses "Periode," but that word corresponds to his use of "Zeitraum" in the previous sentence – the term we have consistently rendered as "era."

37 The closest we come, in the period in question, is Hyrcanus II: Josephus portrays him as unfit for public life and reports that he abdicated in favour of his younger brother (see *Ant.* 14.5–7). However, Josephus goes on to report that Hyrcanus reneged on the agreement and went to war with his brother. Moreover, it is obvious that Josephus' characterization of Hyrcanus was slanted in order to justify the fact that Hyrcanus's Idumean advisor, Antipater (Herod's father), took over in his stead: rather than usurping power illegitimately, he and his sons had stepped in to do what had to be done when no one else was at the helm. See my "Josephus on Hyrcanus II," in *Josephus and the History*, 210–32.

38 Note that Graetz equates the destruction of the Second Temple with the end of the Jewish state, although, as he of course knew well, in fact the state ceased to exist with the Roman annexation of Judea in 6 CE (and one might well make a case that the state's *Untergang* came even seventy years earlier, with the Roman conquest of the independent Hasmonean state). Such an equation, however, is not totally unreasonable, considering the Temple's role as the territorial centre of the Jewish world and axis of hopes to restore statehood – and similar phrasings can be found in the writings of numerous other historians as well. For several examples, see N. Sharon, "Setting the Stage: The Effects of the Roman Conquest and the Loss of Sovereignty," in *Was 70 CE a Watershed?*, 417–18.

39 For other cases in which Graetz deviated from his original scheme, usually (as in our case) without pointing it out or reflecting it consistently in title pages and introductions, see Pyka, *Jüdische Identität*, 234–41; also Dinur, "The Problem." Both focus, however, on the successive changes Graetz made in the division of the period from 70 CE until his own day; neither discusses vol. III in this context.

40 *Geschichte* III, 1st ed., 1 = 2nd ed., 1.

41 *Geschichte* III, 1st ed., 2 = 2nd ed., 2 (*unstreitig ein religiöser*).

42 *Geschichte* III, 3rd ed., xiv (*unstreitig ein vorherrschend religiöser*).

43 Contrast *Geschichte* III, 1st ed., 4 (= 2nd ed., 3) with 3rd ed., xvi.

44 *Geschichte* I, 1st ed., 2.

45 *Geschichte* III, 2nd ed., 2; 3rd ed., xiv.

46 For Hegel's impact upon Graetz, especially via C. J. Braniß, who was one of Graetz's favourite teachers at the University of Breslau between 1842 and 1845 (see Pyka, *Jüdische Identität*, 96, n. 259), i.e., just before Graetz published his *Structure*, see Pyka, ibid., 147–62; also S. Ettinger, "Graetz on

Judaism and the History of the Jews," in *Heinrich Graetz: Essays, Memoirs, Letters* (ed. S. Ettinger; Jerusalem: Bialik Institute, 1969 [in Hebrew]), 14–15.

47 That is, measures taken to prevent people from even coming near to violating the law (see ch. 2, n. 61).

48 *Geschichte* III, 3rd ed., xvi (*hat ihr erst die Unwiderstehlichkeit einer geschichtlichen Triebkraft verliehen*).

49 See above, n. 14.

50 *Structure*, 90–2.

51 *Geschichte* I, 1st ed., 2–3 = 2nd ed., 2–3 = 3rd ed., xiv–xv.

52 "Das Trihäresion," *Geschichte* III, 1st ed., 507–28; 2nd ed., 454–71; 3rd ed., 647–63; 4th ed., 687–703; 5th ed., 689–705.

53 See above, n. 43.

54 See M. Brann's foreword to his second edition of Graetz's, *Geschichte* XI (1900), vii, where he states that it was on the basis of an authentic statement by Graetz, and also on the basis of other writings by Graetz, that he had revised Graetz's harsh judgments ("die harten Urtheile") about Germanism and Germans. A few lines later Brann even wrote that although Graetz was, as is well known, an enthusiastically nationalist Jew, he was also an exemplary Prussian patriot! On *Geschichte* XI, see Michael, *Hirsch (Heinrich) Graetz*, 113–23.

55 See Graetz, *Tagebuch und Briefe*, 431; Michael, *Hirsch (Heinrich) Graetz*, 190–5.

Conclusion

1 See, for example, L. A. Coser, *Masters of Sociological Thought: Ideas in Historical and Social Context* (New York: Harcourt, Brace, Jovanovich, 1977), 223–4, also above, Preface, pp. xi–xii.

2 For the argument that he should indeed be classed as a proto-Sadducee, see J. Klawans, *Josephus and the Theologies of Ancient Judaism* (New York: Oxford University Press, 2012), 28–32.

3 Note that although the Geniza text (Ms. A) of 10:21 states that a wicked person (זד) is glorious if he reveres God, that makes no sense, and the text must be corrected to זר ("foreigner"), as was pointed out by various scholars even before it was confirmed by the reading of a belatedly published page of Ms. B; see J. Schirmann, "Some Additional Leaves from Ecclesiasticus in Hebrew," *Tarbiz* 29 (1959/1960): 129 (in Hebrew). That is, Ben-Sira emphasizes that even a non-Jew can share in the glory of being reverent toward God.

4 For prayers in 1 Maccabees, see ch. 1, n. 21. For 2 Maccabees' pride about the Temple, see 2:19, 22; 3:12; 5:15; 14:13, 31.

5 See ch. 2, n. 10.

6 Contrast Philo's *On Dreams* 2.248 with his *Embassy to Gaius* 186–94; and see my "Philo, His Family, and His Times," in *The Cambridge Companion to Philo* (ed. A. Kamesar; New York: Cambridge University Press, 2009), 24–31.

7 See ch. 2 at nn. 69–70.

8 See ch. 2, at nn. 87–88.

9 See ch. 2, n. 88.

10 See Isocrates, *Panegyricus*, 50; Erastothenes, cited by Strabo 1.4.9; and 2 Macc 4:35 (on which see ch. 1, n. 15).

11 Or "culture." I consider "religion" a part of "culture," but what is important, in the present context, is that both refer to things one does or values, not to physical quantities like pedigree or location. See below, Appendix, n. 40.

12 In this connection, S. Schwartz refers to the use of "Judean" as sometimes having "a salutary defamiliarizing effect" ("How Many Judaisms" [Appendix, n. 1], 223).

13 See D. J. Elazar, "The New Sadducees," *Midstream* 24, no. 7 (September 1978): 20–5; M. Greenberg, "On the Political Use of the Bible in Modern Israel: An Engaged Critique," in *Pomegranates and Golden Bells: Studies in Biblical, Jewish, and Near Eastern Ritual, Law, and Literature in Honor of Jacob Milgrom* (ed. D. P. Wright, D. N. Freedman, and A. Hurvitz; Winona Lake, Ind.: Eisenbrauns, 1995), 461–71; D. R. Schwartz, "Does Religious Zionism Tend to Sadduceeism?" *Eretz Aḥeret* 24 (November 2004): 72–6 (in Hebrew); and Schwartz, "What's the Difference between 1 Maccabees and 2 Maccabees?, or: The Challenging Hyphen in Such Combinations as 'State-Religious,' 'Religious-National,' and 'Zionist-Religious,'" in *Jewish Tradition in a Changing Educational World* (ed. M. Barlev; Jerusalem: Ministry of Education and Hebrew University School of Education, 2005 [in Hebrew]), 11–20. For responses to my characterization of religious Zionism as Sadduceeism, see Y. Bin-Nun, "Seeking the Truth vs. Halachic Formalism: A Note on the Moral Philosophy of the Halakhah and on the Sanctification of the Name," in *Derekh Eretz, Religion and State* (ed. A. Berholtz; Jerusalem: Ministry of Education, 2001 [in Hebrew]), 195–214; and B. Lau, "Against the Time and for the Place," *Akdamot* 17 (Shevat 2006): 212–13 (in Hebrew).

14 For a sociologist's clear review of this classic Zionist self-understanding, see U. Ram, *The Globalization of Israel: McWorld in Tel Aviv, Jihad in Jerusalem*

(New York: Routledge, 2008), esp. 207–14. As he notes on p. 207, classic Zionism maintained the "synthetic Jewish-Israeli national identity," but more recent trends – represented by the shorthand in his volume's subtitle – are more polarized: they "aim at the creation of either a civic Israeli identity or an ethnic Jewish identity, which drift in opposite and mutually hostile directions."

15 For a historical presentation of this issue, see M. Samet, "Conversion and Zionism," in his *Chapters in the History of Orthodoxy* (Jerusalem: Dinur Center of the Hebrew University and Carmel, 2005 [in Hebrew]), 319–40. For an appropriately polarized presentation of the issue in English, which contrasts "Zionists" (including religious Zionists) with "Ultra-Orthodox," see Y. Sheleg, "Zionism Must Reject Ultra-Orthodox View on Conversion," *Haaretz*, March 1, 2011. For other debate, from the standpoint applied in the present volume, see my "The Name 'Israeli' Too Is Respectable," *De'ot* 42 (Sivan 2009): 34–8 (in Hebrew). That article is a response to an interview (*De'ot* 41 [Adar 2009]: 28–33 [in Hebrew]) with the director of the state-supported program that converts immigrants to Judaism, and also responded to a suggestion made by a rabbi at the same institution, who had written that since most immigrants converted through the program would not become members of the religious community, those administering conversions should stop asking for such a commitment: Y. Brandes, "The Renewed Polemics Concerning Conversion," *Akdamot* 21 (Elul 2008): 83–95, esp. 93 (in Hebrew).

16 On "a tendency among some modern Orthodox educators to put all their religious eggs in the Israel basket," and on the tendency of religious Zionists to join the "territorial right wing" as a way of competing for religious authenticity with ultra-Orthodox (but non-Zionist) Jews, see S. Carmy, "A View from the Fleshpots: Exploratory Remarks on Gilded Galut Existence," in *Israel as a Religious Reality* (ed. Ch. I. Waxman; Northvale, N.J.: Aronson, 1994), 34–5. For an example from the other side, see Y. Bin-Nun, "The Obligation of *Aliyah* and the Prohibition of Leaving Israel in the Contemporary Era, According to the Opinion of Rambam (Maimonides)," ibid., 75–104.

Appendix

1 Mason, "Jews, Judaeans," 457–512. The quotation is from the abstract on p. 457. Similarly, for the claims that "there is no Judaism" (in the premodern era) and that "'religions' were invented in the fourth century,"

see D. Boyarin, "Semantic Differences; or, 'Judaism'/'Christianity,'" in *The Ways That Never Parted: Jews and Christians in Late Antiquity and the Early Middle Ages* (ed. A. H. Becker and A. Y. Reed; TSAJ 95; Tübingen: Mohr Siebeck, 2003), 67–8; also – building upon Mason – Boyarin, "Rethinking Jewish Christianity: An Argument for Dismantling a Dubious Category (to Which Is Appended a Correction of My *Border Lines*)," *JQR* 99 (2009/2010): 8–12 and 12–27. However, his claim is quite different from Mason's; see below, n. 40. For a response to Mason and Boyarin, among others, see S. Schwartz, "How Many Judaisms Were There? A Critique of Neusner and Smith on Definition and Mason and Boyarin on Categorization," *Journal of Ancient Judaism* 2, no. 2 (2011), esp. 221–7.

2 See, for a prominent example, the quotation from BDAG cited in ch. 4, n. 29, which moves from problems about "Judaism" to conclusions about translating *Ioudaios*.

3 This is one of the major points made by S. Schwartz in his response to Mason: "How Many Judaisms," 223.

4 See Mason, "Jews, Judaeans," 465.

5 See, in general: J. W. Lett, "Emic/Etic Distinctions," in *Encyclopedia of Cultural Anthropology* (ed. D. Levinson and M. Ember; New York: Henry Holt, 1996), 2.382–3; *Emics and Etics: The Insider/Outsider Debate* (ed. T. N. Headland, K. L. Pike, and M. Harris; Frontiers of Anthropology 7; Newbury Park, Calif: Sage, 1990).

6 Three examples at random from *War* 2 (FJTC 2b): "At this time, too, the audacious actions of those wanting to foment revolution in Hierosolyma became more confident: the powerful [men] were cultivating Albinus with funds to procure impunity for their agitating, whereas, of the populace, the [element] that was not happy with tranquillity was turning away to Albinus' associates" (§274); "Therefore, in order that the nation might be torn off, he intensified their calamities every day" (§283); "Now, at that time, since [matters] had also been stirred up among the others, the [matters] among those ones became all the more inflamed" (§490). In each case, footnotes amplify and illustrate the meaning. On a similar approach to the translation of another ancient Greek work, with similar results, see my *2 Maccabees*, vii.

7 See FJTC 2b, xii ("Our goal has been to render individual Greek words with as much consistency as the context will allow, to preserve the parts of speech, letting adjectives be adjectives and participles be participles").

8 As the matter is formulated by S. Brock, "Aspects of Translation Technique in Antiquity," *GRBS* 20 (1979): 73.

9 As the ancient rabbis put it, "He who translates a verse as it is is a liar, but
   he who adds to it is a blasphemer" (t. *Meg.* 3:41 [ed. Lieberman, 364]//b.
   Qidd. 49a).
10 See Miller, "Meaning of *Ioudaios*," 99: "It is a mistake, however, to combine
   the translation question with the more important and logically prior question of the meaning of *Ioudaios* in the Greco-Roman world ... Studying
   Ioudaios without entering into the question of its translation thus permits a
   more careful analysis of its meaning." For an emphasis upon the breadth
   of the historian's mandate, beyond the study of texts, for historians study
   the reality to which the texts witness, see A. Momigliano, "Le regole del
   giuoco nello studio della storia antica," in *Sesto contributo alla storia degli
   studi classici e del mondo antico* (Storia e letteratura, 149; Rome: Storia e letteratura, 1980), 1.20 (in English in: D. R. Schwartz, *Reading the First Century*
   [WUNT 300; Tübingen: Mohr Siebeck, 2013], 189).
11 For example, at *Ant.* 20.13 Feldman (JLCL) renders διὰ τὸ ἐμαυτοῦ εὐσεβές
   as "because I cherish religion myself," where all the Greek requires is
   "because of my own piety." Similarly, note that the RSV and NRSV
   translations of 1 Macc 1:43 and 2:19, 22 use "religion" to render *latreia*,
   although that word plainly means "worship," just as Josephus, desiring
   to achieve the same end in his version of 2:20, 27, changed the Greek to
   thrēskeia (*Ant.* 12.269 – below, 97–8). It is clear that they all made this
   move from worship to religion because the context required it: at 1:43 *latreia* seems to include observance of the Sabbath (which means "abstinence from labour"), at 2:19 it seems to be very general, and at 2:22
   it comes in the course of an allusion to Deut 17:11 and thus refers
   to Jewish law in general, not just to worship. Thus, it seems that
   1 Maccabees' usage of *latreia*, which – given Septuagintal usage – probably reflects the Hebrew *'avodah*, indicates something of a tendency, of
   the type upon which we shall focus, to look beyond cult toward what
   we would call "religion."
12 On defining "religion" see below, n. 32. That "worship" denotes something that is actively done is a point that will function below, as already in
   n. 11, with regard to passages that refer to *thrēskeia* in connection with *abstinence* from labour on the Sabbath or from eating pork.
13 E. Benveniste, *Indo-European Language and Society* (London: Faber and Faber,
   1973), 516. On the next page Beneviste specifies that the word reappeared
   beginning with Strabo, that "from then on examples multiply both in texts
   and in inscriptions," and that it "became popular because it was the most
   convenient term to designate a complex *of beliefs* and cult practices" (my
   emphasis).

14 Correspondingly, *A Complete Concordance to Flavius Josephus: Study Edition* (2 vols.; ed. K. H. Rengstorf; Leiden: Brill, 2002), 1.898 offers: "(outward) religious demeanour, outward form of worship, religious custom (order), religious precepts, religion (especially the Jewish religion)." And note that although BDAG, 459, offers "expression of devotion to transcendent beings, especially as it expresses itself in cultic rites, *worship*" and does not include "religion" in its opening translations of *thrēskeia*, the body of the entry offers "religion" for several texts that are approximately contemporary with Josephus, including Acts 26:5 (the last in the list of passages below) and 1 *Clem.* 62:1.

15 Note that the *Complete Concordance* (ibid.) specifically relates to *War* 1.146 and 2.456 and offers "for religious reasons" for both.

16 On this verb see also below, after n. 23, on *Ant.* 19.283–4.

17 Only later, in §394, does Agrippa then turn to the omission of *worship* of God, and there he uses another term, which more unambiguously refers to worship – *therapeia*.

18 FJTC 2b, 145, n. 1096. In that note he also offers, for 2.198, "unsurpassable cult." But if we insert that into 2.198, the result seems to make little sense: "Amazement and compassion went into Petronius at these [words] both for the insuperable cult of the men and their ready, ecstatic disposition toward death."

19 As do Thackeray (JLCL) and Feldman (FJTC) in §§223–4. It is accordingly surprising that both translations use "worship" for *thrēskeia* in §222, where Josephus reports that the young Isaac was enthusiastic about the *thrēskeia* of God. See also the next two notes.

20 See, for example, his JLCL translations at *Ant.* 12.269, 271; 13.66; similarly, at 12.320 and 324 he uses "service." Nevertheless, at 12.253 Marcus even uses "religion of the Jews" for the Jews' *thrēskeia*, although the context is indeed restricted to sacrifice. BDAG too (p. 363) cites that passage for "religion" – which shows that many feel no need to make a strong distinction between cult and religion. For the same point, see our next note.

21 Note that Spicq translates it in this passage as "the cult of God" but cites it as an example for the use of *thrēskeia* in the sense of "religion pure and simple" – which he then goes on to gloss as follows: "or better, the liturgy and rites used in the adoration of God, the cult that honors God" (*TLNT* 2.203, n. 14). See the conclusion of our preceding note.

22 On this episode see B. S. Jackson, *Essays in Jewish and Comparative Legal History* (SJLA 10; Leiden: Brill, 1975), 240–3.

23 For doubts about its authenticity, see my *Agrippa I: The Last King of Judaea* (TSAJ 23; Tübingen: Mohr [Siebeck], 1990), 99–106.

24 See van Henten, *Maccabean Martyrs*, 70–3; cf. Schwartz, *2 Maccabees*, 86, n. 197.

25 M. Hadas, ed. and trans., *The Third and Fourth Books of Maccabees* (JAL; New York: Harper, 1953), 171.

26 On this passage, see esp. Spicq, *TLNT*, 2.203–4.

27 Acts 26:5 is of special relevance to us, for the way Paul is made to underscore, here, his adherence to the strictest variety of Jewish *thrēskeia*, functions the same way as Paul's own reference to his zealous adherence to *Ioudaïsmos* in Gal 1:13–14. This point poses a question mark alongside Mason's suggestion (pp. 469–70) that Paul's reference in Galatians refers to his "Judaizing," specifically, to "violent harassment of Jesus' followers" such as is reported in Acts 9:1–3 and 22:3–5, as well as further on in Acts 26 (vv. 9–12). That is meant to support Mason's general case that *Ioudaïsmos* referred to a transitive "Judaizing," an attempt to cause others to do like Jews (see below, at n. 40). However, while Mason is right that Paul was probably alluding to such activity, my sense is that the allusion is made by his reference to his "zeal," not by the word *Ioudaïsmos* itself; one who is "zealous" for Judaism, the way we use the latter term, might well be expected to attempt to force it upon others. Note especially, moreover, that since at Gal 2:14, where Paul definitely refers to the possibility of forcing someone to act like a Jew he does not content himself with *ioudaïzein* but, rather, uses a separate verb for forcing (ἀναγκάζεις ἰουδαΐζειν), it is all the harder to take *Ioudaïsmos* in the sense Mason suggests.

28 The methodological issue here is the same as that raised by critics of H. McKay's claim, in her *Sabbath and Synagogue: The Question of Sabbath Worship in Ancient Judaism* (Religions in the Greco-Roman World 122; Leiden: Brill, 1994), that there was no Sabbath "worship" in ancient synagogues prior to 200 CE. She can claim that by stipulating that reading of the Torah – which is well attested for those early synagogues – cannot be termed "worship" (see ibid., 3–4). However, while above I denied that we might call abstinence from activity "worship," for "worship" entails doing something, reading the Torah *is* an activity and who are we to say – or why might it be useful for us to say – that those who gathered to do it did not consider it "worship"? See van der Horst, *Japheth in the Tents of Shem*, esp. 77–80 (with references on p. 80 to other critics of the narrowness of McKay's definition of worship, such as S. Reif's review in *JTS* 46 [1995]: 611–12); and L. I. Levine, *The Ancient Synagogue: The First Thousand Years* (2nd ed.; New Haven: Yale, 2005), 145–6, n. 59. Beyond that, there are other reasons to doubt McKay's thesis, beginning with the fact that in the

Hellenistic world the usual term for a synagogue was *proseuchē*, which is derived from a verb that means "pray," and with such passages as *In Flaccum* 48, 122, where Philo complains that the destruction of the Jews' synagogues denied them a place to pray, and moving on to a more general question: even if there is no explicit evidence, can we really imagine that Jews who gathered to read the Torah because they believed that God, their all-powerful covenantal partner, wanted them to do so, would not hope that God would take notice of them and requite them in some desired way – and that they at times, or even regularly, voiced that hope?

29 Mason refers here to W. Burkert, *Greek Religion* (trans. J. Raffan; Cambridge, Mass.: Harvard University Press, 1985), 8.

30 *Ag. Ap.* 2.188, trans. Barclay (FJTC 10, 275). As Barclay explains, ibid. n. 746, Josephus is referring here to a "heightened state of holiness – the purification of the worshipper and his/her consecration to the service of the deity. Josephus' point is that Judeans live continually in such a state of holiness."

31 See above, Introduction, n. 18. On Josephus, see esp. S. J. D. Cohen, "Respect for Judaism by Gentiles according to Josephus," *HTR* 80 (1987): 409–30; also my "Doing like Jews or Becoming a Jew? Josephus on Women Converts to Judaism," *Jewish Identity in the Greco-Roman World*, 93–109.

32 Definition of "religion" is notoriously difficult. Even positing a belief in a god-like figure as a necessary condition, which one might think is a sine qua non, founders on the exceptional case of Buddhism, which we nevertheless call a religion. The best approach would seem to be a "polythetic" one that acknowledges that while there is no characteristic that all religions share, they all share a "family resemblance" insofar as they share some of the attributes in a pool considered to typify religions. See, for this approach and lists of such attributes, M. Southwold, "Buddhism and the Definition of Religion," *Man* 13 (1978): 362–79; B. C. Wilson, "From the Lexical to the Polythetic: A Brief History of the Definition of Religion," in *What Is Religion? Origins, Definitions, and Explanations* (ed. T. A. Idinopulos and B. C. Wilson; SHR 81; Leiden: Brill, 1998), 141–62; and M. Hamilton, *The Sociology of Religion: Theoretical and Comparative Perspectives* (2nd ed.; New York: Routledge, 2001), 20–3. My thanks to Dr. Gideon Aran for help with this point. For a polythetic approach toward defining ancient "Judaism," see M. L. Satlow, "Defining Judaism: Accounting for 'Religions' in the Study of Religion," *JAAR* 74 (2006): 837–60.

33 On this passage (*GLAJJ* I, no. 15) see now B. Bar-Kochva, *The Image of the Jews in Greek Literature: The Hellenistic Period* (HCS 51; Berkeley: University of California Press, 2010), 40–89.

34 The implication of the latter passage was pointed out by S. J. D. Cohen, "Ἰουδαῖος τὸ γένος and Related Expressions in Josephus," in *Josephus and the History*, 34.

35 See the introduction to my *Studies*, 5–15; or a similar but later exposition of the same issue: "On the Jewish Background of Christianity," in *Studies in Rabbinic Judaism and Early Christianity* (ed. D. Jaffé; AJEC 74; Leiden: Brill, 2010), 88–97.

36 See also my "'Judaean' or 'Jew'? How Should We Translate *Ioudaios* in Josephus?," in *Jewish Identity in the Greco-Roman World*, 3–27. That study appeared around the same time as Mason's "Jews, Judaeans," so neither could relate to the other.

37 Concerning "nationalism," see D. Goodblatt, *Elements of Ancient Jewish Nationalism* (New York: Cambridge University Press, 2006), 1–27. Similarly, concerning "sovereignty": 1 Maccabees 13:41–2 celebrates the fact that the Seleucid government gave up demands of taxation from Judea, summarizing that as "the yoke of the Gentiles was removed from Israel," and the Judeans began to date documents according to the years of the Hasmonean ruler. Our modern word "sovereignty" seems precisely to denote what the author of 1 Maccabees meant.

38 An example for which I am grateful to J. W. van Henten. Note, for example, that although van Henten begins a discussion of martyrdom in antiquity by noting that "ancient martyrdom is, at least for the period in which no text is specifically dedicated to martyrdom or points to any specific terminology of martyrdom, a construct of research," and goes on to note that the Greek term *martys* begins to denote "martyr" no earlier than the second-century *Martyrdom of Polycarp* and that pre-Christian Jewish texts offer no similar term, he still goes on to discuss martyrdom in the pre-Christian period – just as he uses English and German, which too did not exist in antiquity. See van Henten, "Martyrium II," *RAC* 24 (2011): cols. 301–2, also his volume cited above, ch. 1, n. 18. Concerning the suggestion that chs. 6–7 were added into 2 Maccabees only after the appearance of Christianity, see Schwartz, *2 Maccabees*, 20, n. 51.

39 Which is not to say that it might not be interesting to ask why the ancients did not have – need – a word that we find so useful.

40 Although, as noted above (n. 1), Boyarin builds upon Mason's study, concerning 2 Maccabees he disagrees. As Boyarin puts it, *Ioudaïsmos* in 2 Maccabees means "the entire complex of loyalties and practices that mark off the people of Israel" ("Rethinking Jewish Christianity," 8). True, Boyarin sees in the breadth of that complex reason to deny that *Ioudaïsmos* denotes "Judaism the religion," which he views as something moderns

have "disembed(ded) from the culture of the Jews" (ibid.). I would pose something of a question mark about his assumption that our use of "Judaism" excludes elements that do not pertain to "religion" in a limited sense (whatever that is; see above, n. 32). See, for example, M. M. Kaplan, *Judaism as a Civilization: Toward a Reconstruction of American Jewish Life* (New York: Macmillan, 1934); and note, for another example, the topic of the 2009 annual convention of the British Association for Jewish Studies: "Culinary Judaism." What is essential in the present context, however, is Boyarin's agreement that, in 2 Maccabees, *Ioudaïsmos* denotes the things Jews do and believe qua Jews, not anything they do to others. For an earlier formulation of Boyarin's view, see below, n. 44.

41 See *GLAJJ* I, 566 (no. 263).

42 For a similar discussion of the verb, with similar conclusions, see S. J. D. Cohen, *The Beginnings of Jewishness: Boundaries, Varieties, Uncertainties* (HCS 31; Berkeley: University of California Press, 1999), 175–97.

43 In this following survey I left aside the case of *War* 2.463, where no details about the "Judaizers" are given.

44 Note that, in contrast to his more recent treatment of the issue (above, n. 40), Boyarin first attempted to explain *Ioudaïsmos* in 2 Maccabees as "remaining loyal to the ways of the Judeans and the political cause of Jerusalem." Even there, however, he was forced, by 2 Macc 14:38, to move to glossing the term as denoting "loyalty to the cause of the Jews and fealty to their traditional ways" ("Semantic Differences," 68 and ibid., n. 14).

45 Similarly, with regard to the verb *ioudaïzein* Cohen notes, "In Plutarch the word has a negative valence, as indeed most of the ethnic *-izein* verbs do in classical Greek, but in Jewish Greek the word is used neutrally" (*Beginnings*, 193).

46 "(21) and the heavenly apparitions which occurred for those who nobly fought with manly valor for Judaism, so that although they were few in number they plundered the entire country and chased away the barbaric hordes (22) and retook the temple which was spoken of throughout the entire civilized world and liberated the city, and firmly reestablished the laws that were about to be abolished" (Schwartz, *2 Maccabees*, 170).

47 As opposed to some scholars who have made much of the fact that they are not mentioned in close proximity one to another ("Hellenism" appears at 4:13, "Judaism" in chs. 2, 8, and 14). See, for example, E. S. Gruen, *Heritage and Hellenism: The Reinvention of Jewish Tradition* (HCS 30; Berkeley: University of California Press, 1998), 3–4.

48 On "Medism" see D. F. Graf, "Medism: The Origin and Significance of the Term," *JHS* 104 (1984): 15–30. On p. 15 he explains Medism as "leaning

toward the Medes," just as S. Hornblower renders it as "conspiring with the Persians" (*A Commentary on Thucydides* [Oxford: Clarendon, 1991], 1.142; see also ibid. 455 on "Attikizing").

49 So too S. Schwartz: although he accepts Mason's interpretation of *Ioudaïsmos* in the other passages in 2 Maccabees without any debate, concerning 2 Macc 8:1, as also 4 Macc 4:26, he writes that they "must be subjected to some violence to get them to mean Judaizing rather than Judaism" ("How Many Judaisms," 225).

50 While this passage on p. 467 does not explicitly specify whence or whither the other Judeans are to be brought back, Mason's reference to the goal of "reinstating the ancestral law" shows he is thinking of bringing them back from abandonment of Judean law and custom to observance of them, just as he wrote on the next page, with regard to *Ioudaïsmos* in 2 Macc 14:38: "striving to restore Judean law and custom."

51 See above, ch. 1, n. 31.

52 For the focus of 2 Maccabees on Judas himself, see esp. J. Geiger, "The History of Judas Maccabaeus: One Aspect of Hellenistic Historiography," *Zion* 49 (1983/1984): 1–8 (in Hebrew).

53 For a comparison of these two texts, see Schwartz, *2 Maccabees*, 82.

54 Contrast 1 Macc 2:46, where we read that Mattathias forced circumcision of uncircumcised babies. The closest 2 Maccabees comes to anything like this is very different: a martyr's expression of the hope that his willingness to die nobly will serve as a model for youth (6:28, 31), and mutual words of encouragement among martyrs (7:5–6, 29).

55 See Y. Amir, "The Term Ἰουδαϊσμός (IOUDAISMOS): A Study in Jewish-Hellenistic Self-Definition," *Immanuel* 14 (Fall 1982): 34–41, esp. 39, where he juxtaposes "remained in Judaism" (2 Macc 8:1) to Paul's reference to his former "life in Judaism" (Gal 1:13) and concludes that "Judaism would appear to be a sort of fenced off area in which Jewish lives are led." Concerning Paul's usage in Gal 1:13, and for the rejection of a well-meaning attempt to limit his "Judaism" to law alone, see my "Paul, the Jews, and Well-Meaning Translation: What Price *Einheit*?" *TZ* 69 (2013): 372–84.

56 For Second Maccabees as a work of the Jewish Diaspora, see above, ch. 1, n. 8.

Index of Modern Authors Cited

Index of Names, Terms, and Topics